A History of
EGYPTIAN ARCHAEOLOGY

A History of
EGYPTIAN
ARCHAEOLOGY

FRED GLADSTONE BRATTON

*Illustrated with photographs,
line figures and maps*

THOMAS Y. CROWELL COMPANY
NEW YORK · ESTABLISHED 1834

DT
60
B7
copy2

First published in the United States of America in 1968

68311

Printed in the United States of America

L. C. Card 68-15578

CONTENTS

Contents

ILLUSTRATIONS

Illustrations

Illustrations

LINE FIGURES

Illustrations

MAPS

EGYPTIAN EXCAVATIONS

Maps drawn by T. R. Allen

ACKNOWLEDGEMENTS

I wish to thank the following publishers for permission to quote from the works cited:

University of Oklahoma Press (Joseph Lindon Smith: *Tombs, Temples, and Ancient Art*).

Penguin Books, Inc., Baltimore, U.S.A. (W. Stevenson Smith: *The Art and Archaeology of Ancient Egypt*).

Harvard University Press (W. Stevenson Smith and George A. Reisner: *A History of the Giza Metropolis*, Vol. 2).

Holt, Rinehart and Winston, Inc. (M. Zakaria Goneim: *The Lost Pyramid*).

Crowell-Collier-Macmillan, Inc. (Herbert E. Winlock: *Excavations at Deir el-Bahri, 1911–31*).

Penguin Books, Ltd. (I. E. S. Edwards: *The Pyramids of Egypt*).

G. P. Putnam's Sons (William MacQuitty: *Abu Simbel*).

The George Macy Companies (Harry Carter, ed.: *The Histories of Herodotus of Halicarnassus*).

Curtis Brown, Ltd. (Carter, Howard and Mace, A. C.: *The Tomb of Tutankhamen*).

Oxford University Press (Alan Gardiner: *Egyptian Grammar*).

PREFACE

Jean Capart, lecturing in America in 1924, expressed his surprise that no one had ever written a book entitled *Golden Deeds of Egyptian Excavators*, a book that would tell the story of archaeological discoveries in Egypt over the previous century or more. It would make, he thought, a romantic and exciting detective story. This is what I have tried to do in this volume. It is a presumptuous task but it has been undertaken with the conviction that there is a need for a definitive and complete account of Egyptian excavation. At the risk of oversimplification, unwarranted value-judgements, and some serious omissions, I have attempted, therefore, to present a comprehensive description of Egyptian exploration and discovery from Herodotus to the present time. In doing so I have aimed to steer a treacherous course between the Scylla of statistical and (for the general reader) unintelligible reports from the field and the Charybdis of sketchy popularizations. James Baikie and, more recently, Leonard Cottrell and C. W. Ceram have made the Western world Egypt-conscious by their successful publications dealing with the highlights of Near East archaeology. Public interest in Egypt has in recent years become widespread because of the recent discoveries of new tombs and pyramids as well as the project of the New High Dam.

In the Preface of my *The Heretic Pharaoh* I recorded the names of the most important Egyptian archaeologists. In this volume I wish to tell their story. The book is designed chiefly for the student and layman rather than the specialist. If there is any ulterior motive behind this story of the recovery of the ancient past in Egypt, it is to help the reader recover in this day of frantic immediacy and myopia a greater perspective on life and history, to hear what the centuries say to the hours, and perhaps gain a new appreciation of what the great Egyptian culture bequeathed to us, a culture that existed continuously for three millenniums before Greece came into being. It may be that through this book some of the glorious past may be rescued from the rubbish heaps of oblivion to which many things, good and bad, go. There is only one force that is stronger than death, as Arthur Weigall once observed, and that force is history, for by history and archaeology the dead past lives again. Perhaps there will be found here some cultural preparation for the visitor who will one day make his pilgrimage to the Land of the Nile and thereby be better prepared to listen to the sounds of the past as they echo from the ancient stones of Karnak, Giza, and Deir el Bahri.

The *adjective* may be the enemy of good prose style but any writer who tries to do justice to the wonders of Egyptian excavation finds himself fighting that enemy in every paragraph. Each succeeding discovery is the "greatest". If the reader therefore encounters an overabundance of superlatives, I can only say that they are a reflection of the awe and ecstasy of those who made the discoveries, for let it not be thought that the professional archaeologist, when he walks into a tomb and treads upon the footprints of the last person to leave 4,500 years ago, is without emotion, however restrained.

One of the many famous papyri in the British Museum is "The Tale of the Two Brothers", written in the thirteenth century B.C. The author of the story attaches an interesting colophon to the manuscript: "This book is finished in peace for the *ka* of the scribe and the treasurer Oagabu, of the treasury of the Pharaoh. Life! Health! Strength! The scribe Anena, the owner of this book, has written it. Whoever speaks against this book, may the god Thoth smite him!" This seems to have been the ancient equivalent of a copyright and also an attempt on the part of the author to forestall adverse comment on his work by cursing his critics in advance! I shall not go so far as that but would express the hope at least that my critics will look with forbearance on this attempt to bring the personalities and events of such a vast period of history into perspective and to appreciate the risk of error involved in such a task.

Since this book is a history of Egyptian excavation and is not primarily concerned with an interpretation of Egyptian culture as such, it does not deal, except incidentally, with the work of the writers in the field of Egyptology: the interpreters, the translators, and the historians. These scholars bridge the gap between archaeology and history, and, on the background of the discoveries that are made, put the links of the chain together, establish connections, determine chronological sequence, and interpret the thought and institutions of the ancient Egyptians. Furthermore, their work is just as important as the man in the field, for the final aim of Egyptology is not merely the acquisition of objects for a museum but the acquiring of historical and cultural knowledge. While some of the historians have led or participated in excavations, their work is primarily interpretation. Great names from the past and present immediately come to mind; Alan Gardiner and I. E. S. Edwards in England, Adolf Erman and Kurt Sethe in Germany, and James H. Breasted and John A. Wilson in America, to mention a few from the long list of experts to whom we owe our knowledge of Egyptian life and history.

I am especially indebted to I. E. S. Edwards, whose *The Pyramids of Egypt* is the pyramidologist's bible, to the authors of numerous articles in the UNESCO *Courier* for information on Nubia and the New High Dam, and to contributors to the *Journal of Egyptian Archaeology* through the years for reports of excavations. James Baikie's *Egyptian Papyrus and Papyrus-Hunting*, Alan Gardiner's *Egyptian Grammar*, Stanley Mayes' *The Great Belzoni*, H. E. Winlock's *Excavations at Deir el Bahri*, Howard Carter's *The Tomb of Tutankhamen*, and James H. Breasted's *Ancient Records of Egypt* were valuable aids in specialized fields.

I wish to thank Mr. Gordon Chesterfield of Robert Hale Limited, for his personal interest in the book and for his careful supervision of the long and involved process by which a manuscript becomes a book. I am indebted to Mr. Eric Young, Assistant Curator, Department of Egyptian Art, Metropolitan Museum of Art, for valuable suggestions in the preparation of the final draft. His expert knowledge helped in the avoidance of many inaccuracies. What errors remain are my own. My thanks also to Mrs. Frank A. Warren, who typed the manuscript.

FRED GLADSTONE BRATTON

Prologue

INDESTRUCTIBLE EGYPT

THE GENIUS OF EGYPT

The Egyptian civilization was totally different from any other ancient culture. Its thought-forms and art-style are quite untranslatable. There is a certain take-it-or-leave-it quality in its tenacity of tradition and its refusal to compromise. It is therefore difficult for us to approach the mind of the ancient Egyptian objectively. His way of thinking was based on criteria that are completely foreign to us today. As early as 3000 B.C. there was developed a style of artistic expression that became more enduring than that of any other people in history—a style which in portrait-sculpture, relief, architecture, and calligraphy lasted for over three millenniums. To understand this style one has to go beyond a mere aesthetic appreciation. Egyptian sculpture and painting were symbolic, spiritual representations. They were neither reflective nor complicated. The naiveté of the early Egyptians can easily be misinterpreted. Their very ingenuousness and natural intuition enabled them to portray life and personality with an unequalled clarity and universality. Such concentrated simplicity is likely to escape the modern interpreter who insists on reading into ancient art and writing a perspicacity and an involved meaning that the ancient Egyptians did not have. Both their art and their literature were pragmatic and concrete. They were not philosophical.

Admittedly Egypt did not bequeath to the modern world an intellectual heritage comparable to the philosophy of Greece or the religion of the Hebrews. The Egyptian above all was a practical person, a materialist. His literature shows little ability in the field of speculative thought or abstract ideas. His cosmology, beliefs about the after-life, and his religious and ethical teachings were expressed in terms of the physical and the tangible, the practical necessities of daily life. He had a profound reverence for those natural forces that made life possible. He expressed his beliefs in concrete forms. The genius of the Egyptian was not in theory or inventiveness but in his astounding accomplishments with what he had at his disposal and in his capacity for organization and administration. Such a pragmatic unsophisticated worldview was not without its assets, for it gave him a cheerful outlook on the present life, a confidence regarding the future life, a sense of order and rightness in the universe, and a just attitude towards his fellows.

But while the Egyptian's intellectual contribution to civilization may not compare with that of Greece, his impact on history has been just as important. That impact can be defined as a sense of cosmic order. The basic belief of the ancient Egyptians and the conviction around which all else grew was the changelessness of the universe. Everything in their environment pointed to the one consistent fact that the world was static, and with that observation went the further conviction that changelessness was the only real and unchangeable truth. The modern idea of evolution, flux, and variation had no place in the Egyptian world-view. Implicit in this conception was the idea of immortality. The after-life followed the present life as surely as day followed night. Such a consciousness resulted from the Egyptian's contemplation of two natural forces: the sun and the river. The periodicity of the sun in its ride across the sky each day and the faithfulness of the Nile in its annual flood gave the Egyptian a feeling of cosmic inevitability.

What gives Egypt more archaeological importance than any other ancient civilization is the massive solidity and indestructibility of its pyramids and tombs, statues and temples. These structures reflect the enduring quality of the Egyptian culture. As over against the transitoriness and insubstantiality of our own times, seen, for instance, in the new Manhattan skyline with its glass skyscrapers standing precariously on stilts, the pyramids of Giza, eternal homes of immortalized pharaohs, with their broad base and climactic apex, fittingly symbolize the permanence of Egypt. In order further to understand the mental outlook of the Egyptians we have to imagine a people whose isolated position was a guarantee of their security and whose unchangeable climate suggested eternal stability. It was a proud and self-sufficient civilization, faithful to its own spirit. But different as she was, Egypt's achievements remain for us today an example of the search for self-realization and truth.

Layman and professional alike can only come away from these ancient monuments with a feeling of profound respect and awe. Consider that symbol of mystery, the Sphinx of Chephren, hewn from a single rock in 2650 B.C., sitting with outstretched paws and facing the rising sun, surviving the ravages of Persians, Greeks, Romans, Mamelukes, and Turks as well as the perpetual erosion of wind and sand, dug out of the sand by Thutmose IV, to whom even in the fifteenth century B.C. it was a wonder of the ancient world.

> Inscrutable
> Though mutable,
> Defaced by sands of time
> A cosmos of all things created,
> A union
> Of man and of woman,
> The soul embodied in a beast,
> Longing, unsated,
> Still seeking the east,
> Sublime
> In its wistful endeavor,
> The silence to sever
> Protecting, benignant
> Triumphantly regnant
> It stands there forever.[1]

There was the royal architect Imhotep whom the Greeks looked upon as a god and who lived and worked before the Giza pyramids were made. Today, after almost 5,000 years, his handiwork still dominates the desert landscape at Sakkara—the Step Pyramid of Zoser along with the temples, pavilions, chapels, and capitol buildings of Memphis. Here as early as 2800 B.C. was the fluted column carved out of the wall to resemble a plant with

[1] From Caroline Hazard's "Shards and Scarabs".

leaves at the top, forming a capital. Two thousand years before Athens and Corinth, Imhotep perfected the basic forms of architecture: columns with astragal bases and flowered capitals, wall-niches and projections, portals, ornamental frieze, and pillared halls! Contemplating this tremendous funerary complex is the seated figure of Zoser himself—the earliest life-size statue of a king in existence.

SCULPTURE

No Sumerian, Babylonian or Persian sculpture can compare with the Egyptian in draftsmanship, mastery of form or sense of proportion. No ancient sculpture except possibly the Greek has such a universal appeal. Goethe recognized the classical nature of the Egyptian sculpture in his comparison of the "black basalt" figures with the Greek "white marble". What titanic labour and ingenuity were needed to erect those colossal columns at Karnak, so large in diameter that one hundred men can stand on the top of each papyrus pillar. The walls surrounding the Karnak temple complex could accommodate ten European cathedrals.

Where in all antiquity can be found anything more graceful than the Isis temple at Philae, bravely holding its head above the lapping waters of the lake made by the Aswan Dam, a dreamlike remnant of Ptolemaic and Roman days? At Philae the late style of Egyptian art—as seen in the sculptured plant forms of the colonnades—is combined with the old style. Similar combinations are seen at Edfu, Kom Ombo, Esneh, and in the Sudan.

Standing before the magnificent funerary temple of Hatshepsut at Deir el Bahri makes one almost forget the Parthenon, for no building in all history excels this masterpiece of the architect Senmut in symmetry, proportion, and artistic use of the exterior colonnade. This beautifully proportioned building was carved out of the limestone cliffs in a bay of land on the western bank of the Nile at Thebes. Its three terraces were approached by long gentle ramps. The basic design is horizontal, accentuating the heights of the cliffs towering above it. To the left, neglected by most visitors, are the ruins of the temple of Mentuhotep from the Eleventh Dynasty. Across the river at Karnak stands Hatshepsut's obelisk, a column of pink granite, 98 feet high, quarried in one piece at Aswan and incised with inch-deep hieroglyphs. In the long reign of Ramses II, with his preoccupation with the colossal and pure massiveness, sculpture reaches the point of exhibitionism. Abu Simbel, gargantuan monument to Pharaonic pride, carrying the familiar forms to new heights of grandeur, is, to be sure, an architectural overstatement. But grandiose as it is—described by an early French traveller as "the Cathedral of Notre Dame carved out of a single block of stone"—the Ramses temple and the adjoining one of Nefertari the Queen are undeniable evidence of the continued vitality of Pharaonic culture and of the ability of the Egyptians, as Kurt Lange says, "to master the incomprehensible".

The temples of Egypt from Zoser to the Ramesside Dynasty were not just places of worship, forms of architecture conceived by individuals such as Imhotep and Senmut. They were living expressions of cosmic truth (*maat*), symbolic manifestations of deity (*neter*) as incarnated in the royal person. They followed a set plan from first to last. Their colossal character indicates that they represented something that transcended man. Like the pyramids, they pointed to eternity.

Egyptian sculpture may be seen as an extension of the hieroglyph. In fact, it has been described as a "three-dimensional hieroglyph". And, like the sacred writing itself, it has a spiritual significance. Much has been said of the immutability and changelessness of Egyptian sculpture, especially as illustrated in representations of royalty which almost always showed the king seated with august unbending dignity or, if standing, with the left leg advanced, arms hung taut at the sides, fists clenched and inscrutable face looking straight ahead. It is argued that the idea of the god-king, the constancy of the natural forces, the isolation of Egypt itself all combined to produce a static art. And this in the main is true. The one outstanding exception to the generalization is the Amarna revolution with its modernism in art and its monotheistic reform in religion. But Amarna was a mutation, an heretical movement and did not leave any permanent marks. If any other change is to be recognized it was in the status of the Pharaoh. The immortalized god-king was not always a ruthless dictator, as some scholars have pictured him, and the people were not always abject slaves of the royalty. True, the king as god was far removed from the people and even his court, but he was also hailed as "beneficent", "kind", and "merciful". There is discernible a gradual weakening of the centralized, all-powerful rule of the Pharaoh. The vulnerability of the king and his feeling of insecurity may be inferred from the appointment of the co-regent, a procedure probably aimed at the continuance of his power. In spite of the achievements of the Golden Age of the Thutmosid and Amenhotep lines one detects even at that time the beginning of the feeling of insecurity and loss of assurance.

PAINTING

Engrossed in the sculptures and reliefs of ancient Egypt modern art lovers have been inclined to overlook the field of painting—the earliest art in Egypt. The excellently preserved wall paintings are found in every period of Egyptian history. The life and culture of prehistoric and predynastic ages are illustrated in the painted pottery. From the beginning, Egyptian painters showed how relief work could be embellished by painting in colour, the best examples of which are the wall paintings of the Eighteenth and Nineteenth Dynasties. They represent painting and sculpture in perfect combination.

Egyptians generally used four colours: red, blue, green, and yellow, but at times they were mixed. Many of the tomb and temple scenes were carved in high relief or incised and were afterwards coloured. Otherwise the painting was on a flat surface. One conspicuous characteristic of Egyptian artists was their handling of the profile, the conventional pose of gods and royalty. Their philosophy of graphic art demanded that the individual could best be portrayed only in that form. On the other hand, the desire to reproduce as many parts of the body as possible led them to give at the same time a front view of the shoulders and abdomen while the hips and legs remained in profile—a method that disturbs the modern viewer until he becomes accustomed to it. Males were shown with the left foot forward and females with the legs almost together.

The typical decorative scheme was based on the belief that the future life was like the present and that the dead must be provided with the same possessions and indulge in the same activities as in this life. For this reason, as we have indicated earlier, the tomb paintings have given us detailed information about the social and cultural life of the ancient Egyptians. Along with the secular scenes were depicted the funerary theme and ritual of the dead. Eighteenth-dynasty tomb paintings tend to deal chiefly with the religious motif: the king or queen making offerings to the god or worshipping Osiris. Whatever the scene, it was based on the desire for a happy after-life.

In Egypt the precious patina of history lies heavy, for no other civilization can boast of such a long continuous history. In no other place can one see such evidence of high culture, such splendid examples of technical skill and artistry. Greece, the only rival, reckons her cultural history in centuries but Egypt reckons hers in millenniums. The Greeks, and later the Romans, looked to Egypt as the source of all wisdom and transmitted that wisdom to posterity. To Egypt we owe our system of dividing time into twenty-four hours to the day, twelve months and 365 days to the year. The Egyptians invented the clock. They were the first to record historical events and the first to use practical writing materials. Their penchant for recording events is one reason for our extensive knowledge of their history, literature, theology, ritual, and medicine.

Much of our knowledge of ancient Egyptian life comes from tomb paintings. The reason for the elaborate paintings and reliefs on the walls of tombs arose out of the desire to assure the deceased of the continuance of all his earthly activities in the next life. The tomb reliefs have given us an accurate picture of Egyptian architecture, horticulture, clothing, eating, farming, fishing, and hunting, as well as religious practices. The custom of placing in the tomb of a dead person his personal possessions and household treasures has made it possible for archaeologists to reconstruct accurately the daily life of an Egyptian in any period of history. The elaborate care with which the Egyptians provided for the material needs of the deceased testifies to their insistent belief in a personal existence in the hereafter. The body was preserved for eternity, equipped with everything—not only food, drink and clothing, but all those things necessary for recreation and enjoyment. This belief in the future life, it must be admitted, was thoroughly materialistic. It was the physical life which continued in the realm of Osiris. Yet we must say in his defence that the Egyptian's exaltation of the physical life and the individual personality, both in the present world and in the next, is more to be admired than the nihilistic and self-negating religions of the Far East. For the archaeologist, at least, the pragmatic materialism of the Egyptian's view of the future life has meant the difference between knowledge and ignorance of this ancient race of people. Another reason for our detailed knowledge of Egyptian thought is a climatic one. Because of the excessively dry climate of the Nile valley, the papyri, stelae, monuments, and tomb paintings have been preserved in a condition otherwise impossible. The sands and rubbish heaps of Egypt have held intact for us for 5,000 years not only papyri, which have given us accurate information about Egyptian astronomy, physics, medicine and engineering; but also organic materials such as wooden objects, flowers, and even cooked food. Tomb paintings and incised hieroglyphs on obelisks from 1500 B.C. are as fresh and clear as the day they were created. It was not just the careful process of mummification that is responsible for the remarkable preservation of the mummies of kings for 4,000 years but the climate itself. Excavators have found excellently preserved bodies of pre-dynastic Egyptians who lived before the practice of embalming came into use. These mummies were not in coffins and were not eviscerated. The exceptionally dry climate and the absence of bacteria in the air and sand had kept the cadavers in a better state of preservation than carefully prepared mummies. The climate is, of course, not the only explanation of the abundance of cultural remains. Another factor was the availability of writing materials both in the form of papyri and the unending supply of limestone for building materials.

RELIGION

The Egyptians were religious but they were never mystical. Their religion was strictly utilitarian—a reverence for the two natural forces that made their life possible: the sun and the river. Indeed it is not too much to say that their entire religious, political and cultural history was determined by these two forces. They have left us little or no abstract thought. Their *Weltanschauung* was defined by the dualism of light and darkness, aridity and fertility, night and day, life and death. Just as there was no twilight in Egypt, neither was there any middle ground of thought. From the earliest times the sun and the river were identified with the two chief deities, Ra and Osiris. The daily rising of the sun in the east brought renewed life to the soil and to the soul of man after the night of cold and darkness. The regularity of the sun's ride across the sky, bringing warmth and life, had its counterpart in the annual flooding of the Nile which, depositing the black silt in the fields, was also a guarantee of life. Sun and river gave the Egyptian a reassuring sense of security and stability. Ra, the sun-god, represented life in the present; Osiris, the god of vegetation, represented life in the future. Thus the insistent facts of life and death were blended in the Solar and Osirian faiths.

The most impressive literature dealing with the river is that which has to do with Osiris in his function as god of the Nile and the ritualistic formulae of the Book of the Dead. "Thou, Osiris, art indeed the Nile, great on the fields at the beginning of the seasons; gods and men live by the moisture that is in thee." The annual cycle of death and birth in nature was personified in the death and resurrection of Osiris. To celebrate the resurrection of Osiris, an annual Passion Play was held at Abydos. Here the burial of the god was re-enacted and his death was mourned with great drama. Then the stones were removed from the tomb and the people shouted, "The Lord is risen!" In this rebirth of Osiris the people saw their own triumph over death. The risen Osiris entered his realm as the king and judge of the dead.

The Book of the Dead was the guide book for the deceased and contained the requirements for entrance into the realm of Osiris together with magic formulae that would assist the soul in its passage. Upon entering the Hall of Truth, the deceased must testify that he has consciously done no wrong. If he satisfies the God of Truth on moral grounds, he enters the judgement hall where his heart is weighed on a scale over against a feather, the symbol of righteousness. If they balance, he is received into the kingdom of Osiris. It is important that these judgement scenes exhibit a distinct moral quality. The idea that each individual bears a definite moral responsibility exerted a profound influence upon the common people as the Osirian faith became the religion of the masses. A man had to prove his worthiness of eternal life by the way he lived on earth. Through the worship of Osiris, moral goodness became a paramount consideration.

The worship of Ra, the sun-god, on the other hand, was more aristocratic since it had originally been the religion of kings. But because both religions had to do with the cycle of death and re-birth, the two were often compounded. Ra was the god of creation, the primal force, the father of kings and author of the cosmic order. The name Ra was often linked to the names of other deities to invest them with greater importance: Ra-Harakhti, the god of the Eastern horizon, and Amon-Ra, the god of Thebes. At Heliopolis where the official Egyptian religion took its rise in the Pyramid Age, a temple cult developed with an organized priesthood devoted to the worship of the sun. In the Holy of Holies of the temple was a symbol called the *benben*, a pyramid-shaped stone representing the sun-god. This stone fetish may provide the key to the religious significance of the pyramid itself which seems to have been an enlargement of the *benben*. If this were the case, the pyramid must have been built to represent the rays of the sun slanting towards the earth. Some of the early Pyramid Texts refer to the pyramid as "a staircase to heaven" and "a place of ascension". There can be no doubt that the pyramid, whose apex was the first object in all the land to catch the sun's rays each morning, was associated with the solar faith.

For a period of twenty-five or thirty years there was an inter-ruption in the traditional priestly religion of Egypt—a pheno-menon without parallel in history. It was the religious revolution of Amenhotep IV who, in order to symbolize his worship of a new god, called himself Ikhnaton. The Atonism of the heretic Pharaoh died with him—a radiant interlude in history—and yet, while it made little difference in the total history of Egypt, it looms large in the history of humanity. Ikhnaton brushed aside the powerful Amon priesthood and instituted a monotheistic religion. He made a clean break with the stereotyped forms of Egyptian art to create a new and dynamic naturalism. Taking his stand against 2,000 years of tradition, he taught a cosmic theism that has much to say to the present world with its parochial and provincial concepts of God. He recognized the vast creative force of the sun as a symbol of deity. Aton was the source of all energy, the primal power behind all things, a formless essence, an intelligence permeating the universe. This was man's first attempt to define God in intangible terms and idealistic qualities —a conception of God vastly superior to the anthropomorphisms of the later Western religions. Ikhnaton's God was both transcendent and immanent, original causation and continuous presence. His religion was not only monotheistic but universal. God was the "father and mother" of all creation, the guiding spirit of the universe.

The idea of God bestowing his blessings upon his creatures is most graphically represented in the Amarna paintings and reliefs which portray the solar disc, from which descend long rays terminating in human hands which hold the *ankh* or sign of life. Such a symbol suggests the power of deity in the affairs of men through the life-giving rays of the disc. In so picturing the deity, Ikhnaton formulated the profound idea of God's immanence, a concept which anticipated the modern liberal theology of the nineteenth century in Germany.

One of the most conspicuous elements in the religion of Ikhnaton is the joy of life, the sheer delight in God's creation. Here was a poet finding God in the contemplation of nature, in the enjoyment of sunshine, and in the simple life. God is the loving Father who caused the birds to flutter in their marshes, the sheep to dance in the fields and the fish to leap in the river. Such an elemental appreciation of nature has characterized all creative periods of history. The feeling of ecstasy and rapture in being a part of life, the *joie de vivre*, so prominent in the Amarna hymns, recalls a line of Browning: "How good is man's life, the mere living."

Aside from the short-lived Amarna heresy, the religion of Egypt, like the language and the social life, was for three millenniums a homogeneous and virtually unchanging tradition. This unchanging continuity was based on the metaphysical conviction that the universe is static, that there never was and never will be any change in this world or the next. It was this conviction that dictated the Egyptian's art, his morals and his literature. Moreover, he reasoned that only as the world was conceived as changeless could there be real meaning or ultimate reality. This conception, of course, is opposed to the modern philosophy of change but it assured the Egyptian of stability and reliability in the universe. It is therefore imperative that the modern interpreter of the Egyptian civilization see it *sui generis* and not comparatively. The rationalism of the Greeks and the evolutionary theism of the Western world are both irrelevant as regards Egyptian cosmology. The *a priori* principle of static changelessness is clearly manifest in the immortality of the god-king, the eternal rising and setting of the sun, and in the constancy of the Egyptian climate. All this was a permanent part of creation. The isolation and self-sufficiency of the country tended to support this belief. This is not to say, however, that Egypt was without international relations and foreign influences. But as far as the Egyptians were concerned, Egypt was not one among many, a land to which they had once migrated and might some day leave. It was an eternal fact. The state was not just a political organization, the product of man's devising; it was foreordained from the beginning, a part of creation. The king was God and as such had cosmic significance. Since he ruled by divine right as a part of the permanent order of things, no thought was ever given to rebellion against that rule. The cosmic consciousness in Egyptian thought, the concern for eternal values, and the oneness of life and death meant that life was to be lived *sub specie aeternitatis*, to use Spinoza's expression.

A thousand years before Ikhnaton, the Egyptians had found a term which summed up for them all that was highest and best in human life. It was the word *maat*, a term which stood for righteousness, justice, and truth. In the Old Kingdom it referred also to national order under the dominion of the sun-god. It signified the enduring state, organized under the god-king. With Ikhnaton *maat* came to denote the moral order, the realm of universal values under God. It was this cosmic principle that produced the Amarna monotheism or solar monism. The connotation of cosmic harmony found in *maat* resembles the Vedantic *Ananda*, which is equated with the Ultimate Reality or inner universal harmony, but even more closely with the Chinese *Tao* which represents the order and constancy of the universe, the cosmic system, the perfect way.

With the Egyptians *maat* referred to the divine order of nature, the eternal process established at the time of creation. In the Creation Story found in the Pyramid Texts *maat* replaced chaos; order took the place of disorder—an idea later echoed in the Genesis account of creation. It was the Pharaoh's function as a divinity to maintain *maat* in the sense of justice, truth, and order. Egyptian officials, in turn, representing the king, were guided by this same principle of order. It is therefore clear that the word *maat* had both ethical and metaphysical implications. In the latter sense, it expressed the basic Egyptian belief in the changelessness of the universe. Modern ideas of evolution, progress, flux, and revolution are completely foreign to this concept. The ethical aspect is seen in the attempt of man to enter into harmony with *maat* in all his doings. This meant respect for one's superiors, respect for another's property, fair dealing with inferiors, avoidance of arrogance and pride, moderation in all things, generosity, self-restraint, humility, and integrity.

LITERATURE

Our discussion of *maat* brings us finally to the literature of the Egyptian sages whose writings were devoted to the cultivation of the above-mentioned virtues. The philosophy behind the practice of these virtues was essentially utilitarian and pragmatic. The same can be said, to be sure, of the teachings in the biblical book of Proverbs which seems to have been based on the sayings of the Egyptian wise men. Perhaps the best known of these is Ptah Hotep, vizier of the Pharaoh Isesi (Fifth Dynasty). His proverbs were written for the guidance of his son in his administrative career, but they have also a universal appeal as instruction in the life of common sense, practical wisdom and humility.

Be not proud because of thy learning. Take counsel with the unlearned as with the learned, for the limit of a craft is not fixed and there is no craftsman whose worth is perfect. . . . A listener is one whom the god loves. . . . The good fortune of a man is his understanding. . . . How worthy it is when a son hearkens to his father! How many mishaps befall him who hearkens not! As for the fool who hearkens not, there is none who has done anything for him. He regards wisdom as ignorance, and what is profitable as useless.

If thou hast become great after thou wast little, and hast gained possessions after thou wast formerly in want, be not unmindful of how it was with thee before. Be not boastful of thy wealth, which has come to thee as a gift of the god. . . . Be not avaricious in dividing. . . . Be not avaricious towards thy kin. Greater is the fame of the gentle than [that of] the harsh. . . . Repeat not a word of hearsay. . . . If thou art a strong man, establish the respect of thee by wisdom and by quietness of speech.

Incline thine ears to hear my sayings,
And apply thine heart to their comprehension.
For it is a profitable thing to put them in thy heart,

But woe to him who transgresses them.
Remove not the landmark on the boundary of the fields.

. . . .

Be not greedy for a cubit of land,
And trespass not on the boundary of the widow.

Weary not thyself to seek for more,
When thy need is [already] secure.
If riches be brought to thee by robbery,
They will not abide the night with thee.

Better is poverty in the hand of God,
Than riches in the storehouse.
Better are loaves when the heart is joyous,
Than riches in unhappiness.

Better is praise as one whom men love,
Than riches in the storehouse.
Eat not bread in the presence of a great man,
Nor open thy mouth in his presence.
If thou sate thyself with unpermissible food,
It is but pleasure of thy spittle.
Look [only] upon the dish that is before thee,
And let it furnish thy need.

Consider for thyself these thirty chapters,
That they are satisfaction and instruction.

The wise sayings of Imhotep, the Grand Vizier of King Zoser of the Third Dynasty, and creator of the first stone architecture, were quoted for centuries after his death. His maxims and medical lore were known by the Greeks among whom he was known as the patron god of medical science. A popular treatise in praise of the profession of the scribe was the *Instruction of Akhthory, son of Duauf.* Outstanding among Egyptian literary masterpieces is the *Tale of Sinuhe*, an official under King Amenemhet (2000 B.C.). Upon the death of the king, Sinuhe fled to Palestine and Syria. The story is a record of his travel experiences and his return to Egypt and the royal palace. Other examples of secular literature are the *Admonitions of Ipuwer*, the *Prophecies of Neferti*, *The Miracles which happened in the Reign of King Cheops*, *The Tale of the Two Brothers*, *The Eloquent Peasant*, *The Foredoomed Prince*, *The Shipwrecked Sailor*, and the *Story of Wenamon*, envoy to Syria.

Outstanding in the non-religious literature are the Medical Papyri, some of which go back to the Twelfth Dynasty. The two most important are the Ebers and Edwin Smith Papyri of the Eighteenth Dynasty. These documents contain instructions for the treatment of many diseases and wounds. The Book of Surgery, probably handed down from the Pyramid Age, was copied by scribes in later centuries.

It remains for us to consider briefly the religious literature of the Old Kingdom which is concerned altogether with the hereafter and which set the standard of the Egyptian grammar and literary style. The oldest religious documents are the Pyramid Texts. These were wall-inscriptions found in the pyramid tombs of kings of the Fifth and Sixth Dynasties, but which were apparently derived from writings as remote as 3500 B.C. These texts contain incantations and prayers designed to guarantee the future happiness of the king. They constitute our oldest source of information about Osiris and the heavenly realm. They were written by the priests of Heliopolis who exalted Ra as the chief deity of Egypt and ruler of Heaven, but it was the Heaven of Osiris. The Pyramid Texts were copied and changed in the Ninth and Eighteenth Dynasties. New ideas were added to the old to stand side by side even though contradictory. Grossly materialistic conceptions are found together with more ethical teachings. Some of the texts, particularly those of Unas, are devoted to the ritual connected with the daily offerings in the pyramid temples.

The Coffin Texts were a collection of spells used for the protection of non-royal persons from the dangers encountered in the journey to the realm of Osiris, and incantations which would assure the deceased of the continuance of the pleasures and friendships of this life.

The so-called Book of the Dead, containing the same type of material as in the Coffin Texts, is more elaborate and really represents an accumulation of funerary spells over various periods as well as hymns to Osiris and Ra. These incantations were written on papyrus and placed in the tombs of nobles and officials throughout the history of Egypt. Those of the Eighteenth and Nineteenth Dynasties are the best examples of Egyptian calligraphy and colouring.

Other religious texts are The Ritual of the Funerary Cult, The Magical Papyri, The Litany of the Sun, and various hymns to the gods. Under the last might be included the Hymn to the Nile, Hymns to Amon-Ra, and the well-known Amarna hymns to Aton, written by Ikhnaton. It is surprising that so much of the literature of ancient Egypt has survived and what we have is probably only a fragment of the original intellectual output of this great civilization, which was already a legend when Greece came upon the world scene.

Unlike the Babylonian and Greek, the Egyptian literature, on the whole, was not so much an art form as a record of facts. There was myth but it was not of an epic quality. There was poetry but it was perhaps lacking in artistic value. The quality that characterizes the architecture and sculpture of Egypt also dominates the literature, and that is the sense of permanence and changelessness. But what is lacking in aesthetic worth is made up in the realm of moral values, a fact which Breasted more than any other Egyptologist recognized long ago. Here the Egyptians made a lasting contribution in spite of the fact that at times the moral criterion was dominated by the utilitarian motive. The Egyptians were concerned with a high way of living. True, their ideas underwent little change. Intellectual evolution is seldom if ever perceived in their literature. Nevertheless the feeling of serenity and divine authority seen in all the "teachings" is in some respects superior to the apprehension of the Hebrews and the uncertainty of the Babylonians.

In this introductory chapter we have made some generalizations about the culture of the ancient Egyptians, noting along the way some of their achievements in sculpture, painting, architecture, philosophy, religion, and literature. These achievements placed the Mediterranean civilization and the Western world forever in their debt. But the cities and their inhabitants that lined the banks of the river were an unknown quantity for the first eighteen hundred years of the Christian era. We would still know nothing of this great culture if it were not for the work of the archaeologist; and that is the burden of this book.

Chapter One

THE LOST LANGUAGE

AN UNKNOWN SOLDIER'S DISCOVERY

Napoleon, standing before the great pyramids of Giza, exhorted his legions: "Soldiers, forty centuries are looking down upon you!" This famous remark has by this time become somewhat shopworn. The reason for quoting it here is that it provides the clue to the history of Egyptian archaeology, which was dominated in its earlier phases almost completely by the French.

In Napoleon's plans, Egypt was just a stepping-stone to India, but his ill-fated invasion miscarried when Nelson, having finally caught up with the French fleet, dealt a telling blow in the sea battle of Abukir. The French army struggled on for a year but on 19th August 1799, Napoleon deserted the cause and sailed back to France.

What started as a military conquest, however, ended as a scientific achievement. Embarking with Napoleon when he started from Toulon for Egypt was a carefully chosen brain-trust of 175 scientists. These scholars—orientalists, cartographers, engineers, chemists, astronomers, geographers, artists, historians, physicians—took with them a vast library and a boat-load of scientific apparatus. They explored Egypt from Alexandria to the Sudan. They analysed the Nile mud; they inquired into the causes of oriental plague and trachoma; they investigated the possibility of cutting a canal through the Isthmus of Suez; they unearthed temples in Upper Egypt; they collected specimens of animals, plants, and minerals; they made plaster models of statues and transcripts of inscriptions.

One day a French soldier stumbled upon a slab of polished

black basalt bearing a polyglot inscription. Officers standing nearby were quick to surmise its value and had it transported to Cairo. This strange stele, found in 1799 near the town of Rosetta and therefore called the Rosetta Stone, became the key that unlocked the door to the mysteries of Egypt. It measured 3 feet 9 inches in height, 2 feet 4½ inches in width, and 11 inches thick. It was considerably damaged on three sides. It was made up of three panels, each in a different type of writing. Actually, it was inscribed in two languages but in three scripts. Plaster copies of the stone were made and sent to Paris for study. The stone itself was supposed to follow but in 1802 the British took possession of Egypt and also all the antiquities acquired there by the French, including the Rosetta Stone—but not before one of Napoleon's generals, who was also a scholar, translated the bottom register, which was in Greek. He found that the stone contained a message, inscribed in 196 B.C. by some Memphite priests, praising King Ptolemy Epiphanes for his benefactions and granting him divine honours. It was inferred from the Greek text that the other two panels carried the same message and might be deciphered by means of a comparative analysis. But that turned out to be a tough problem, requiring twenty-three years and the intensive study of many scholars for its solution.

The upper register was written in hieroglyphic or pictograph style, examples of which had been observed previously by explorers in Egypt, but the script was still a completely unknown quantity. The middle panel was in Demotic, a form developed from the Hieratic writing, which was in turn a short-hand or cursive development of the hieroglyphic form. It was also learned from the Greek version that other copies of the edict were to be set up in all the chief temples of Egypt. How many copies were made is not known but some actually have been found, one of them at Nubayrah in Lower Egypt in the latter part of the nineteenth century. After the arrival of the Rosetta Stone in the British Museum, scholars from France, Italy, Germany, and England attacked the problem of the two upper panels but with no results.

The first important name connected with the decipherment was that of the French orientalist Sylvestre deSacy who in 1802, concentrating on the Demotic text, recognized several names, chiefly that of Ptolemy. Beyond the observation that the Demotic was an "alphabetic writing", he made no progress and gave up the problem as insoluble.

Following deSacy, the Swedish diplomat J. D. Akerblad took up the task and succeeded in identifying in the Demotic version all the proper names that occurred in the Greek section as well as a few other words. His mistaken conclusion that Demotic was entirely alphabetic led him into a blind alley and he also capitulated. For a decade thereafter, work on the Rosetta Stone was monopolized by charlatans and mystics whose deductions, needless to say, resulted in confusion worse confounded.

THOMAS YOUNG AND THE "ROYAL RINGS"

Real progress towards the goal was made in 1814 when the attention of Thomas Young was drawn to the problem. Young, a Cambridge physicist and physician, was already famous for his discoveries in the field of optics and particularly his wave theory of light. He was also an Egyptologist by avocation and had mastered a dozen Near Eastern languages before he was thirty. Observing that the Demotic was the most complete version, the top and bottom panels having been greatly damaged, Young concentrated on the middle section. He knew that the Egyptian script ran from right to left. He then tried to relate the Greek words to their Demotic equivalents. The starting-point for such a procedure would be to find words in the Greek panel that were repeated. Noticing that the names Alexander and Alexandria were repeated in two different lines of the Greek, he found in the corresponding section of the Demotic version two groups of signs that were alike. It was logical, therefore, to assume that he had found the Demotic signs for Alexander and Alexandria. This procedure was facilitated by the fact that the word "king" occurred thirty-seven times in the Greek; so it was not difficult to locate the Demotic equivalent by finding the word in that panel which was constantly repeated. In like manner the name "Ptolemy", appearing eleven times in the Greek, was ascertained. Furthermore, it was seen that royal names in the Demotic were surrounded by the cartouche or oval in abbreviated form.

Young's research resulted finally in the publication of a Demotic vocabulary and a translation of the middle register. This
translation was later shown to be faulty because the two Egyptian
versions of the original Greek text of the decree were not literal
translations but only paraphrases. Passing to the study of the
hieroglyphics, Young reasoned that this form of writing would
be partly phonetic. On that basis it should be possible to determine the phonetic value of royal names since they were identified
by the cartouche. Such was the case with the name ''Ptolemy''
which appeared in the hieroglyphic panel.

He also learned that the hieroglyphs were partly alphabetic and
that the sign for Ptolemy varied both in the Demotic and the
hieroglyphic writing. Beyond this, Young could not go. His contribution was highly significant. He had found that the cartouches
contained royal names, that they should be read from the direction which the signs faced and that the language was a combination
of phonetic and alphabetic characters to which at times determinatives (a picture of a complete word) were added.

THE GENIUS OF CHAMPOLLION

The final chapter of the mystery of the Rosetta Stone, like the
first, was written by a Frenchman. When Jean François Champollion (1790–1832) was a boy of eleven, he met the famous
mathematician Jean-Baptiste Fourier, who showed him some
papyri and stone tablets bearing hieroglyphs. ''Can anyone read
them?'' he asked. When he was assured that no one could, the
boy promptly replied: ''I will do it.'' The announcement proved
to be prophetic for it was he who later finished the task begun
by Thomas Young.

Champollion wrote a book when he was twelve and at thirteen
he was reading Arabic, Syriac, and Coptic. From this point until
he died, everything he did was related to Egyptology. At seven-

teen he compiled a chronology of the Egyptian kings and in the same year, 1807, he was made a member of the faculty of the Lycée of Grenoble. The one thing that haunted him perpetually was the enigmatic Rosetta Stone, a copy of which he had seen at the home of Fourier. In Paris he buried himself in oriental studies and perfected his Coptic and Arabic. During those years of intensive study it was only the devotion and constant financial help of his brother, Figeac, that kept Jean François alive. He was continuously in poor health and was barely able to keep body and soul alive. Unable to appear in public for lack of decent clothes, he wasted away in his damp cold room while his brother sought ways of finding money to aid him.

In 1808 Champollion decided that he was ready to start work on the Stone. He had succeeded in deciphering a few words and had begun to feel the warm glow of success when the news came to him of the complete reading of the hieroglyphic inscription. The shock upon hearing this soon gave way to relief as he realized that the so-called decipherment was the work of a quack and was sheer nonsense. He plunged feverishly into his task but it was to take fourteen years or more for its completion.

Returning to Grenoble, he began lecturing in history. He compiled a Coptic dictionary and wrote plays and political satires. He became a reformer and went about the country preaching the doctrines of academic freedom and political liberty. The itinerary of Napoleon's triumphal return to Paris included Grenoble. Figeac, a loyal supporter of the emperor, was made Napoleon's private secretary. Champollion was present at the formal appointment. Napoleon was impressed with his accomplishments and later called upon him at the university. The meeting had its own dramatic irony: the one having attacked Egypt and failed; the other about to wage his Egyptian campaign and win. With Napoleon's downfall and the restoration of the Bourbons, Champollion was dismissed from the university on charges of treason. He left the city and resumed his hieroglyphic studies.

Following Horapollon's description of the hieroglyphs in the fourth century as purely picture writing, all later untrained investigators were inclined to interpret the Egyptian writing in fanciful symbolic terms. Scholars and laymen alike, giving full rein to their imagination, saw in the Rosetta Stone apocalyptic

prophecies, cabalistic signs, Gnostic revelations, medieval astro-
logy, and biblical references. Profiting by Young's research,
Champollion now showed that the purely ideographic interpretation, at least in Middle and Late Egyptian, was erroneous. His
treatment of the problem began with the theory that the hieroglyphs were both alphabetic signs and phonetic symbols. His
starting-point was the royal cartouche of Ptolemy which was found
in the hieroglyphic section of the Stone. His work was given a significant boost at this time by the discovery of an obelisk at Philae.
This obelisk fortunately carried a message in Greek and hieroglyph
and, like the Rosetta Stone, bore the name of Ptolemy in a
cartouche. It contained also another oval ring which, when compared with the Greek inscription, was seen to represent the
hieroglyphs for the name Cleopatra.

The Philae obelisk, inscribed by the priests of the island, was
addressed to King Ptolemy VII, Queen Cleopatra II, and Queen
Cleopatra III, all three of whom reigned simultaneously. It requested the discontinuance of raids made upon the temple funds
by army officials. The request was granted and the priests consequently erected the obelisk in front of the Isis temple as a warning
to all future offenders. The fallen column was found in 1815 by
W. J. Bankes who later had it shipped to England. The Philae
obelisk therefore played a role in the story of the decipherment
almost as important as that of the Rosetta Stone because Champollion, by comparing the Ptolemy and Cleopatra ovals, was able

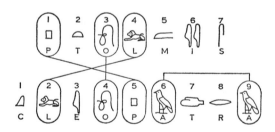

to confirm immediately his reading of three hieroglyphic signs, for it was now clear that the first, third, and fourth signs in the name Ptolemy coincided with the fifth, fourth, and second signs in the name Cleopatra.

This left the other signs in each name unconfirmed. The "aio" of the Greek *Ptolemaios* or the "i" of *Ptolmis* was represented in the hieroglyphics by the signs "⟨⟨⟨⟩"; and the "e" of Cleopatra by "⟨⟩". The "t" (⌒) of Ptolemy apparently differed from the "t" (⊂⊃) of Cleopatra, but by inserting the English letters, of which he was sure, Champollion could easily guess the others, at least for the time being. He assumed that since *Ptolemaios* ends in "s", the sign "⟨⟩" must stand for "s", and since the sixth and ninth signs in the Cleopatra cartouche were the same, it followed that the two signs must stand for "a". The extra signs at the end of the Cleopatra cartouche (⌒ over ○) had been identified by Young as a feminine termination and usually appeared at the end of the name of a goddess or queen.

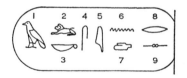

Encouraged by this progress, Champollion continued to add to his hieroglyphic vocabulary. This he did by means of two additional cartouches that came to his attention.

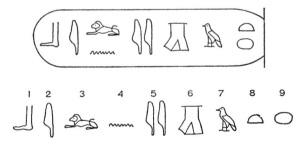

In the above cartouche of nine signs Champollion recognized all but three and that was enough to suggest to him the name Alexander. From the Greek ALKSENTRS he surmised that 3, 6, and 9 were K, N, and S. In the second cartouche: numbers 2, 3, 4, 5, 7, 8, and 9 had already been identified. The last two signs indicated a royal lady. Since the Greek inscription that accompanied this text mentioned BERENIKE, it was concluded that 1 was B and 6 was K.

Proceeding thus, Champollion was able in a short time to read the hieroglyphs for many Greek and Roman rulers of the Ptolemaic period. His attention was then drawn to a hieroglyphic text from a date preceding the Hellenistic period. It contained the following cartouche:

The first sign stood for the sun, which was pronounced Ra in Coptic, and the last two signs were recognized as the double S. He connected the middle sign with the Coptic "MS" which means "child of" or "to be born". The whole cartouche, he concluded, meant Ramses, born of Ra. By the same method he identified

as "Thutmose" or "Thotmes, Child of Thoth" or "Thoth is born", the ibis being the sign for the god Thoth.

The farther back in history he went, the more Champollion realized that the hieroglyphs were not entirely phonetic but symbolic or ideographic as well. He also found that some English letters had two different equivalents in the hieroglyphic system.

Champollion had never left his studio but he knew Egypt from one end to the other. As the director of the newly formed Egyptian section of the Louvre and professor of Egyptology at

the Collège de France, the great decipherer at last came into his
own and was privileged to see Egypt first hand. His expedition,
which lasted from July 1828 to December 1829, was a fitting
climax to his life of study as one after another of his theories
were confirmed by investigations in the field. He discovered
buried temples, deciphered unknown inscriptions, stood speech-
less before the gigantic columns of the Isis temple at Dendera
and astounded his companions with his knowledge of Egyptian
chronology.

Three years after his return to Paris Champollion died. His
posthumous publications, *Grammaire Egyptienne* and *Dictionnaire
Egyptienne*, were bequeathed to later scholars as a foundation
upon which to build. Some nineteenth-century authorities rejected his theories but others came to his support. It was only
towards the end of the century that he was accorded his proper
niche in the history of Egyptology. Richard Lepsius in 1866 discovered another "Rosetta Stone" in the Decree of Canopus, and
his study of this tri-lingual inscription resulted in the first important validation of Champollion's work. Incidentally, this
decree, addressed to Ptolemy III Euergetes I in 238 B.C., proposed that a day be added to the calendar every fourth year, since
it was clear that there was a discrepancy or time-lag in the exist-
ing chronology. Hieroglyphic study was greatly advanced by the
later contributions of Gaston Maspero, Adolf Erman, Kurt Sethe,
Elmar Edel, and Sir Alan Gardiner.[1]

HISTORY OF EGYPTIAN WRITING

It had been apparent to Champollion that the hieroglyphs of
the pre-Hellenistic period were different from those of the
Ptolemaic era. Further investigation now showed that there were
three distinct periods: Old, Middle, and Late Egyptian. It also
became clear that the first elaborate hieroglyphs, which were in

---

[1] Gardiner's *Egyptian Grammar* (Third Edition, London, Oxford University
Press, 1957) is unequalled as an introduction to the Middle Egyptian language.
For a systematic account of the work done on the Rosetta Stone and a study
of the early Greek references to the hieroglyph, see E. A. Wallis Budge: *The
Mummy; Chapters on Egyptian Funereal Archaeology*. New York, Biblo and Tannen,
1964, pp. 108–53.

existence as early as 3000 B.C., gradually lost much of their pictorial character and very early assumed an abbreviated or shorthand form called Hieratic. This transition was occasioned by the necessity of speed in writing government documents, letters, and business transactions. Hieroglyphs were cut in stone and wood with unbelievable accuracy, the depth ranging anywhere from $\frac{1}{16}$ of an inch to 1 inch. They were also sculptured in high relief and painted. The sky and heavenly objects were coloured blue; animals and birds were painted as far as possible in their original colours; men were painted in red and women in yellow or light brown. Contemplating a lengthy inscription on an obelisk or temple wall today, one can imagine the time and effort that went into such magnificent work, in which every sign was perfectly carved. Inscriptions in stone for official state or religious purposes, designed to remain stationary, were cut with bronze, copper, or iron chisels.

Correspondence, official documents, texts of the Book of the Dead, preliminary drafts of messages to be cut in stone, and personal documents of all kinds naturally required something other than stone. For such things papyrus was used from the earliest times. Papyrus was a plant which grew to a height of 12 feet or more. Strips of the pith or inner part of the stalk were placed vertically side by side upon a board and upon these other strips were placed horizontally. The two layers were glued together with the juice of the plant, pressed, dried, and rubbed smooth. The result was a practical and durable sheet of writing-paper. The horizontal side was used as the writing surface. If more than one sheet was required, others were joined to it. The width of papyri sheets varied from 3 to 17 inches. One of the longest rolls known is the Harris Papyrus (from the time of Ramses II) which measures 135 feet in length. The scribes used a reed brush-like pen and an ink made of vegetable substances of coloured earth mixed with gum and water.

Obviously it was impossible to achieve on papyrus the clarity and precision of the stone hieroglyphs. The scribe in time naturally resorted to a modified form of the hieroglyph, especially in view of the quantity of things to be written and the short time he had to write them. Hence, the appearance of the Hieratic or cursive form, used at times by priests (*hieros*, Greek, meaning "sacred") in copying religious and literary texts. Its rounded forms resulted from the rapid use of a reed-pen on papyrus as contrasted to the pictorial and more sharply defined hieroglyphic characters made by chisel on stone. The Hieratic writing was in existence during the First Dynasty and continued to function along with the hieroglyphic form throughout the history of ancient Egypt. The use of Hieratic seems to be paralleled by the Babylonian cuneiform and also the Chinese writing. All early cultures probably started with the pictograph system of writing which tended to disappear in favour of the simplified method. The hieroglyph, however, continued in use through the first four centuries of the Christian era.

About 800 B.C. a new style of writing appeared called Demotic —a modification of the Hieratic script, which rapidly disappeared. Originally designed for commercial purposes and private letters, the Demotic eventually attained prominence in priestly circles and was used as a second script in important public documents, stelae and obelisks. It was used after the fifth century A.D.

Champollion's approach to the problem of the hieroglyphs was facilitated by his expert knowledge of the Coptic language. This script dates from the early third century of the Christian era when Christianity appeared in Egypt. With this occurrence, what little knowledge of hieroglyphics existed at that time vanished when the scribal schools and temples were closed. The Egyptian language then took the form of Coptic, a script written with the Greek alphabet plus six Demotic characters and sustaining a relation to the ancient Egyptian somewhat similar to that of Italian to Latin. The Coptic script used vowels but while it is the only connecting link with the pronunciation of the ancient Egyptian language, it was greatly influenced by Greek and contains many biblical and theological expressions. This language, which owes much to the early Church Fathers in Egypt, represents, as far as scholars can ascertain, sounds of the original Egyptian words. The Christian Egyptians, called Copts, continued to live in Egypt, survived the Arab conquest in the seventh century, and today number more than a million. The Coptic spoken language, however, gave way to Arabic in the sixteenth century. Roughly speaking, aside from a hieroglyphic fragment from the fourth century, found near Aswan, hieroglyphics was a lost language from the second until the nineteenth century A.D.

Hieroglyphics were used in four ways: (1) alphabetic, a uni-lateral sign indicating a single sound; (2) syllabic, the combination of two or three consonants, usually without vowels; (3) word-signs, a picture of an object which in itself stands for one word; and (4) determinatives, the picture of an object which has been spelled by separate signs and which comes after the alphabetic or syllabic signs as a summary. In simpler terms, the language might be described as consisting of two classes of signs: (1) sense-signs or ideograms which signify the object depicted (⊙ – sun; ᨾ – hill country) or, less obviously, ⌑⍦, a scribe's palette, water, and reed-holder, all representing "scribe"; (2) sound-signs or phonograms, which have sound values (⬭ r). What makes hieroglyphics not the easiest language to read is the absence of vowels or, if expressed, their changing position in relation to the consonants. A further difficulty is presented by the variety of sign arrangements. Hieroglyphics appear both in perpendicular columns and in horizontal lines. As a rule, if they appear in a horizontal line, they are to be read from right to left as in most Semitic languages, but frequently the reverse is found. Occa-sionally they follow the boustrophedon forms (turning like oxen in ploughing) in which case the lines run alternately from right to left and from left to right. Sometimes the lines begin in the middle and go outwards. Generally, one reads an inscription in the direction which the characters face; that is, the signs face the beginning of the line.

Although the hieroglyphic writing throughout the 3,000 years of its existence was chiefly in the hands of the conservative scribal caste, there was nevertheless considerable change both in the vocabulary and the characters or signs. The history of the language can be divided roughly into three stages: Old Egyptian, Middle Egyptian, and Late Egyptian (to which may be added the later development of Demotic and Coptic). Middle Egyptian is considered the definitive classical style chiefly because of its con-sistent orthography. As far as literary compositions and monu-mental inscriptions are concerned, it was used from the Ninth through the Eighteenth Dynasties (2240–1314 B.C.) and was revived by scribes in the Saite Period (715–525 B.C.). Strictly

Rosetta Stone. Key to the decipherment of the hieroglyphic writing.
(*Courtesy, British Museum*)

Slate palette of King Narmer (recto). (*Courtesy, Metropolitan Museum of Art, New York*)

Scribe's equipment. Scribe's palette; wood, Ptolemaic; from Gerza. Scribe's ink saucer; obsidian; Twelfth Dynasty; from Lisht. Palette and writing utensils; wood; from Sheik Abd el-Kurna. Inkwell; wood, Middle Kingdom; from Thebes. (*Courtesy, Metropolitan Museum of Art, New York*)

speaking, Middle Egyptian belongs to the Middle Kingdom (Dynasties 9–13) but it continued to be used for official inscriptions in the Eighteenth Dynasty. However, starting with the Amarna period, literary texts and business documents were written in what can only be described as New Egyptian. Despite the dialectical differences and changes in the spoken form, the written language of Egypt, scholars are agreed, remained essentially the same from 3000 B.C. to the Ptolemaic period.

The family relationship of the Egyptian language is still a controversial problem with some authorities claiming a Hamitic background, others, Semitic, and still others, Afro-Asiatic.[1] All three, of course, are closely related. The rigidity and formality of Egyptian art is reflected in the hieroglyph itself as is also the objective, concise character of Egyptian thought. The hieroglyphic system was a derivation of an earlier pre-dynastic art form used for recording history. This pictorial representation took the form of a rebus containing pictures of objects which suggested certain words, a good example of which is the slate palette of Narmer from the First Dynasty. In this early illustration of the transition from the purely pictorial form to the real hieroglyphs, the king's name is represented by a picture of a fish (nar) and a chisel (mer); and the god Horus is symbolized as capturing the people of the Delta region. The picture, in other words, was used to indicate the name of somebody or something which had the same sound. The hieroglyphics retained the pictorial element (the ideogram) but combined with it the phonetic sign (the phonogram). In the first, the sense-sign, the object is pictorially shown; in the second, the sound-sign, the object is indicated by a sign that carries a certain sound. An ideogram, therefore, is a picture of the object itself; whereas a phonogram is a sign or combination of signs having a phonetic value. The phonogram consists of one, two, or three consonants and occurs without vowels, thus permitting a variety of word possibilities

[1] Thomas O. Lambdin in his bibliographical study of the question concludes that "Egyptian consists of an early level of Hamitic, itself related to Semitic, to which has been added at several distinct periods a large amount of Semitic speech material as a result both of actual invasion and of commercial content." "Egypt: Its Language and Literature" in *The Bible and the Ancient Near East*; ed. by G. Ernest Wright (New York, Doubleday, 1961), p. 290.

for the same combination of consonants. The English letters b t, for instance, could stand for bat, bet, bit, bot or but. This often leads to guesswork on the part of the translator but context usually helps. At times it is quite impossible to determine the vowel. The Coptic often provides a clue but since Coptic is related only to the last stage of Egyptian, it is not always reliable. This predicament explains why some authorities use the spelling Ikhnaton, while others prefer Akhnaton, or Nefertiti and Nofretete.

The uniconsonantal phonograms numbered about thirty if one includes some half-vowels that have no English equivalents. The chief signs are as on opposite page:[1]

The mysterious writing of the ancient Egyptians was a source of awe and wonder to the Greeks and they called the figures "hieroglyphs" or "sacred signs". Their vividness and clarity are just as amazing to modern man as they were to the Greeks. Where else does one find such perfection of form? But there is more than meets the eye in this precise calligraphy. It was symbolic as well as aesthetic and it is no wonder that hieroglyphics was regarded as magical writing.

The modern Chinese artist with his brush and black ink regards his painting as a form of writing. The ancient Egyptian scribe saw his pictorial writing conversely as a work of art and himself as an artist. The Chinese painting in fact is calligraphy while the Egyptian writing is decorative art. The hieroglyphs, so cleanly incised in stone or gracefully stroked on papyrus, are unquestionably the most beautiful system of writing ever devised by man.

[1] After Gardiner.

Hieroglyphic Sign	Transliteration	Object Depicted	Approximate Sound Value and Remarks
	3	vulture or hawk	glottal or aspirate A; like Hebrew Aleph
	'	reed	consonantal y; like Hebrew yod
or \\	y	reeds or strokes	y
	'	forearm	guttural sound corresponding to Heb. ayin
	w	quail chick	w or u
	b	foot	b
	p	stool	p
	f	horned viper	f
	m	owl	m
	n	water	n
	r	mouth	r
	h	reed shelter	h as in English; Heb. he
	ḥ	twisted flax	rough or emphatic h
	ḫ	placenta	like German ch
	ẖ	animal's belly	similar to above sound
	s	bolt or folded cloths	voiced and unvoiced s
	š	pond, lake	sh
	ḳ	hill-slope	like English Q; Heb. qoph
	k	basket with handle	k; Heb. kaph
	g	a stand for jar	hard g
	t	loaf	t
	ṯ	tethering rope	like Ger. tsch
	d	hand	
	ḏ	snake	ds or dj
	w		abbreviation for above hieroglyph w
	m		alphabetic m
	t		biliteral used with i

Chapter Two

EARLY EXPLORATION

HERODOTUS: FOREIGN CORRESPONDENT

Modern archaeology in the sense of scientific excavation, Egyptian or otherwise, started with W. M. F. Petrie in 1880, but from the standpoint of exploration and discovery our story must start with Herodotus, "the Father of History", who was born in 480 B.C. in Halicarnassus (now Bodrum).[1] Although his home was on the coast of Asia Minor, like Hippocrates and Thales who were born there also, he was thoroughly Greek. In connection with a new translation of *The Histories*, Harry Carter describes Herodotus as follows:

> The character of Herodotus emerges from his book: a lovable man, cheerful, eager to learn, self-reliant in his judgments, tolerant and broad-minded, respectful of virtue, magnanimity and delicacy, humorous and peace-loving, always ready to admire and wonder. The strength of his intellect and memory are attested by the way he marshals his material and puts in the right place so much that he must have carried in his head—only once does he have to add a postscript to something he had said earlier (VII, 239). Nearly all his faults are likeable too: he is careless in describing battles, is grossly superstitious, but believes in good rather than evil spirits and heartening rather than gloomy prophecies, muddle-headed where philosophy and civil engineering are concerned, discursive, vague and given to exaggeration, indulgent towards plausible rogues.[2]

[1] Mention must be made of Solon, the Athenian law-giver, who, even before Herodotus, visited Egypt during the reign of Amasis in the Saite period.

[2] *The Histories of Herodotus of Halicarnassus* (New York, Heritage Press, 1958), Vol. I, Intro. p. XVII.

This appraisal of the character of Herodotus provides the key to his writings, which admittedly are not as accurate as those of our best modern historians; but his stock has gone up rather than down with present-day scholars and, when checked by archaeological evidence, his history turns out to be fairly reliable.

Herodotus travelled in Egypt as far south as Aswan. He picked up much information as well as misinformation from guides, priests, and tomb robbers, but he seems to have discriminated rather well between the historical and the apocryphal. It is in personal observations that he gives the impression of authenticity. He discusses in detail such varied items as the Egyptian calendar of twelve months, Egyptian astronomy, the geography of Egypt, the Delta region, agriculture, village life among the ancient Egyptians, methods of capturing a crocodile, medical practices, and the annual flooding of the Nile. In regard to the last topic he regarded as questionable but somewhat plausible the report that the melting snows from the mountains of Central East Africa were the cause. It is known now that the monsoons are a further cause of the inundation.

Herodotus' description of mummification coincides well with what we know today of this ancient Egyptian art.

> The most painstaking manner of embalming goes by the name of one whom it would be unseemly to mention in this connexion; the second way that they offer is not so good or so costly, and a third is cheaper still. Then they ask the mourners in which fashion they will have the body prepared. And these, having agreed on a price, go their ways; leaving the body with the embalmers. To do this work in the most thorough fashion they first draw out part of the brain through the nostrils with an iron hook and use drugs to dissolve the rest. Next, they make an incision in the side, using a sharp-edged piece of Ethiopian stone, and take out all the intestines. They clean the inside of the corpse by washing it with palm-wine and again with pounded spices. Then they stuff the belly with pure myrrh, pounded fine, and cassia and other such spices, excepting frankincense, and sew up the vent. After this, they keep the body buried in saltpetre seventy days to embalm it; for it is forbidden to embalm it longer. At the end of the seventy days they wash the whole body and bind it with bandages of fine linen and coat it with gum, which the Egyptians commonly use instead of glue. The relatives, when they receive the mummified body, make for it a wooden case, shaped like

a man; and having put the body inside and sealed it up, they stand it in a sepulchre, upright against a wall.

That, then, is how they treat the dead for those who choose the costliest fashion. For those who would avoid so great an expense, choosing the second manner, they act thus. They charge syringes with oil of cedar and with them fill the belly of the corpse without making an incision or taking out the intestines, but injecting the oil through the vent and stopping it from returning. Then they embalm the body for the due number of days; and on the last of these they let the oil run out again. By its peculiar virtue the oil brings out all the intestines and the vitals liquefied, and the flesh being meantime consumed by the saltpetre, nothing remains but skin and bones. In this state they give back the body and do no more to it.

The third way of embalming is used for poor men. It consists simply in cleansing the belly with a purge of radish-oil and the embalming for seventy days, after which those who brought the body fetch it away.[1]

Even today we have no completely authentic knowledge of mummification.[2] We do know that the excellent state of preservation was due both to climate and embalming. By the Nineteenth Dynasty (1305–1200 B.C.) the process of embalming was so advanced that mummies of kings like Seti I and Ramses II have preserved perfectly the facial likeness and individual features. An important procedure not mentioned by Herodotus was the placing of the viscera and the heart in vases or "canopic jars" which were placed near the mummy in the tomb. After the removal of the internal organs, the abdominal cavity was washed and cleansed with wine and spices and filled with aromatic substances and then sewn up again. The cheeks and breasts were padded and the orifices of the body were plugged and sealed. The corpse was then washed and soaked in brine, as Herodotus notes, for seventy days. At the conclusion of this period the body was washed again and wrapped in linen strips which were smeared with gum on the under side. The embalmers were most meticu-

[1] Ibid., pp. 123, 124.

[2] The word mummy comes from the Arabic mumiya meaning "pitch". The Arabs used the word to indicate a mixture of pitch and myrrh, which was sold for medical purposes in Europe in the sixteenth century and later. In ancient Egypt pitch or some bituminous substance was poured on the mummy wrappings.

lous and artistic in the designing of the linen wrappings. The corpse was then placed in a nest of wooden coffins, each one being covered with inscriptions from the Book of the Dead.

The most elaborate observations of Herodotus were those dealing with the pyramids of Giza.

For first he (Cheops) closed all the temples and prevented the people from making sacrifices, and then he made all the Egyptians work for him. Some he allotted to haulage from the stone-quarries in the Arabian mountains called Libyan. One hundred thousand men at a time worked for three months. Ten years of this forced labour were consumed merely in making the causeway along which the stones were hauled, which work, I consider, was hardly less than building the *pyramid*; for it is five furlongs in length, ten fathoms wide, and its height, where it is highest, ten fathoms; and it is all made of stones dressed and carved with images. Ten years, they say, were taken by this work and the making of underground chambers for the king's burial in the hill on which the pyramids stand, which he turned into an island by cutting a canal from the Nile. The pyramid itself took twenty years to build: it is square, each face being eight hundred feet wide, and the height the same, and made of dressed stones most exactly laid, none measuring less than thirty feet.

This pyramid was built after the manner of steps, which some call "ramparts" and others "altar-steps". When this first stage of the construction had been completed, the remaining stones were raised by means of contrivances of short logs of wood, being lifted first from the ground to the first tier of the steps, and from there to a second contrivance erected on the first tier, and from that to the second tier and onto another of the contrivances. Either they made one of these contrivances for every tier, or else they had only one of them so made as to be easily carried from one tier to another: I record both methods, for both are reported. The highest part was the first to be finished, and then the part next below it, and last they finished the lowest part that rests on the ground. There are inscriptions in Egyptian characters on the pyramid telling how much was spent on radishes and onions and garlic for the workmen, and if I remember rightly what the interpreter told me when he read me the inscriptions, they cost a thousand and six hundred talents of silver. Now, if that is so, how much must have been spent on the iron used for the work and on food and clothing for the workmen? For I have said how long a time was taken by the building, and I am sure the hewing of the stones and the haulage and the digging of the underground works took no little time.[1]

This passage is followed by a description of the building of the pyramids of Chephren and Mycerinus. The modern reader will notice several inaccuracies in the above quotation. There was no canal to the pyramids and no water under them. The measurements, like those of later explorers, are also wrong and the method of construction only partially correct. The builders may have used such machines or "rockers" to elevate the stone blocks but today the principle of the long inclined plane and rollers would seem to be more satisfactory. His reference to "dressed stones" indicates that in his time the casing of polished limestone was still intact on the Cheops Pyramid.

Brief mention must be made here of three other Greek travellers. The first was Diodorus Siculus, an historian who was in Egypt during the Roman occupation from 60 to 57 B.C. Diodorus had evidently read what Herodotus wrote about the pyramids and contributes little in addition except to mention "mounds" of sand or long ramps used in the construction of the pyramids. He says that 360,000 men worked on the Cheops Pyramid which took twenty years to complete.

The seated colossal statues of Amenhotep III at Thebes were mistakenly called the Colossi of Memnon by the Greeks (the Homeric hero Memnon). They also called the nearby mortuary temple of Ramses II the Memnonium. Diodorus, however, came a little closer in calling it the tomb of Ozymandias (Greek for *User-maat-Re*, the real name of Ramses).[2] Diodorus describes the courts of the temple and quotes "an inscription found on one of the statues of Ramses. 'My name is Ozymandias, king of kings; if any would know how great I am and where I lie, let him surpass me in any of my works.' " The largest of the three statues of the Ramesseum in the time of Diodorus lay broken on the ground, as it was so described by many later explorers. Originally it was almost as high as the "Colossi of Memnon".

Strabo, a contemporary of Diodorus, accompanied the Roman prefect of Egypt, Aelius Gallus, on his expedition to Upper Egypt in 25 B.C. His observations are recorded in the seventeenth

[1] *Ibid.*, pp. 140, 141.
[2] The probable source of Shelley's poem *Ozymandias*.

book of his *Geography*. He estimated that there were some forty royal tombs in the Valley of the Kings. He also records that he entered the Great Pyramid but his description is brief and somewhat inaccurate.

Finally, there was the Greek geographer, Pausanius, of the second century A.D., whose travels took him to Egypt where he saw the pyramids, stood among the columns of Karnak, and heard the "singing" of the Colossi of Memnon.

Pliny the Elder (A.D. 23–79), a Roman military officer and naturalist, was interested chiefly in the Giza Pyramids, which he describes in his *Natural History*. He apparently thought that the pyramids were treasure vaults rather than just tombs, for he observes that "the only motive for constructing them was a determination not to leave their treasures to their successors or to rivals". He emphasizes the ostentation of the Pharaohs in constructing these monuments and refers to them as "stupendous memorials to their (the kings') vanity". He entered the Cheops Pyramid and mentioned a "deep well which communicates with the river, it is thought". He speaks with awe and mystery of the Sphinx which "is looked upon as a divinity by the people".

Throughout the Middle Ages many Arab travellers explored Egypt but were concerned mainly with the pyramids of Giza. Their legendary accounts reveal only an interest in treasure-hunting and have little scientific or historical value.[1]

EUROPEANS AT THE PYRAMIDS

In the period from 1500 to 1800 there were sporadic invasions of Egypt by English and European explorers but few of them ventured beyond the pyramids of Giza. In 1553 a European by the name of Bellonius is reported to have entered the Great Pyramid as far as the burial chamber and mentioned that the Chephren Pyramid had no opening. Both had been entered by the Arabs in the Middle Ages but the opening of the Second Pyramid had probably been covered by the desert sand. In the middle of the sixteenth century the limestone casing of the

[1] For quotations from Arab writers see Leonard Cottrell: *The Mountains of Pharaoh* (New York, Rinehart, 1956), pp. 46–60, and R. W. Howard-Vyse and J. S. Perring: *Operations Carried on at the Pyramids of Giza in 1837*, 3 vols. (London, J. Fraser, 1840–42).

Cheops Pyramid was only partly missing while that of the Second Pyramid was practically intact. A few years later a Frenchman, Jean Palmerme, explored the Giza group but his observations duplicate those of his predecessor. In 1610 Sandys, an Englishman, in his "Travels" relates in great detail how he entered the First Pyramid and correctly notes that it was not a treasure vault but the tomb of the king.

A more important contribution to pyramidology was made by John Greaves of Oxford who was in Egypt in 1638 and later wrote his *Pyramidographia*. This book contains not only the first scientific measurements of the Great Pyramid but also the first accurate drawing of the interior. The sketch, entitled "The Inside of the First and Fairest Pyramid", shows the entrance passage, the ascending corridor, the first gallery, the well, the grand gallery, the king's chamber, the descending corridor, and the queen's chamber, all of which were carefully measured.

Greaves was also the first explorer to cut free from the Arab legend and European mysticism which surrounded the Great Pyramid. (This esoteric interpretation of its dimensions and angles has continued among various groups and individuals down to our day.) His conclusions regarding the function of the pyramid as a royal tomb and symbol of immortality and its particular form as being most conducive to endurance need no modification today.

One of the most distinguished of the eighteenth-century pyramidologists was Richard Pococke, his distinction being that he investigated not only the Giza pyramids but those at Dashur and Sakkara and was probably the first European to describe the Step Pyramid of Zoser.[1] Pococke's importance is also seen in his identification of the mastabas of Giza as the tombs of nobles and princes. His experiences in Egypt make exciting reading but we pass on to name one more early European traveller—a Mr. Davison, who was the first to descend the "well" at the entrance to the Grand Gallery of the Cheops Pyramid. This shaft was found to be about 150 feet deep.[2]

---

[1] *Travels in Egypt* (London, 1755).

[2] The "well", further explored by Caviglia in 1817, extended, in fact, to a depth of 200 feet and apparently served as an escape route, connecting with the descending or entrance gallery.

EARLY ARTISTS IN EGYPT

When Napoleon sailed to Egypt he was accompanied by Dominique Vivant Denon, whom Josephine had recommended as a draftsman and illustrator. Thus it turned out that while the French troops were engaged in a campaign to conquer the Mamelukes, a campaign of a different sort was being waged with the pencil and brush, the result of which was the monumental *Description de l'Egypte*.[1] This vast project, consisting of ten volumes of text and fourteen of plates, indeed proved to be more significant than the French military operations, for, although all the antiquities taken from Egypt by the French had to be surrendered to the British, everything had been faithfully copied and reproduced in plaster cast; but most important of all were Denon's drawings which revealed to Europe for the first time the hitherto undreamed-of wealth of Egyptian antiquities and which served as an invaluable base for future work in Egyptology.

Baron Denon (1745–1825) had once served Louis XV as a cataloguer of Madame Pompadour's gems, coins, and antiques. He had been reportedly a favourite of Pompadour as well as Catherine of Russia in whose court he had occupied the position of embassy secretary. He had been entertained frequently by Voltaire at the latter's villa in Ferney. His drawings had won for him membership in the Academy. He had acquired considerable wealth and was well known throughout Europe, but, with the outbreak of the French Revolution, he lost all his property and was reduced to poverty. Through his drawings and etchings (some of which were highly pornographic even by French standards) he gradually won his way back to court favour and through Josephine, as we have said, was commissioned to go to Egypt with Napoleon.

It was through Denon's realistic sketches that the eyes of Europe became focused on Egypt. He rushed back and forth from battles and skirmishes the length of Egypt, sketching such

[1] This important work (Paris, 1802–25) was edited chiefly by Edmé François Jomard. Prior to its publication, and as a source for it, Denon wrote *Voyage dans la Basse et la Haute Égypte, pendant les Campagnes du Général Bonaparte*, 2 vols. (Paris, 1802); English translation by A. Aikin: *Travels in Upper and Lower Egypt* (London, Heard and Forman, 1803).

monuments as the Step Pyramid of Zoser, the columns of Karnak, the temples at Philae, the Ramesseum, and the Chapel of Amenhotep III at Elephantine. Of the temple at Dendera he wrote: "I had the presentiment that I should meet with nothing finer in Egypt; and, after having made twenty journeys to Dendera, I am confirmed in this opinion." However, he made the same enthusiastic comment after visiting Edfu and Esneh—and with good reason. At Thebes he noted that "on the leg of the southernmost Memnon are the names of the illustrious and ancient travellers who came to hear the sound of the statue of Memnon; these are written in Greek". Although he earlier characterized the temples of Karnak as "merely large masses loaded with uncouth bas-reliefs and tasteless hieroglyphics", he remained to admire the chaste, clear-cut beauty of the Hatshepsut obelisks and concluded that Karnak was of such magnificence that "one has to rub his eyes to be sure he is not in a dream".

The publication of the *Description de l'Egypte* by Jomard (1777–1862) was a turning-point in the early history of Egyptology and established Jomard as an authority on Egyptian antiquities. It must be held in mind, of course, that none of these artists and explorers of the first two decades of the nineteenth century understood the inscriptions on obelisks, temple walls, and tomb reliefs. It was enough for them to have called the world's attention to the objects themselves. It would not be long, however, before the puzzle of the hieroglyphic symbols would be solved, at least partially. Jomard was a member of Napoleon's scientific staff in Egypt and had helped to lay the foundation of the *Description* in Cairo before returning to Paris. Among his drawings are a panorama of Karnak as it was at the beginning of the nineteenth century, the Luxor obelisks which were later given to France by Mohammed Ali, and the Ramses statue which guards the entrance to the Hypostyle Hall of Karnak.

Two other artists, whose work were never published, should be named here. The first was Robert Hay who travelled throughout Egypt between 1820 and 1840 and who made extensive drawings, architectural plans, and travel notes. This voluminous collection is in the manuscript room of the British Museum. The sketches of Hay's assistant, Edward William Lane, represent the best workmanship of any artist in this early period. Notable among his pictures were those of the king's burial chamber in the Great Pyramid, the interior of the Ramses temple at Abu Simbel, and a remarkable view of the Second Pyramid from the top of the First, all of which were taken with the *camera lucida*, an instrument which, by means of mirrors, or a prism, causes a reduced image of an object to be projected upon a plane surface so that the outlines can be traced.

BELZONI: THE PATAGONIAN SAMSON

On Easter Monday in the year 1803, the Sadler-Wells Company of London advertised a new show featuring "Signor Belzoni and the Human Pyramid". His performance, to quote an old playbill, consisted in "carrying twelve men in a manner never attempted by any but himself. He clasps round him a belt to which are affixed ledges to support the men about him. Thus encumbered, he moves as easy and as graceful as if in a minuet and displays a flag in each hand." The harness itself weighed 127 pounds. With twelve members of his company perched on this apparatus, the giant would walk about the stage without the slightest show of strain. Belzoni was 6 feet 7 inches tall and was well-proportioned. As "The Patagonian Samson" he delighted London audiences with the spectacle of the biblical hero standing between the pillars of a stage temple and pulling down the columns with a great roar and confusion. His feats of magic and strength took him to the famous Bartholomew Fair, Astley's Circus, and other carnivals in England and on the Continent.

This mountebank and magician of the English music halls, whom Sir Walter Scott described as "the handsomest man for a giant I ever saw", was also in Howard Carter's estimation "one of the most remarkable men in the entire history of archaeology". As an Egyptologist, he would have to be classified as an amateur —but so was Schliemann! Both were pioneers in archaeology. Both had the drive, the colour, and the eccentricity of genius. It is only in recent years that Belzoni has been recognized as anything but a freak and adventurer. His accomplishments in Egypt make Carter's comment look like an understatement.

Giovanni Battista Belzoni was born in Padua in 1778, one of a brood of fourteen. At the age of sixteen he went to Rome, spent a few years in a monastery but abandoned the religious life when the French invaded the city. In the monastery school he had made a study of hydraulics and had become expert in his knowledge of the science. There was little chance of earning a living in that field, so he took to the road as a juggler, strong man, and magician. He made his way through France, Germany, and Holland and finally went to England, where he spent the next ten years. As the Great Belzoni he thrilled audiences throughout the land. During this period he married an English woman. Sarah was a remarkable person in her own right and had much to do with her husband's subsequent ventures.

In 1814 Belzoni and Sarah went to Sicily and from there to Malta which was the turning-point of his career. The magician had turned himself into an inventor and his hydraulic device, a water-lifting wheel, attracted the attention of the Moslem governor of the island who suggested that he seek an audience with Mohammed Ali, the governor of Egypt. The thirty-seven-year-old Belzoni who presented himself to the Pasha in Cairo was a different man from the strolling entertainer who had arrived in England a decade before. He was now an Englishman in speech and manner, knew life and people, and was a student of history and archaeology. He had accumulated a fair knowledge of Egyptology probably through Salt's books as well as the works of Denon, Norden and Pococke.

It turned out, however, that Mohammed Ali was not interested in the invention. As that door was being closed to him, another opened, when an old friend, John Lewis Burckhardt, persuaded the British Consul-General, Henry Salt, to send Belzoni on a mission up the Nile. Burckhardt had found a colossal granite head of Ramses II, lying in the sand at Thebes, and wanted it transported down the Nile and shipped to the British Museum. The head measured some 6 by 8 feet and weighed over 7 tons. Belzoni accepted the challenge, not as "the strong man" but as an engineer and with some home-made apparatus succeeded in the undertaking.

In connection with the mortuary temple of Ramses II there were originally three colossal statues. The largest of the three still lies in the outer court of the Ramesseum, toppled perhaps by the earthquake of 27 B.C. The other two had stood in the second court near the Hypostyle Hall. Belzoni found the head of the Pharaoh "near the remains of its body and chair, with its face upwards, apparently smiling at me at the thought of being taken to England". The head had to be moved to the river bank before the Nile was in flood in which case the flooded field would be too shallow for a barge. The work was accomplished with great delay but, inching along day after day, the wooden "car" with its precious cargo finally arrived at the river's bank, was floated down to Cairo, and shipped to England.

The removal of the Ramses head was followed in turn by an investigation of the tomb of Ramses III, an exploration of the Valley of the Kings, and an inspection of the temples of Esneh, Edfu, and Kom Ombo. At Aswan he saw the lovely temples of Philae before they were drowned by the dam. Here also he saw the Philae obelisk which figured so significantly in the decipherment of the hieroglyph. Philae had been the terminus for practically all previous Egyptian explorers. Belzoni, accompanied by his wife, now undertook the dangerous voyage beyond the First Cataract and after many days of hazardous sailing arrived at Abu Simbel. He found the colossal seated statues of Ramses II buried in the sand with only their heads protruding above the debris. Burckhardt, who had been at Abu Simbel a few years earlier, had surmised that underneath the sand lay a vast temple which no one had seen for centuries. The Italian giant determined to extricate the statues, a seemingly insurmountable task since natives, ignorant of coins, refused to work for "small pieces of metal". Finally, with the permission of the local Kashif and with a few labourers whom he succeeded in persuading, he began the work. After clearing some twenty feet on the façade of the temple, he left Aswan to get funds. The interval was occupied with the removal of many monuments and the discovery of several mummies in Thebes. Several months later he returned to Abu Simbel and resumed the almost endless task of uncovering the Ramses figures. The climax came when, early one morning, 1st August 1817, he and his party found themselves in the long hall of the temple walking down the entrance passage between two rows of Osiride statues of the king. Brilliant multi-coloured reliefs, now seen for the first time in 3,000 years, overawed the party. As they further penetrated the temple, the rising sun cast its beams to the innermost sanctuary illuminating the awesome figure of the god Amon. Elaborate reliefs covering the temple walls described the foreign campaigns of Ramses. Surveys of the interior were made and some statues were removed.

Two years later, further work was done at Abu Simbel by William Bankes and Henry Salt. Belzoni now returned to the Valley of the Kings. Here, after discovering the tombs of Amenhotep III, Ramses I, Merneptah, Ay, and those of several princes, he detected indications of another royal tomb near that of Ramses I. Eighteen feet below the surface he found the entrance to the most magnificent sepulchre in Egypt—that of Seti I. Modern visitors to the electrically-lighted tomb, awestruck by the vastness of the chambers and halls and the wealth of coloured high reliefs throughout, can well imagine the feelings of the first man to set foot in this tomb since the ancient tomb robbers left it 3,000 years before. The body of Seti I, found later, is the best preserved and most life-like mummy in the Cairo Museum. Seti I initiated the foreign conquests continued by his son, Ramses II. His building enterprises at home included the gigantic columns in the Hypostyle Hall at Karnak and his beautiful temples at Abydos and Qurna. His tomb in the Valley of the Kings was cut 100 yards into the rock. Practically every inch of wall and ceiling is covered with brilliantly painted hieroglyph in high relief. The first corridor measures 36 feet in length and 8 feet 6 inches in width. The corridor continues on successively lower levels and ends in a square pit 30 feet deep and 12 feet across. This pit was made to look like the end of the tomb but Belzoni noticed a hole in the painted wall. In all Egyptian tombs the various devices to mislead robbers had failed to accomplish their purpose. Here also it was clear that the corridor beyond the pit had been entered by plunderers and then walled up again. Belzoni, walking over the deep pit on a beam, forced his way through the hole to come upon "a beautiful hall, 28 by 26 feet in which were four pillars 3 feet square". These pillars were carved out of the rock and were covered with reliefs in many colours. But that was not the end. Descending from this hall, Belzoni entered another room. Here the artists had been abruptly stopped in their work, for one wall contains only the preliminary drawings. From this room he descended another corridor lined

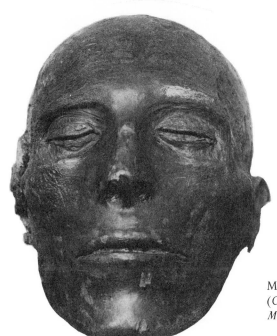

Mummy of Seti I.
(*Courtesy, Metropolitan Museum of Art, New York*)

Egyptian Hall in Piccadilly in which Belzoni exhibited his model of the tomb of Seti I.
(*Courtesy, British Museum*)

Colossi of Memnon, Thebes. (*Courtesy, Hirmer Verlag, Munich*)

Step Pyramid of Zoser, tomb area and temple.

with even more beautiful reliefs and this led to still another hall, which proved to be only the ante-chamber to the burial hall, a room that was more magnificent than even the first great hall. Here the picture story of painted hieroglyphs reached its climax. What Belzoni saw in the middle of this vaulted chamber could only be equalled by the sight that greeted the eyes of Carter and Carnarvon in the nearby tomb of Tutankhamon a century later. What he saw was the resplendent alabaster sarcophagus, translucent and beautifully formed from a single block. It was 9 feet long, 4 feet wide and the sides were 3 inches thick. The cover lay on the floor in scattered pieces. Both interior and exterior were carved with an inlay of blue paste.[1] To his surprise, the exhausted Belzoni found, below the burial chamber, a 300-foot tunnel which must have led almost through the mountain. Adjoining the burial chamber were five additional rooms, one of them being 40 by 20 feet.

Henry Salt with the Earl and Countess of Belmore and other dignitaries came to see the tomb and congratulate the Italian in his finest hour. Reports reaching England were not always clear and often confused him with someone else. Six months later we find Belzoni at Giza remarking to a friend, as they contemplated the Cheops Pyramid, that it was strange that the Second Pyramid had never been opened and he resolved to do something about it. "The idea," he wrote at the time, "seems a little short of madness;" but he could not rid himself of the challenge. Standing before the solid mass of stone, he must have asked himself: "How does one approach such a task? Where do you strike first?" Taking into account first of all that the entrance to the Great Pyramid was on the north side, he noticed that just under the centre of the north face of the Chephren Pyramid there was a pile of debris which looked as if it might conceal the entrance. His workmen began clearing the ground between the temple and the pyramid as well as the debris on the northern slope. After several weeks of digging they struck a small open slit in the stones. Removing the outer stone blocks, Belzoni found a passage 3 feet wide filled with rubble. This passage led to a tunnel. The rejoicing over the discovery was short-lived when it soon became clear that this was a forced entrance, made by ancient robbers,

[1] The sarcophagus is now in the Soane Museum in London.

and ended in a pile of rubble. Returning to a study of the Great Pyramid, Belzoni noticed that the entrance was not in the centre of the northern face but some 30 feet to the east of centre and connected with the eastward end of the burial chamber. This observation turned out to be the key to the solution of the riddle. More weeks of digging at the corresponding spot on the northern face of the Second Pyramid followed and on 1st March 1818 the real entrance was found. The passage was 4 feet high and 3 feet 6 inches wide and descended into the centre of the pyramid. After crawling 100 feet, Belzoni and his helpers came to a solid wall of granite. "At first sight," he wrote, "it seemed like a fixed block of stone which stared me in the face and said 'Ne plus ultra', putting an end to my project, as I thought." But he discovered that one of the barrier stones was a portcullis which could be raised with crowbars. The giant led the way, followed by Chevalier Frediani, a friend who had been invited to stay for the opening. A long passage opened on a deep pit which they descended by a rope. More passages followed, one of them ending at the burial chamber. There was the empty sarcophagus of the Pharaoh Chephren. Who had entered the chamber in the Middle Ages or earlier, no one knows.

Returning to London in September 1819, Belzoni began work on his "Exhibition" which contained reproductions of two chambers in Seti's tomb, the sarcophagus, and other attractions. After its completion, the Wanderlust drove him on again. This time his destination was Timbuktu. It is not difficult to imagine the hazards of such a journey in the early decades of the nineteenth century. He made his way as far as Benin where he died of dysentery and was buried by natives at Gwato in Africa.

The accomplishments of this improbable, astonishing genius— the removal of the Ramses head, the clearing and exploration of the Ramses temple at Abu Simbel, the discovery and exploration of the tomb of Seti I, and his entrance into the Chephren Pyramid —were incredible, considering the period and the lack of modern tools and knowledge. He was motivated, like most nineteenth-century explorer-archaeologists, by the fanatical desire to find treasures and sell them to collectors.[1] His methods were at times

[1] Belzoni's funds for his undertakings in Egypt came from the sale of antiquities and gifts from Burckhardt and other friends.

destructive, caring, as he did, more for the intrinsic value of an object than for its archaeological importance. Granted that these criticisms have much truth in them, the fact remains that his investigations prepared the way for the later and more scientific work on Egyptology.[1] It is only in our time that the Great Belzoni has been given proper recognition for his pioneer work as an Egyptologist.[2]

ENGLISH PIONEERS

In the first three decades of the nineteenth century there were in Egypt several English travellers whose paths crossed that of Belzoni and who, while they were not primarily archaeologists, were involved in this mad scramble for antiquities and who turned out to be amateur Egyptologists. One of these was Henry Salt. In 1816 he was appointed British Consul-General in Egypt. He had received a somewhat spotty training in art and was trying unsuccessfully to make a living by painting portraits when he met Viscount Valentia. Lord Valentia was arranging a tour to India and reluctantly consented to take Salt along as draftsman and artist. This reminds one of Captain Fitz-Roy's decision to take the young Darwin on his world encircling voyage of the *Beagle*. Both trips had far-reaching results, determining the entire career of each, although there is no comparison in their importance. In India Lord Valentia and Salt were asked by the Governor-General to explore the coast of Africa along the shores of the Red Sea with the idea of developing trade with Ethiopia. Salt was sent into the interior where he was given letters from the Emperor of Abyssinia to the King of England. Salt returned to London with a reputation as both artist and diplomat. The Foreign Office commissioned him to go to Africa and cultivate good relations with Abyssinia and with tribes along the Red Sea coast. It was on his return trip from Africa that he replaced

[1] The catalogue of the British Museum lists some twenty important items which were acquired through Belzoni.

[2] Stanley Mayes: *The Great Belzoni* (London, Putnam, 1959) is an up-to-date, scholarly and most readable volume. See also Colin Clair: *Strong Man Egyptologist* (London, Oldbourne, 1957) and M. Wilson Disher: *Pharaoh's Fool* (London, Heinemann, 1957).

Colonel Missett as Consul-General in Egypt. He was stationed in Cairo and became a close friend of Mohammed Ali. His diplomatic office was not too demanding and he soon found himself engaged in "extra-curricular activities". This work consisted in collecting antiquities for his friend Sir Joseph Banks, a trustee of the British Museum. As the Consul-General and friend of Mohammed Ali, he was free to undertake such missions. His first find was a granite sarcophagus at Sa el Hagar (ancient Sais). He made a sketch of the coffin and came to the important conclusion that the hieroglyphs should be read from the end of the line which they faced.

Salt's next project was the removal of the colossal head of Ramses II which lay in the dust at Thebes. Burckhardt, the Swiss explorer, had seen it and discussed the matter with Mohammed Ali and English friends. Burckhardt then approached Salt for funds. The Consul was intrigued by the project and commissioned Belzoni, as we have learned, to remove the head and have it transported to England.

We find Salt later subsidizing the work of one Captain Caviglia, a Genoese shipowner, in exploring the Pyramid of Cheops. Caviglia in 1816 succeeded in descending the 20-foot "well" and finding that it was connected with the main corridor. He also cleared the Sphinx of sand and excavated some of the Giza mastaba tombs. Meanwhile Salt sent Belzoni to Karnak to excavate the colossal statue of Ramses II. Belzoni was on the point of excavating further in the temples at Karnak when Drovetti, a naval explorer, hired all the available natives and proceeded to dig there on a large scale. Belzoni left Karnak for the time being and conducted expeditions to Philae and the Valley of the Kings. It was Salt who sponsored Belzoni's second expedition to Abu Simbel. Belzoni felt that Salt was exploiting him and trying to get credit for all of his accomplishments. They met in the Valley of the Kings and the Italian declared that he was not in Salt's employ but was an independent agent. Salt insisted that he always gave Belzoni full credit for his discoveries. This led to an estrangement, but a reconciliation was later reached whereby Salt made certain concessions. While they remained good friends on the surface, misunderstanding and bitterness continued to the end. The rest of Salt's life was devoted to expeditions with Drovetti,

William John Bankes, and Belzoni at Philae, Thebes, Karnak, and Abydos.

William John Bankes, a friend of Byron and former M.P., went to Egypt in 1815 to confer with Burckhardt about the removal of the Ramses head from Thebes, a project completed by Belzoni. We first encounter Bankes at Philae where he partially excavated the Isis obelisk, a beautiful granite monolith containing a Greek inscription of some twenty lines. The inscription was a complaint of the priests of Isis to Ptolemy IX and his queen Cleopatra that government officials were usurping temple funds for their own purposes.[1] Bankes was the first to copy this inscription and later identified an Egyptian cartouche on the obelisk as the name of Cleopatra. He had previously noticed on a temple wall near Dendera the same cartouche along with another which he surmised was that of Ptolemy. The Philae obelisk contained the same two cartouches. This discovery was greatly instrumental in the decipherment of the Rosetta Stone.[2]

Bankes is next found at Abu Simbel, accompanied by the Italian artists, Finati and Ricci, copying and reproducing the hieroglyphic reliefs in the Ramses temple. They cleared the southernmost statue of Ramses II on the façade, discovering at its base the figures of three of the Pharaoh's daughters. He also found some Greek graffiti or scratchings on the legs of the king. Upon excavating the legs of the headless statue, Bankes discovered more Greek defacing, this one being the work of a soldier in the sixth century B.C.—proof that the temple was at least that old. (Later excavation of the interior established the date of completion at 1260 B.C.)

Not the least significant of Bankes' contributions to Egyptology was his discovery at Abydos in 1818 of a list of kings which he found while excavating a temple of Ramses II. Inscribed on a wall of the temple was a series of cartouches which he guessed must have been a chronological list of royal names. This catalogue was used by Young and Champollion in their work of deciphering.

---

[1] See p. 42.
[2] The obelisk was finally removed and erected on the Bankes estate in England.

The name of Col. Richard Howard-Vyse (1798–1853) merits our attention, for it is through his writings that we learn much about all previous travellers in Egypt.[1] His work takes on added importance, however, because it came after Champollion's decipherment of the hieroglyph—a fact which enabled him to approach the subject of Egyptology somewhat more intelligently than his predecessors. On the other hand, although he carefully surveyed the pyramids and made precise records, he was not above using the crude method of blasting with gunpowder.

Vyse, who had been an officer under Wellington, went to Egypt in 1835 and immediately began work at Giza. Discarding the mass of superstition and pseudo-scientific explanations which had attached to the pyramids for centuries, Vyse insisted that they were simply the tombs of the Pharaohs. His interest in the pyramids was aroused by a conversation with Caviglia with whom he collaborated until they quarrelled and parted company. He was fortunate in obtaining the services of John Shae Perring, a civil engineer in the employ of the Khedive, Mohammed Ali. Together they surveyed not only the Giza complex but also the pyramids of Sakkara, Dashur, and Meidum. When Vyse and Perring set up camp on the desert, the interior of the Cheops Pyramid had been pretty thoroughly explored, the Second only partly, but the Third had not been opened. Although previously ascribed to Mycerinus, no confirmation of this had ever been found. It was the achievement of Vyse not only to enter this pyramid but to confirm the identification of the name of Mycerinus which he found inscribed in the burial chamber of an adjacent small pyramid. It was in his attempt to find the entrance to the Third Pyramid that he resorted to his blasting technique. His efforts with this method were fruitless. After bombarding his way through the top and side almost to the centre of the pyramid, neither burial chamber nor entrance was found, but great damage was done. On 29th July 1837 he succeeded in discovering the true entrance by the simple removal of a few loose blocks of stone on the northern side. These stones had probably been loosened centuries before by Arabs. "After passing through various passages," he writes, "a room was reached wherein was

[1] *Operations carried on at the Pyramids of Giza in* 1873; with an Appendix by J. S. Perring. 3 vols. (London, J. Fraser, 1840–42).

found a long blue vessel quite empty. . . . They found in this basin, after they had broken the lid of it, the decayed remains of a man, but no treasures, except some golden tablets inscribed with characters of a language which nobody could understand.'' In addition to the human bones, Vyse found parts of the royal anthropoid wooden sarcophagus of the king. Part of the lid of the sarcophagus was discovered nearby. It bore the inscription: ''Osiris, King of Upper and Lower Egypt, Menkure, living for-ever.'' Vyse managed to get the sarcophagus out of the pyramid and transported it to Alexandria, where he put it on a ship bound for England. The ship touched at Leghorn and after leaving that port ran into a storm and was never heard of again. Perhaps some under-sea archaeologists will some day salvage the sarcophagus of Mycerinus from the bottom of the Mediterranean off the coast of Spain. The fragments of the wooden coffin and the human remains were later taken to the British Museum. Whether the bones are those of the king or one of the Arab tomb robbers who entered the pyramid in 1226 remains an unsettled problem.

Vyse found why his attempt to find a passage by boring through the side and down from the top was unsuccessful. The burial chamber and the corridors leading to it were not in the pyramid itself but under it and the entrance passage, which is just above the surface of the ground, descends abruptly to a long granite-walled corridor, ending in an ante-chamber. As Edwards shows, the first architectural plan called for an entrance nearer the centre of the pyramid at the base and descending to the ante-chamber.[1] This was abandoned in favour of the second plan described above. A third plan involved the addition of two chambers, the second and deeper of which was the burial chamber itself.

Before leaving Giza, Vyse discovered the chambers in the Cheops Pyramid which had never been entered and also found a lower entrance to the Chephren Pyramid. Digging down to the foundation of the First Pyramid, he uncovered some of the polished limestone casing blocks which had originally covered the entire pyramid. He also cleared a section of the pavement or apron which extended outwards from the base of the pyramid. Vyse's partner, John Shae Perring, measured and charted not

[1] I. E. S. Edwards: *The Pyramids of Egypt* (London, Penguin, 1947), pp. 126, 127.

only the Giza group but some thirty other pyramids including an extensive survey of the Zoser Step Pyramid. The two men then combined their efforts to produce their book of "Operations", the diagrams, drawings and descriptions of which are most detailed, including the hieroglyphs and their translation.[1] Most of these pyramid inscriptions were names and titles of kings made by quarry workers when they cut the blocks in the Mokkatam Hills.

The period of early exploration comes to an end with the work of Ippolito Rosellini, Gardner Wilkinson, Joseph Bonomi, and James Burton, who represent a somewhat more advanced stage of systematic study in view of the fact that they operated with at least a partial knowledge of the hieroglyphs.[2] Their drawings and descriptions, many of which are still unpublished, served as valuable sources for all later investigators. But, like all previous explorers, even these late contemporaries of Champollion and Belzoni were consumed with the idea of collecting rather than preserving *in situ*. Before the middle of the nineteenth century, excavation for the most part was still haphazard and unscientific. Infinite damage was done by these amateur archaeologists who ransacked tombs for gold, ruthlessly trampled mummies, hacked reliefs from tomb walls, and made off with priceless statues from temples. Valuable objects of all kinds were being removed and shipped to European museums and private collectors. Belzoni admitted to mutilating mummies and looting tombs in order to get papyri of the Book of the Dead. His narration of one such occasion in which he sat down on a mummy is both naïve and sad. "But when my weight bore on the body of an Egyptian," he writes, "it crushed it like a band-box. I naturally had recourse to my hands to sustain my weight, but they found no better support; so that I sank altogether among the broken mummies, with the crash of bones, rags, and wooden cases, which raised such a dust as kept me motionless for a quarter of an hour, waiting till it subsided again."

Such incidents are shocking but they were common enough—

[1] The translations were made by Birch, a prominent linguist of the time and adviser to Perring.

[2] See Sir John Gardiner Wilkinson: *The Manners and Customs of the Early Egyptians*, 3 vols. (London, J. Murray, 1879, Revised).

not to mention the reckless vandalism of the natives in their search for gold and papyri. It was a grim scene: foreign travellers by the score frantically jumping from one site to another, up and down the country, fighting each other and resorting to all kinds of intrigue in their mad race for the antiquities of Egypt.

Chapter Three

ORDER OUT OF CHAOS

LEPSIUS AND CLASSIFICATION

In 1842 King Friedrich Wilhelm IV of Prussia subsidized an Egyptian expedition and appointed as its leader Richard Lepsius (1810–84), a lecturer in philology and comparative linguistics at the University of Berlin. This event virtually marks the end of the wasteful and destructive period of amateur archaeology and the beginning of a transition to modern Egyptology. Lepsius went to Egypt not with loot in mind but to catalogue, classify, and fix dates. Lepsius the scholar was the first to bring order out of chaos, to attempt the almost impossible task of establishing a chronology and initiating the process of interpreting Egyptian history as a cultural continuity.

Interpretation, however, came later, for the three-year Prussian expedition was filled with one dramatic find after another. The difference between the work of Lepsius and all those preceding him was the difference between the haphazard and frantic ransacking of ancient sites and the deliberate, careful analysis of each discovery in the light of its bearing on Egyptian history. The expedition made an auspicious start with the excavation of the remains of thirty previously unknown pyramids and 130 mastabas from the Old Kingdom. Lepsius continued the exploration of the Giza Pyramids, begun by Vyse and others, as well as the Step Pyramid of Zoser. From the latter temple enclosure he removed a door and some blue faience tile which he sent to the Berlin Museum.

In regard to the pyramids, Lepsius proposed a theory that the size of a pyramid was determined by the length of the owner's reign. This has been called the accretion theory and, while it is true that certain pyramids such as Zoser's underwent changes and were enlarged during the king's lifetime, the idea does not necessarily hold true. If his theory were true, the Pyramid of Pepi II, who reigned for ninety-four years, should have been the largest, but it is one of the smaller structures; and by the same reasoning the Pyramid of Cheops, who reigned only twenty-three years, should have been relatively small.

In 1844 the expedition surveyed the entire Valley of the Kings and excavated at Tell el-Amarna, the Fayoum, Thebes, Silseleh, Philae, Abu Simbel, and other Nubian sites. Lepsius' work in making copies of reliefs, cartouches, and his translation of tomb and temple inscriptions resulted in his twelve-volume *Monuments of Egypt and Ethiopia* (1849–59). The subject of dating was given its first great impetus by Lepsius' publication of *Egyptian Chronology* (1849) and his *Book of Egyptian Kings* (1850). On his return to Germany after the expedition he was appointed professor of Egyptology at the University of Berlin, the first to hold that position.

While the career of Lepsius changed the character of Egyptian excavation, it did not by any means put a stop to the wholesale exportation of antiquities. Lepsius himself sent some fifteen thousand objects to Berlin, including three tombs from Memphis, an obelisk, and a pillar from the tomb of Seti I at Abydos. At the time of the Prussian expedition there was no Director of Antiquities, no museum, and very little supervision of foreign excavators. What laws existed against exportation were set aside in favour of Lepsius by Mohammed Ali, who charged all local authorities to give him every possible assistance and who enforced compulsory labour so that there was no trouble with the fellahin. Lepsius rationalized his own policy by the statement that only by rescuing the antiquities and sending them to a European museum could they be preserved from destruction. Until recently this was partly correct but a fine ethical question persists. Georg Ebers, his biographer, wrote naïvely as follows:

With full authority to take possession of all that might embellish the Berlin collection, Lepsius appropriated what was most desirable and most interesting wherever he found it, and ventured, as we have seen, to remove whole tombs from the necropolis of ancient Memphis to the Spree (meaning Berlin). This could not be done without injury to the adjoining tombs, as they had consisted of a number of rooms collectively, and envy, illwill and stupidity were quickly at hand to accuse the Prussian expedition of having, like impious vandals, plundered and injured the monuments in pursuit of their own purposes. But this accusation was entirely unfounded, and anyone who knows the condition of Egypt at that time can only rejoice that so many treasures, which were neglected and exposed to wanton destruction in their native country were at a favourable moment removed to Europe and preserved in a fine public museum.[1]

The study of the hieroglyph was greatly accelerated by Lepsius' discovery of a bilingual decree at Philae containing the names of several Ptolemies. He also anticipated Petrie in discovering a number of Old Kingdom monuments, thereby acquiring more information about the third and fourth dynasty dating. Not the least important of his expeditions was his journey to the Sinai Peninsula where he discovered, and later published, inscriptions made by Egyptians who for centuries worked the copper mines at Maghareh and Serabit el-Khadem. This discovery, along with his findings in the Sudan, revealed the extent of the commercial activity and foreign exploration of the ancient Egyptians.

MARIETTE AND CONSERVATION

Organization and supervision came to Egyptian archaeology for the first time with the appointment in 1858 of Auguste Mariette as Director of the Service of Antiquities, a position which was held by Frenchmen until 1952. (The Anglo-French *Entente* of 1904 provided that the post of Director-General of the Egyptian Antiquities Department along with the Directorship of the Cairo Museum be held by a Frenchman.) Mariette had been Assistant Curator in the Louvre for ten years when he was sent to Egypt to buy papyri and Coptic manuscripts. Arriving in Cairo, he was appalled at the shameful traffic in antiquities. Amateur and professional alike were consumed with the mad search for buried treasures. Cairo was one grand bazaar with archaeologists, collectors, and travellers bargaining with natives for antiquities to

[1] *Richard Lepsius, a Biography* (New York, Gottsberger, 1887), pp. 145, 146.

take home. Smaller objects disappeared by the thousands as Arabs, assisting in the digs, pocketed jewellery, scarabs, ushabties, and statuettes and sold them to tourists. Tombs were being plundered and their valuable contents ruined. Mariette forgot momentarily his mission to buy papyri and sought to find a way to bring some semblance of governmental control to the situation.

His appointment as Director of the Department of Antiquities was made by the Khedive, Said Pasha, who was probably urged to do so by Ferdinand de Lesseps, a prominent French diplomat and promoter of the Suez Canal. It was not easy, however, to convince the Egyptian authorities of the necessity of properly housing the antiquities, but Mariette was a forceful person and Said finally came around to his side. He provided the means for building a museum at Bulak. The newly appointed Director insisted that Egyptian treasures were to remain in Egypt and he did his best to enforce this rule. In his determination to enforce discipline and combat the unprincipled trading in valuable archaeological objects he went so far as to forbid any other person to excavate in Egypt. Such drastic measures did not add to his popularity. In fact, the mere mention of his name in some circles was occasion for vehement cursing. During his tenure of office Mariette conducted excavations at thirty-seven different sites. It goes without saying that he defeated his own ends in attempting such widespread operations, for it was impossible either to supervise properly all these "digs" or to catalogue the results. Consequently the record of his work has remained woefully incomplete.

In spite of the hurried and inadequate cataloguing, however, Mariette's accomplishments represent a milestone in Egyptian archaeology. He exhumed some 15,000 objects from Abydos, the site of the royal cemetery of the early dynasties and the holy city of the Osiris cult. In the course of this excavation, he predicted that the tombs of the First Dynasty Pharaohs would be found there, a prophecy which was later fulfilled. He made important contributions in the continuing excavations at Karnak, Thebes, Tanis, Abu Simbel, and Edfu. He it was who discovered the temple of the Second Pyramid which contained the statue of Chephren himself, one of the most prized masterpieces in the Cairo Museum today.

Perhaps the chief thing for which Mariette is known today was his discovery of the Serapeum in 1851. In his walks about Cairo and visits to Alexandria he had noticed the presence of identical sphinxes in the gardens of high officials and in front of villas. He determined to find out where these sphinxes came from, for they were obviously very old. One day on a visit to Sakkara he stumbled upon a sphinx which was half-buried in the sand near the Step Pyramid of Zoser. He immediately recognized it as a duplicate of those in Cairo and Alexandria. Uncovering the sphinx, he found an inscription which connected it with the Apis cult, a prominent religion of the early Egyptians. Apis, the sacred bull, was worshipped chiefly in Memphis, the capital. Mariette had heard of the Lost Avenue of the Sphinxes and his guess was that this and the other sphinxes were part of that mysterious causeway. He hired some Arabs and when they were through digging they had uncovered 140 sphinxes. This avenue had once connected two temples the excavation of which became the object of Mariette's next project. This whole site is what is known as the Serapeum, named after the god Serapis, who embodied the attributes of Osiris and Apis. In early Egypt, deities were represented in animal form—Horus, the Falcon; Thot, the Ibis; Sebek, the Crocodile; Knum, the Ram—and Memphis was the centre of the worship of Apis, the sacred bull, who was the servant of Ptah. The reigning bull was kept in the temple where priests ministered to his needs. When he died he was embalmed with great ceremony and was buried in the Serapeum.

The first room to be excavated was the Mortuary Chapel which was connected by a steep shaft with the burial chamber. From this room for 320 feet ran a corridor from which extended many chambers containing the mummified remains of bulls. The total length of this passage, as later excavated, was some 1,200 feet. Proceeding from one burial chamber to another, Mariette came upon the sarcophagi in which the bulls had been buried. They were made of black and red granite, each one having been quarried in one piece, weighing about 72 tons and measuring 9 feet in height, 6 feet in width, and 12 feet in length. All but two of the sarcophagi had been plundered by ancient robbers. The tomb chambers of the Serapeum were built over a long period, extending into the Ptolemaic period. One of the sarcophagi, perhaps the last one to be made, was not taken to a burial chamber but lay near the entrance of the temple.

Mariette credits Strabo with the clue that led him to the discovery of the Serapeum. "One finds also at Memphis," wrote Strabo, "a temple of Serapis in a spot so sandy that the wind causes the sand to accumulate in heaps, under which we could see many sphinxes, some of them almost entirely buried, others only partially covered." According to Mariette the Tomb of Apis consisted of "three distinct parts which have no direct communication with one another", the first dating from the Eighteenth Dynasty and Amenhotep III, the second part from the Twenty-second, and the third part from the Twenty-sixth. Concerning the importance of his discovery for chronology Mariette wrote as follows:

> It is well known that the exploration of this tomb has furnished science with unhoped-for results. For what the traveller now sees of it is merely its skeleton. But the fact is that, although it had been rifled by the early Christians, the tomb, when first discovered, still possessed nearly all that it had ever contained that was not gold or other precious matter. There existed a custom which had especially contributed to enrich the tomb with valuable documents. On certain days in the year, or on the occasion of the death and funeral rites of an Apis, the inhabitants of Memphis came to pay a visit to the god in his burial-place. In memory of this act of piety they left a stela, i.e. a square-shaped stone, rounded at the top, which was let into one of the walls of the tomb, having been previously inscribed with an homage to the god in the name of his visitor and his family. Now these documents, to the number of about five hundred, were found, for the most part, in their original position . . . and as many of them were dated according to the fashion of the time, that is with the year, month and day of the reigning king, a comparison of these inscribed tablets must necessarily prove of the greatest importance, especially in fixing chronology.[1]

Another great discovery of Mariette was the Tomb of Ti which was not far from the Serapeum. Ti was a nobleman and rich landowner of the Fifth Dynasty. His tomb was one of the most elaborate in Egypt and, along with the Serapeum, is a show-place

[1] *The Monuments of Upper Egypt.* English translation by Alphonse Mariette (Boston, Mansfield and Dearborn, 1890), pp. 120–1.

for tourists today. In addition to the stone statue of Ti, the tomb is known for its rich, well-preserved reliefs which are unusually realistic and detailed. These wall paintings and narrative friezes portray the daily life of Ti, the activities of the court, his family, and the people on his estate. Here one sees farmers mowing, threshing, and winnowing grain; the preparation of flax; the building of a ship from the felling of the tree to the fitting of the planks; the process of smelting gold; sculpturing; leatherwork; masonry; the family life of the king—dining, hunting, boating on the Nile; offerings being taken to the palace for Ti; bulls being slaughtered for sacrifice; and tenants bringing their payments to the palace. These reliefs are valuable, not only for their artistic excellence, but also because they depict in vivid fashion the daily life of the ancient Egyptians at work and at play.[1]

Mariette's excavations of the Serapeum and Ti's tomb are two of the most significant contributions in the history of Egyptian archaeology, but he himself regarded his founding of the Bulak Museum as his most important work. In 1891, during the administration of Maspero, Mariette's successor, the Museum was moved to Giza and in 1902 to Cairo where the collection was permanently housed and carefully catalogued. Tourists today, upon entering the great museum, pass the statue of Mariette which was erected by the Egyptian government in recognition of his work in rescuing the wealth of ancient Egypt from the hands of plunderers and in keeping what was left on Egyptian soil. It was in that soil that Mariette's body was buried.

PETRIE AND METHODOLOGY

With all deference to Lepsius and Mariette, it is William Matthews Flinders Petrie (1853–1942) who marks the real turning-point in Egyptology and who justly deserves the title of "founder of modern archaeology". As Leo Deuel writes: "Egyptian archaeology became respectable with Mariette; it came of age with Petrie."[2]

---

[1] For the best photographs and descriptions of the Ti reliefs see Kurt Lange-Max Hirmer: *Aegypten* (Munich, Hirmer Verlag, 1955), Plates 66–71 and pp. 50, 51 in Explanatory Notes.

[2] *The Treasures of Time* (Cleveland, World Publishing Company, 1961), p. 56.

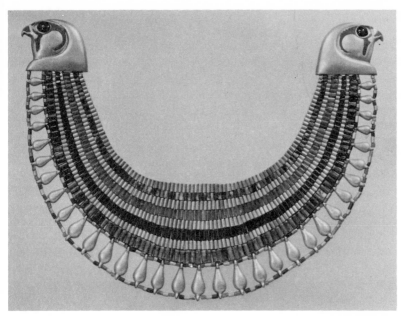

(*Above*) Twelfth Dynasty collar of carnelian, felspar, gold leaf, green faience; from the tomb of Senebtisi at Lisht. (*Below*) Pectoral (Twelfth Dynasty) of Princess Sat-hathor-iunut of gold and inlay, from Lahun.
(*Courtesy, Metropolitan Museum of Art, New York*)

Mycerinus and Queen. (*Courtesy, Museum of Fine Arts, Boston*)

Flinders Petrie is regarded as the "father of scientific archaeology" because it was he who established the laws by which modern excavations are carried on. When Sir Leonard Woolley was exploring the Death Pit on the site of ancient Ur, he came across a hole about an inch and a half in diameter. Three feet away he saw another. He promptly poured liquid plaster cast into one hole and to his surprise it came up and filled the other hole. Waiting until the cast solidified, he carefully scraped away the dirt with a fine brush and knife and there *in situ* lay a harp of the Sumerian king Meskalumdug with the gold head of a bull attached to the sound-box in its original position, the plaster filling the space made by the decayed wood. In this way a royal harp was recovered after 5,000 years. The arm bones of the court harpist lay across the instrument, showing that he was playing even as he was put to death along with the whole retinue of the king in the funeral ceremony. In his excavation of Lahun, Guy Brunton describes the process of recovering 9,500 beads and other specimens of Egyptian craftsmanship: "The whole of the clearing, except in certain areas where the mud contained no remains whatever, was done with a small penknife; or with a pin when there was a chance of finding small beads in position. The work of picking out the minute beads (there were over 9,500 of them) was so laborious, that eventually any detached scraps of mud were examined in camp." After the discovery of the tomb of Tutankhamon, Howard Carter tells of going to Cairo and purchasing "thirty-two bales of calico, more than a mile of wadding, and as much again of surgical bandaging", not for the excavators (!) but for the careful handling of the treasures of the tomb—all of which had been photographed and recorded before being touched. These three incidents could have happened only after Petrie's initial work in Egypt and not before. The camel's hair brush and dental pick were a far cry from the battering ram and the dynamite blasting of Vyse and Belzoni. The modern archaeologist can only speculate on the tremendous wealth of remains that might have been preserved if the earlier explorers could have known and used the scientific methods inaugurated by Petrie.

In a circle of scholars whose historical horizon was bounded by either the Bible or classical Greece, the publication of *Inductive Metrology* was nothing less than a bombshell. That was in 1877 and with it the author, Flinders Petrie, transformed archaeology from an undocumented collection of antiquities to a deliberate reconstruction of history by the location of artifacts.

The method introduced by Petrie was called "Sequence Dating", a technique by which a relative time scale or chronology could be established through the observation of different styles of pottery on successive levels and particularly by association of materials. The changes in the type of pottery-fragments indicate a sequence of human cultures. This method was used even more successfully in Palestine at Tell el-Hesi and at Kish and Ur in Babylonia where the pottery remaining in the mounds clearly differentiated a dozen distinct periods of occupation. By the process of cross-dating a system of comparative archaeology was achieved whereby Petrie was able to date the Aegean civilization for example through the discovery of layers of Cretan and Mycenaean pottery in Egypt in the Middle and New Kingdom periods. He discovered foreign pottery at Lahun and proved that it was Aegean and was from the Twelfth Dynasty (1991–1786 B.C.). The later discovery of similar ware by Sir Arthur Evans in Crete, together with the Lahun excavation, helped provide a chronology for the early Aegean civilization.

Thus with Petrie a potsherd was as important as a pyramid in reconstructing Egyptian cultural history and the unglamorous research among the scattered bits of pottery becomes quite as significant as the more spectacular discoveries.

Petrie's expedition to Meidum is an illustration of his scientific method of establishing cultural history. The importance of the Meidum Pyramid lies in the fact that it represents the first true pyramidal form. Petrie's investigations revealed the various stages in the evolution of this type of structure. Originally planned as a mastaba tomb, it was converted into a step pyramid and later took the form of a true pyramid, as it appears to have been cased from top to bottom in smooth limestone. The Meidum Pyramid has always been considered to be the work of Seneferu, the first king of the Fourth Dynasty (c. 2680 B.C.) and the father of Cheops. When Petrie discovered it in 1891 it was badly mutilated and consisted of only three of the original eight stages. It may be, as W. Stevenson Smith suggests, that its initial form as a mastaba step pyramid was built by Huni, the last king of the

Third Dynasty, and that Seneferu merely completed it in the form of a true pyramid.[1] Such a pyramidal form had previously been built by Seneferu at Dashur. On the east side of the Meidum Pyramid, Petrie discovered a small funerary temple, probably the first complete Egyptian temple. Its early date is indicated by the simplicity of the architecture and the total absence of decoration. The whole complex resembles that of the later Giza group. A causeway with two walls but no roof was discovered. This led into the plain by the river. In the tomb-chamber of the Pyramid Petrie found fragments of a wooden coffin but no mummy or inscriptions. Graffiti on the walls of the funerary temple, scribbled by visitors (or thieves) in the Eighteenth Dynasty, mentioned Seneferu by name. Here also were found the mastaba-tombs of Nefermaat and Rahotep and the famous seated figures of Rahotep and Nofret, now in the Cairo Museum. Petrie describes his search for the temple as follows:

> The most promising means of ascertaining the age (of the Pyramid) was to search for any remains of the pyramid temple. But where was it? No sign of such a building could be seen anywhere to the east of the pyramid. . . . Marking out a space which would have held two or three good-sized London houses, and knowing that we must go as deep as a tall house before we could get any result, I began a work of several weeks with as many men as could efficiently be put into the area. . . . At last we uncovered the court-yard, and found two steles; and moreover instead of a mere court there appeared a doorway on the east side, and crawling in I found a chamber and passage still roofed over and quite perfect. We had in fact, an absolutely complete, though small, temple. Not a stone was missing, nor a piece knocked off. The steles and the altar between them stood just as when they were set up; and the oldest dated building in the land has stood unimpaired amidst all the building and the destruction that has gone on in Egypt throughout history.[2]

More than one biographer has written of Petrie in terms of genius rather than great talent—and with considerable justification. He was a child prodigy, exhibiting a keen interest in Egypt at the age of ten. As a youth he had a profound respect for the

[1] See *The Art and Architecture of Ancient Egypt* (Baltimore, Penguin, 1958), p. 39.
[2] *Ten Years' Digging in Egypt* (New York, Revell, 1893), pp. 139–40.

inductive method and mathematical measurement. His first publication was a book on Stonehenge and its unit of measurement.
That was the first of some ninety volumes which he wrote before
his death at the age of eighty-nine. He went to Egypt in 1880 and
stayed for half a century, unearthing three millenniums of Egyptian history. Not the least of Petrie's contributions to Egyptology
was his research in pre-history and his research on the dates of
the pre-dynastic periods. Later Egyptologists, however, have
questioned his pre-dynastic dating. Excavating in 1894 at Nagada,
a few miles north-east of Thebes, Petrie found some 3,000 graves
of people who seemed to be different from those of the dynastic
periods. The skeletons lay on their sides with arms and legs in
the embryonic position. The pottery was entirely different from
that of dynastic Egyptians. He concluded that these people belonged to the Sixth and Seventh Dynasties, about which little or
nothing was known at the time. Later at Dendera this theory was
disproved when he found cemeteries with no objects of the
previous type. It was clear that "the new race" was pre-dynastic
and the people were the ancestors of the Egyptians. Still later
(1898) the French archaeologist, Amelineau, discovered the
missing tombs of the kings of the First and Second Dynasties.

Although Petrie's greatness can be attributed to his ceramic
method of dating and his inauguration of the scientific method, it
must not be forgotten that he made some of the most sensational
discoveries in the history of Egyptian excavation. In the Delta
area he found three important sites: the sixth-century B.C. Greek
trading colony of Naucratis; Daphnae, a frontier fortress of
Psamtik I, where Greek mercenaries had been stationed; and
Tanis, where he discovered fragments of a colossal statue of
Ramses II along with many others. He discovered the Temple of
Amenhotep III to which the Colossi of Memnon had once been
connected. One of his greatest finds was the Pyramid-Tomb of
Amenemhet at Hawara, which yielded the portrait statue of the
king, one of the greatest works of sculpture ever found in Egypt.
He discovered many funeral portraits and vast collections of
papyri in the Fayum. They include sections of the *Phaedo* of Plato
and the *Antiope* of Euripides from 300 B.C. Lahun is famous as
the site of Petrie's discovery of the treasures of the princess
Sat-hathor-ant, exquisite examples of Egyptian craftsmanship in

2000 B.C. The crown of gold is one of the most remarkable specimens of technical skill in Egyptian history. At Gurob, another Fayum site, he found much Greek and Mycenaean pottery, which provided definite dating for the earlier stages of Greek civilization.[1]

Like many previous explorers, Petrie's first interest was the Pyramids. His operations at Giza, Abydos, and other pyramid sites will be included in the following chapter.

[1] Petrie's Delta and Fayum excavations are reported in his *Ten Years' Digging in Egypt* (New York, Revell, 1893).

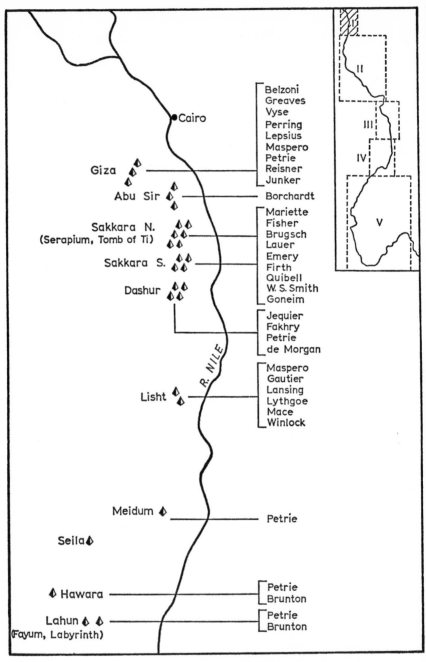

EGYPTIAN EXCAVATIONS Part I

Chapter Four

PYRAMIDS

Among all the structures ever erected by man on this earth, the most famous are the pyramids of Egypt. For most people, this means the Giza group, for, as far as size is concerned, no other of the seventy-odd pyramids can be compared with the gigantic mausoleums of Cheops, Chephren, and Mycerinus. These three for the average person represent Egypt and hold for him the alluring mystery of the Land of the Nile. Of the Seven Wonders of the Ancient World, the Giza Pyramids alone have survived the ravages of time and the destructive hand of man. They are still the most massive and impressive buildings in the world today.

As with astronomical measurements where the scientist has to resort to comparisons in order to demonstrate the immensity of the universe, so it is with the Pyramid of Cheops. No other building in history has called for so much study of construction, dimensions, and purpose as this pile of thirty million cubic feet of limestone. It has been estimated that the Great Pyramid, built forty-six hundred years ago, is large enough to accommodate St. Paul's Cathedral, Westminster Abbey, St. Peter's in Rome, and the Cathedrals of Milan and Florence. It consists of 2,300,000 limestone blocks, each one weighing 2½ tons and measuring 3 feet in each direction. Originally it was 481 feet high but now is 451 feet. The average length of the four base lines is 755 feet. A careful survey by J. H. Cole for the Egyptian government in 1925 indicated that the original measurements on the four sides at the bases were: north, 755·43 feet; south, 756·08 feet; east, 755·88 feet; west, 755·77 feet. The difference between the longest and the shortest base line was therefore only 7·9 inches. By using one of the celestial bodies, the Cheops builders were able to orient the Pyramid to the four cardinal points, the errors being only in the following fractions of one degree: north side, 2' 28" south of west; south side, 1' 57" south of west; east side, 5' 30" west of north; west side, 2' 30" west of north. The four corners were almost perfect right angles with the following measurements: 90° 3' 2"; north-west, 90° 59' 58"; south-east, 89° 56' 37"; and south-west, 90° 0' 33".[1]

In the absence of any precise information on the subject, the question of how many men were required to erect the Pyramid would seem to be an idle one. Petrie, followed by Edwards, calculated that 100,000 men were used in the transportation of the blocks to the base of the Pyramid and some 4,000 in its actual construction. The latter probably worked all year but the former could work only during the inundation period—from the latter part of July to the end of October.

The problem of construction is equally baffling. At best we can only make a conjecture but it is one which seems inescapable. The builders of the Cheops Pyramid worked with such precision that, as Petrie says, any errors in the angles and degrees "can be covered with one's thumb". The stone blocks were fitted together so well that a knife cannot be inserted in the joints, an observation made by Abd al-Latif some eight centuries ago. How was this accomplished without modern machinery or even the pulley? The first part of the answer is, as we have already intimated, sheer man-power. The second part is the incline plane. The limestone blocks were quarried in the Mokkatam Hills by driving into the rock sharp sticks which, when water was poured around them, cracked open the rock. Of course, the Egyptians had the adze along with copper tools for starting the wedge-slots as well as saws and chisels for cutting. The rough blocks were pulled on wooden sledges to the Nile where they were loaded on barges. On the west bank they were dragged up a long causeway to the site of the Pyramid. Meanwhile, workmen at Aswan were quarrying granite for chamber-walls, doors, columns, and the

---

[1] Measurements from I. E. S. Edwards: *The Pyramids of Egypt* (Baltimore, Penguin, 1947), p. 87. For an explanation of the most probable method used to determine true north, see *ibid.*, p. 210.

sarcophagus. The location of the site for the Pyramid was determined by several factors: like all tombs, it had to be on the west bank (the side of the setting sun); it had to be built on a floor of native rock which was even and perfect; and it had to be built near the capital and not far from the river. First the bed-rock was cleared of sand and then made level by chipping off high spots and filling in low ones—a task which the masons performed well, for only a half-inch discrepancy is found anywhere on the outside edge of the rock floor. This well-nigh perfect job of levelling was achieved by means of an irrigation technique in which the square surface of the Pyramid base was surrounded by mud and then filled with water. Trenches were dug in the rock floor at equal depth from the surface of the water. After the water was run off the protruding sections of rock were chipped off.

The limestone blocks were hauled along the inclined causeway on wooden sledges. A block could have been placed on the sledge either by use of a lever or by a short ramp. Each block was then roped to the sledge. As to the problem of raising the blocks to the required height so as to fit them into the Pyramid, the answer could only be by the use of a long ramp made of stone, rubble, and sand. Just how the interior of the Great Pyramid was put together is still unknown, but we may gain an idea from the earlier pyramids at Dashur, Abu Sir, and Meidum, which contained vertical columns of core masonry. These upright columns were encased in limestone to make a stepped effect. The steps in turn were filled with "packing blocks" and finally the whole structure was covered with a smooth outer casing. Such may have been the method used in the Great Pyramid.[1] Herodotus suggests that the blocks were raised from one level to the next "by means of machines formed of short beams of wood". But Clarke and Engelbach hold to the ramp method. According to Edwards the supply ramp was constructed to cover the whole of one side of the Pyramid. With the raising of each level, the ramp would be raised and made longer and narrower. The masons could move the blocks and mount them on the other three sides as each level was raised. For this purpose a narrow

[1] See S. Clarke and R. Engelbach: *Ancient Egyptian Masonry* (London, Oxford University Press, 1930).

embankment could serve as a scaffolding. The work proceeded from the centre outwards, the packing block being inserted last. Much of the fitting of the joints was done previously by masons on the ground. Apparently mortar was used in fitting the joints of the larger casing and packing blocks. The chambers and corridors would have to be built at the proper levels before the outer blocks were put in place. The granite slabs would be cut, pre-fitted, polished and numbered beforehand. The top having been reached, a polished cap-stone of granite was put in place on a bed of mortar. Then the process of dressing was begun and the outer casing was applied as the ramp was gradually lowered and taken away.[1]

A still more puzzling question has to do with the purpose and meaning of the pyramid. We have already established the fact, that whatever else it stood for, the pyramid was primarily a royal tomb. For its more symbolic meaning we must look to the solar faith of the early Egyptians. At Heliopolis, where the official religion took rise in the Old Kingdom, a temple cult developed with an organized priesthood devoted to the worship of the sun. In the Holy of Holies of the temple was a symbol called the *benben*, a pyramid-shaped stone, representing the sun-god. This stone fetish may provide the key to the religious significance of the pyramid itself. The king was buried under the sun-god symbol, which was placed in the centre of the pyramid. The pyramid dominated the landscape for miles and its apex was the first object in all the land to catch the sun's rays each morning. Some scholars believe that the pyramid was simply an enlarged reproduction of the similarly shaped solar symbol in the temple. If this were the case, the pyramid must have been built to represent the rays of the sun slanting towards the earth. It is interesting to note that at times, especially in winter when late afternoon clouds form, if one stands by the Nile and looks towards the Giza pyramid complex, he can see the impressive spectacle of the sun's beams shooting downward through a cloud at the same angle as the sides of the pyramid.

There is no doubt then that the pyramids were definitely con-

[1] The above reconstruction of the method of building the Pyramid is based largely on Edwards, Engelbach, and Petrie. What has been suggested on the problem of construction would apply naturally to all other pyramids.

nected with the solar faith. In most ancient cultures the god was
conceived as transcendent, and towers or temples were built to
bring the worshipper nearer to the god. The ziggurat of Babylonia
(the biblical Tower of Babel), enclosed within the temple area,
was one such high pyramidal building which the people ascended
to be nearer heaven. Some of the early pyramid texts indicate
that the kings saw the pyramid in this light. Several of these
inscriptions speak of the pyramid as "a staircase to heaven being
laid for the king". The Egyptian word for pyramid in its deriva-
tive sense is not clear, but there is reason to think that it refers
to "a place of ascension".

The fact that the pyramid, associated symbolically with the
sun, was also used as a burial place for the Pharaohs is eloquent
testimony to the profound influence of the solar faith in early
Egypt. The cap-stone from the pyramid of Amenemhet III at
Dashur (now in the Cairo Museum) illustrates this influence. On
the side that had faced the east is pictured an ascending falcon
with the sun-disk on his back. Under the sun-disk are the eyes of
the king facing the rising sun. Under the falcon is an inscription:
"The face of King Amenemhet III is opened that he may behold
the Lord of the Horizon when he sails across the sky." The Book
of the Dead frequently pictures the sun-god in the form of a
falcon, with the sun-disk on his head, rising from the desert together with the deceased and his friends bowing in reverence
before Ra.

The pyramid was called the "House of Eternity"; its sides
were "ladders to heaven"; and the solar boat was the "Divine
Barque" for the journey across the sky. Edwards sees possible
confirmation for this interpretation in the Egyptian name for
pyramid—*M(e)r*, which can be translated "Place of Ascension".[1]

The determinative for *M(e)r* is the sign $\triangle$. The step pyramid
is usually attached to the sign *r*, thus pointing to the same explanation; i.e., a stairway to heaven. As the king's "Castle of Eternity", his permanent home, the pyramid had to be built to last
forever.

---

[1] *Ibid.*, p. 234.

THE EVOLUTION OF THE PYRAMID

There were three classes of pyramids: the mastaba, the step pyramid and the true pyramid. It would seem that one form simply grew out of the other, as illustrated in the Step Pyramid of Zoser, which started as a mastaba tomb, followed by the Pyramid of Meidum, where the stepped-form was transformed into the true pyramid. Strictly speaking, however, the developmental or evolutionary theory is not foolproof since a step pyramid from an earlier period and a mastaba from a later period have been found; but generally the theory can be followed.

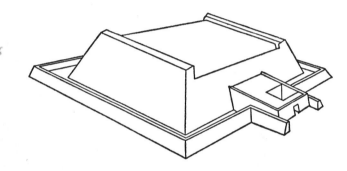

Fig. 1. A mastaba (reconstruction)

In pre-dynastic times the body was buried in an oblong flat-bottomed pit and was covered with a skin or woven fabric. Weapons and food were deposited in the grave for the deceased to use in the after-life. A pile of sand covered the grave. In the First Dynasty the burial pit was covered by a rectangular structure made of brick. Its flat roof and slanting sides led later Egyptians to call it a mastaba (the Arabic word for bench; but actually it resembled an Egyptian house). One of the earliest known mastabas was that of Aha, the second king of the First Dynasty. This tomb, found by W. B. Emery at Sakkara, had a wooden roof and a row of five rooms in the centre of the structure. The body of the king was placed in the middle chamber; and the other rooms housed his possessions. The five rooms were completely surrounded by magazines or storage chambers for food-offerings and funerary furniture. Around these and covering the entire tomb was a brick superstructure which in turn was enclosed by two brick walls.

The Egyptian tomb, it might be explained at this point, had two functions: to house the body and the *ka* and to provide a means of supplying the *ka* with its daily necessities. It was necessary also to provide chambers for the equipment to be used in the after-life. The tomb of the Old Kingdom consisted of a substructure containing the mummy and a superstructure or offering-place which contained the funerary equipment.

Interest in the excavation of the early periods centres in Abydos where the royal tombs have thrown much light on early Egyptian culture. As the holy city, Abydos from earliest times was connected with the Osirian faith and became the site of the Passion Play of Osiris in which the death and resurrection of the god was celebrated annually. For this reason perhaps Abydos was chosen as a royal cemetery.

Some examples of the early pyramidal form—small brick tombs covered with mud plaster—were found by Mariette. The tomb of the Pharaoh Khent, discovered by M. Amélineau, may serve as a typical example of the early royal tombs. It consisted of a pit, 28 feet square, floored and buttressed with brick, and surrounded by smaller chambers. Adjoining the king's tomb enclosure were seven rows of shallower graves, presumably those of the royal retinue. The discovery in these graves of seventy stelae, practically all of which had to do with women, would indicate that the tombs were those of the royal harem. This would suggest the possibility that all the members of the king's household, including his wives, were put to death and buried with him, a practice which, if it did exist, was shortly afterwards discontinued. Clearer evidence of such a custom is found in the early Sumerian culture.

Work at Abydos was continued in 1899 by Petrie whose discovery of the tomb of Den-Setui, the fifth king of the First Dynasty, served to show the progress of tomb construction. This tomb was more elaborate than earlier ones, being not only lined with brick but floored with blocks of granite. It was surrounded by 137 graves, belonging presumably to the family and nobles of the dead Pharaoh. Petrie also found the tomb of Khasekhemui, the ninth king of the Second Dynasty. This tomb measured 223 feet by 54 feet and consisted of three rooms, the middle one being the royal burial chamber in which were found fragments of the royal sceptre made of sard and gold. While clearing the tomb of King Zer, Petrie's workmen noticed the arm of a mummy in a hole in the wall of the chamber. Removing the wrappings, they found on the arm four beautiful bracelets of gold, turquoise, lapis lazuli, and amethyst. How this arm, probably that of Zer's Queen, escaped the attention of the ancient robbers and later Coptic fanatics is still a mystery. The bracelets testify to the high taste and consummate skill of the early Egyptian craftsmen.

Sakkara is perhaps the most important site for our knowledge of early private tombs. The Archaic Cemetery here was discovered and partially excavated by James E. Quibell whose work was continued by Cecil M. Firth.

Added light has been shed on the chronology and the reigns of the First Dynasty by the expedition to the Archaic Necropolis of Sakkara directed by W. B. Emery in the 1950s for the Egypt Exploration Society. These excavations were a continuation of Emery's pre-war work on the same site. In 1953 he discovered the tomb of Uadji, the fourth king of the First Dynasty. This tomb, typical of the others found by Emery, measured 165 feet by 70 feet. Its original height was about 40 feet. The sides were made of panelled buttresses and the walls were painted in many colours. Outside the enclosure wall were sixty-two small tombs containing the bodies of the members of the royal retinue— another instance, perhaps, of the mass burial of the family, servants, and attendants, who were killed and buried with the king to accompany him into the after-life. The superstructure of the tomb contained forty-five magazines which were filled with funerary equipment. The substructure consisted of a large burial chamber surrounded by additional storage magazines and auxiliary rooms.

The fate of Uadji and his tomb was, needless to say, no different from that of any other king. The tomb robbers did a thorough and systematic job and, after taking the valuable objects from the burial chambers, set fire to it. The tomb was repaired and refurnished during the reign of Ka'a, the last king of the First Dynasty, and, of course, the new funerary equipment was also stolen. In spite of the successive robberies, the Emery expedition found thousands of treasures in the magazines: alabaster vases, and pottery and stone vessels, many of which were filled with food, some inscribed with the seal of Uadji and others with that of Ka'a.

In 1954 Emery discovered another elaborate tomb and, nearby, a smaller one. A stele and several seals found there indicate that they were the tombs of King Ka'a and a priest or nobleman by the name of Mer-ka. In the following season Emery found two more royal tombs of the First Dynasty. Adjoining one of them was the almost intact funerary boat of King Udimu, the earliest example of such in Egyptian history.

In the Third and Fourth Dynasties, the mastaba became more elaborate and was made partly or wholly of limestone instead of mud-brick. The burial chamber, deep in the mastaba, was closed off by a limestone portcullis and the vertical shaft leading to it was filled with rubble and sealed at the entrance.

The first step pyramid was that of Zoser, the second king of the Third Dynasty, and was located at Sakkara, the cemetery of Memphis. Mention has been made of the early surveys of this site by Pococke, Perring, and others. The identification of the name of Zoser was made by two German Egyptologists, Emil Brugsch and Georg Steindorff. Through their research it was also found that the famous architect and physician, Imhotep, whom Manetho had mentioned as "the inventor of the art of building in hewn stone", was the builder. Zoser's Step Pyramid, erected probably between 2800 and 2700 B.C., was the archetype of all later pyramids and the first great stone structure in history. The importance of the transition from brick and wood to hewn stone is indicated by G. A. Reisner:

> Whatever the architectural forms developed in the earlier stone buildings which I have inferred, the buildings of Djoser present a wonderful transition [translation] of the older brick architecture with wooden accessories into dressed limestone. This work is associated with the name of Imhotep, famous as a scribe, wise man, physician, and prime minister, but now revealed as a great creative

architect. . . . This wonderful tomb and its overwhelmingly abundant funerary equipment reveals an astonishing mastery over the hard materials of the earth and an opulence in power without precedent in Egypt before this time. It shows the civilization of Egypt approaching its climax.[1]

Imhotep apparently had intended to build a stone mastaba tomb. He first built a burial chamber of granite in the bed rock and sealed it with a heavy granite block. The superstructure took the form of a terrace, thus making a mastaba tomb. This was 26 feet high and was square at the base rather than oblong, each base measuring about two hundred feet and oriented to the cardinal points. Two horizontal extensions of the first step were made, making the base oblong instead of square. At this juncture the architect changed his plan. He now added three terraces to the base, thus making a four-stepped pyramid. Still later a new superstructure was added so that the final enlargement made a total of six huge steps. This was covered with dressed limestone. The final structure rose to a height of 204 feet and measured 411 by 358 feet at the base. A rectangular wall, 34 feet high, was built around the pyramid, making an enclosure of 597 yards by 304 yards. The perimeter of the enclosure measured over a mile.

Excavations of the Zoser complex by C. M. Firth, J. E. Quibell, and J. P. Lauer have added much to our knowledge of the entire complex and especially of the interior of the Pyramid itself. The builders, they found, had sunk a shaft some 90 feet in the bed rock, at the bottom of which was the burial chamber. This chamber was built of pink granite which had been quarried at Aswan. After the body of the king had been placed in the burial room, a large granite block, weighing several tons, was lowered to seal the entrance. The tomb was surrounded by a maze of ramps leading to galleries which were cut out of the rock a hundred feet below the surface. These rooms were beautifully decorated with reliefs in limestone and green-blue faience tiles. That some of these corridors were tombs of the royal family is proved by the discovery of alabaster coffins in one of which was the skeleton of a child.

The buildings within the enclosure formed the most elaborate

[1] *The Development of the Egyptian Tomb Down to the Accession of Cheops* (Cambridge, Harvard University Press, 1936).

Giza Pyramids from the south (Fourth Dynasty). From left to right: Mycerinus, Chephren, Cheops. (*Courtesy*, *Hirmer Verlag*, *Munich*)

Funerary Temple of Mycerinus with the Chephren Pyramid in the background. (*Courtesy*, *Hirmer Verlag*, *Munich*)

Wall relief (Eighteenth Dynasty) in the tomb of vizier Ramose depicting a funeral procession. (*Courtesy, Hirmer Verlag, Munich*)

pyramid-complex in Egypt.[1] These buildings consisted of the Mortuary Temple on the north side of the Pyramid; a court with the Serdab, which contained a limestone statue of Zoser; the Great Court with the Altar (near the south wall of the Pyramid) and two stones around which it was the custom of the king to walk (or run) in the Heb-sed ceremony; the Entrance Hall with porticoes; the Heb-sed Court with its two chapels; a smaller temple; the North and South Palaces; the South Tomb, containing coloured reliefs; and the Great Altar on the north side just inside the wall.[2] The notable feature of the North and South Palaces is the use of the plant-forms in half-columns carved in the wall, with the capitals formed of leaves, and also the engaged papyrus, rib and fluted columns. The engaged fluted columns of the entrance colonnade represent bundled reeds.

The forty-year campaign of Professor Walter B. Emery at Sakkara had brought him by 1965 to the threshold of what may be one of the most significant discoveries in the history of Egyptology—the unearthing of the tomb of Imhotep himself. Working on the theory that the tomb of the great genius must be near that of his king, Professor Emery discovered a temple contemporary with Imhotep, a vast underground chain of labyrinths, passages that he identified as parts of the tomb, and thousands of mummified ibises and bulls which could be clues to the tomb area. Imhotep was venerated as the god Aesculapius, "the Great One of Ibis", by the Greeks who made annual pilgrimages to the site and sacrificed to him bulls and ibises by the thousands. Pilgrims from all the ancient Mediterranean lands visited the tomb seeking wisdom and miraculous cures. They also brought with them stelae and inscribed slabs describing their own countries and their times. The discovery of Imhotep's tomb would undoubtedly provide new information about medicine, surgery, and disease in Third-dynasty Egypt.

Between the Step Pyramid of Zoser and the True Pyramid there were several transitional stages. The first is the unfinished

---

[1] For a discussion of the architectural design of the buildings see W. Stevenson Smith: *The Art and Architecture of Ancient Egypt* (Baltimore, Penguin, 1958), pp. 34–5.

[2] See Kurt Lange and Max Hirmer: *Aegypten* (Munich, Hirmer Verlag, 1955), Plates 7–17 and Figures 3–6 on pp. 42–3.

"Layer Pyramid" at Zaniyat el-Aryan near Giza, excavated first by Alessandro Barsanti and later more thoroughly by Reisner. So little remains of the Layer Pyramid that it is difficult to determine the exact type of building, but the inner core, like the usual stepped pyramid, was constructed of inclined layers of masonry against which layers of casing blocks leaned. This pyramid is

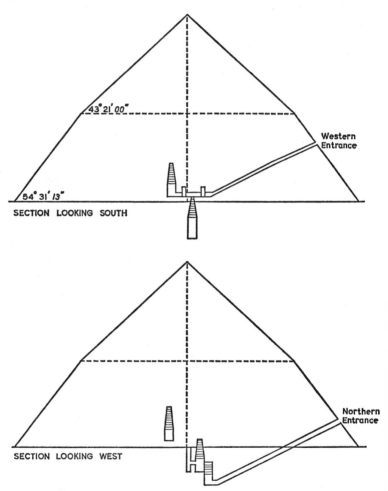

Fig. 2. Diagram of a Bent Pyramid, showing change of angle, the two separate entrances, and the chambers with corbelled roofs

assigned to an obscure king of the Third Dynasty named Kha-ban. Here one can see the preliminary work for a great pyramid lying unfinished just as the workmen left it nearly five thousand years ago. What Barsanti saw was a huge rectangular pit, 73 feet deep, 82 feet long and 46 feet wide, cut into the limestone bed and approached at one end by a stairway 28 feet wide and 360 feet long. The floor of the pit was paved with blocks of dressed granite, each weighing about nine tons. In the middle of the pit on a 45-ton block of polished granite lay an oval sarcophagus with its lid in place.

More important in the transitional period was the Bent Pyramid of Dashur, which now is thought to have been built by Seneferu rather than by Huni, his predecessor. When the structure was half finished, the angle of incline was changed from 54° 14′ to 42° 59′, thus giving rise to its name. The reason for this change is not known. One suggestion is that the builder changed his mind about the height and therefore cut back the angle of inclination. Another is that the masons, discovering that there was too much stress, altered the exterior angle with a view to reducing the weight that the lower chamber would have to bear. In either case it was probably designed originally as a true pyramid.

The sides at the base measure 620 feet and its original height was 320 feet. It was oriented, like the Great Pyramid, on the four cardinal points. It is the best preserved of all the pyramids, the reason for which, as Edwards observes, is that the casing stones rather than lying in flat courses "incline inwards, thus giving the superstructure greater solidity".[1] An odd feature of the Bent Pyramid is that it has two independent entrances which lead to separate chambers, one in the Pyramid itself and the other below the surface. It is not known which of the two chambers housed the body of the king. Originally, it could be safely assumed, there was the usual complex with Mortuary Temple, other tombs, enclosure walls and a causeway.

In 1924 Jéquier did some exploratory work on the Enclosure and Causeway of the Bent Pyramid, establishing the existence of walls and remains of buildings. In 1951 Ahmed Fakhry of the Department of Antiquities excavated the Funerary Temple to the

[1] *Op. cit.*, p. 69.

east of the Pyramid. Altars and offering bowls were still in place. In the days that followed the discovery of the Valley Temple, Fakhry found hundreds of blocks covered with reliefs, statues, stelae, and vases. Outstanding among these finds was the beautiful crowned statue of Seneferu, still retaining its colour. The walls of the Temple were covered with reliefs which recorded Seneferu's endowment for the support of temple and priests.

The Meidum Pyramid constitutes the last stage in the transition, containing, as it does, both the stepped form and the true pyramidal form. The importance of this Pyramid as shown in

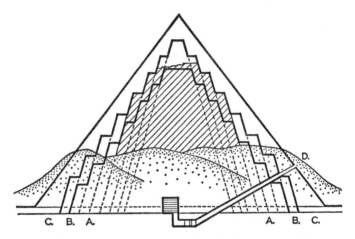

Fig. 3. The Pyramid of Meidum: last of the forerunners of the true pyramid. A, Originally a seven-stepped pyramid. B, Top step raised and each succeeding step built up to a higher level. C, The steps were filled in with stone and the entire structure was then overlaid with smooth casing of Tura limestone, thus eventuating from a step to a true pyramid. D, Entrance and corridor. E, Vertical shaft leading upward to tomb chamber made of limestone. This pyramid was excavated by Petrie, 1891; later by Wainwright, Borchardt and Rowe. (After I. E. S. Edwards, *The Pyramids of Egypt*.)

Petrie's excavation has already been discussed.[1] Completing the transition was another pyramid at Dashur built by Seneferu not far from the Bent Pyramid. This was designed as a true pyramid

[1] See pp. 82, 83.

and was built simultaneously with the one at Meidum but is much larger, measuring 719 feet at each base.

Such was the ancestry of the true pyramid, the best example of which is of course the Great Pyramid of Cheops, son of

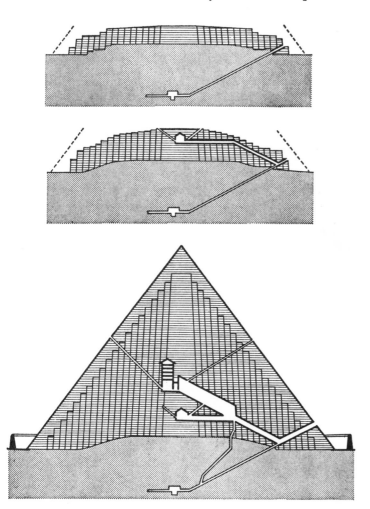

Fig. 4. Sectional view of the Cheops Pyramid showing successive changes of plan

Seneferu. Cheops chose a perfect site on a rocky plateau overlooking the Nile at Giza. We have previously dealt with its construction and some of its architectural details.[1] Vyse, Perring,
and Greaves had worked on the solution of several construction
puzzles; it remained for Borchardt and Petrie, if not to solve
these mysteries, at least to come close to a solution.

As with the Step Pyramid of Zoser, changes were made in the
Great Pyramid during the course of construction. The architect
originally planned to have the burial chamber underneath the
Pyramid. The entrance is on the north side, 24 feet east of centre
and 55 feet from the base. The entrance corridor descends at an
angle of twenty-six degrees, first through the Pyramid itself and
through bed-rock for 345 feet from the entrance, then continues
on the level for 30 feet and ends in a chamber. This chamber was
left unfinished, as was a corridor leading away from the room on
the south side. According to Edwards, this passage, if completed,
would probably have led to a second burial chamber on the same
level. After the core masonry of the superstructure had advanced
substantially, it was decided to build the burial chamber in the
centre of the Pyramid. Consequently a passage was cut through
the core joining the Descending Corridor about 60 feet from
the entrance. This Ascending Corridor, 129 feet long, was built
in the same dimensions and gradient as the Descending Corridor.
At its top was a horizontal passage leading to a room which is
usually called the Queen's Chamber. This chamber was also left
unfinished, indicating that what had probably been intended as
the king's burial chamber was abandoned. With this further
change in plans, the Ascending Corridor was continued as the
Grand Gallery which measured 153 feet in length and 28 feet in
height.[2] At the end of the Grand Gallery a narrow passage led
to the King's Chamber. This impressive room was built of granite
and measures 34 by 17 feet and is 19 feet high. The granite sarcophagus of the king still stands on the west side of the room.
Since its width exceeds that of the Ascending Corridor, it must
have been put in place before the passages and the room itself
were built. The roof of the King's Chamber presents an unusual

[1] See pp. 87-91.
[2] For a detailed description of the Grand Gallery see W. M. Flinders Petrie:
The Pyramids and Temples of Giza (London, 1883), p. 72.

architectural phenomenon. The ceiling consists of nine slabs of polished granite weighing altogether about four hundred tons. Above the ceiling are five superimposed chambers, the thick roofs of the first four being flat and that of the fifth pointed, so constructed as to guard against the collapse of the structure over the tomb. The first of these "relieving compartments" called "Davison's Chamber", probably because he was the first to mention it, is connected by a passage to the top of the Grand Gallery. The other four "relieving compartments" were discovered by Vyse and Herring.

In the case of the Great Pyramid with its Ascending Corridor, the blocking of the passage after the body had been placed in the Burial Chamber has presented a problem. It is now thought that the plug blocks were placed in the Grand Gallery in the course of construction and held in place by slots on the sides. After the funeral, the plugs were released, slid down the Ascending Corridor, which narrowed at the end, and filled up the passageway. That being accomplished, the workmen made their escape through the shaft or well which led down almost vertically from the end of the Grand Gallery to the entrance of the Queen's Chamber. From that point they climbed up the Descending Corridor which was afterwards closed with rubble. Finally, the entrance to the Pyramid was covered with casing stones so as to make it look exactly like the rest of the Pyramid wall.

Little remains of the Cheops Complex except the limestone pavement, running from the Pyramid to the enclosure wall and the ruins of the recently excavated Mortuary Temple. The Cheops Temple, situated at the eastern base of the Pyramid, consisted of a court paved with basalt and surrounded by granite pillars with a roofed portico. Fragments of reliefs from the walls of this temple have also been found. On the south side are three small pyramids and beside one of them is a large stone pit, which according to Reisner, its discoverer, once contained the funerary boat of the queen.

It was not until 1954 that Cheops' funeral barque was discovered and then purely by accident. Towards the end of May of that year Kemal el Malakh, an architect employed by the Department of Antiquities, was clearing the sand along the south wall of the Great Pyramid in order to make a road for the convenience of tourists. The workmen came upon an ancient wall, shovelled away a layer of sand and exposed a row of forty-two limestone blocks, each one weighing 15 tons, and all tightly sealed with gypsum. Malakh surmised that these blocks might be the roof of an underground chamber. He tapped on the stones repeatedly with a bamboo stick and heard a resonant sound. He then chiselled a 6-inch hole through one of the blocks. He had forgotten to carry a flashlight, so he transferred sunlight into the darkness below by using a mirror—just as the ancient tomb builders had done. He smelled a strange fragrance like incense drifting up through the hole, perhaps the aroma of cedar beams from Lebanon. When his eyes became adjusted to the scene, he gazed upon a fabulous find that had not been seen or touched since it was placed there 4,600 years ago. It was the sacred solar boat of Cheops! The hull, 125 feet long and 17 feet wide, was carved out of bed-rock. What appeared to be a series of decks had shrunk away from the stone sides, but the wood was in excellent condition due to the fact that the gypsum sealing had never been broken. The remarkable thing about this boat is that it is one of the few objects from ancient Egypt that was not wrecked by thieves. The top deck was covered with a frayed fabric. Near the bow lay a wooden steering oar. Part of the decorated prow lay on the deck along with a rope 300 feet long. Also of interest were several 5-foot poles similar to those found in the tomb of Queen Hetepheres. They were probably used to support the roof of the deck cabin.

The solar ship may be one of two, or possibly four, funerary ships required by the king to transport him in his voyage over the heavens in his role of sun-god. At present writing the pit remains closed and sealed, awaiting further scientific investigation.

Surrounding the Great Pyramid on all but the north side were rows of mastabas which were the tombs of the royal family and high officials. Today these tombs are unimpressive but originally were cased in limestone. Such an arrangement carried out the idea of the king being surrounded in the after-life by his relatives and retinue. The difference between the god-king and his mortal subjects is emphatically emphasized in the contrast between the towering Pyramid and the low flat-roofed mastabas.

We have already described the early excavation of the Second
and Third Pyramids by Belzoni and Vyse. The Chephren Pyramid
is distinguished by its original limestone casing which has with-
stood erosion, earthquake, and other destructive elements, both
natural and human. This dressing remains on the top fourth of
the Pyramid and also at the base but the casing at the base is red
granite. The Second Pyramid originally was 471 feet high but at
present measures 447 feet. The sides at the base were 708 feet.
The angle of inclination is 52° 20′ as compared with that of the
Cheops Pyramid which is 51° 52′.

The visitor today is apt to overlook the Pyramid of Chephren
in his preoccupation with other remains that belonged to the
Complex, notably the Sphinx, the Funerary Temple, and the
Valley Temple. Surviving wind, sand erosion and mutilation by
the Mamelukes and others, the Sphinx still holds its enigmatic
head high above the desert floor. Guarding the entrance to the
Causeway, which runs straight back to the Pyramid, this recum-
bent colossus is 66 feet high and 240 feet long. It was carved
out of the living rock in the form of a lion with a human head.
It is a portrait of Pharaoh Chephren during whose reign it was
sculptured. In later times it was worshipped as a representation
of the sun-god. According to an inscription on a granite slab that
stands between the paws, Thutmose IV, 1420–1411 B.C., before
he ascended to the throne, cleared away the sand that surrounded
the paws and body. Later clearings were made by Caviglia in
1818, Maspero in 1886, and the Egyptian Service of Antiquities
in 1925.

The Valley Building was discovered by Mariette in 1853. It
was further cleared by several later expeditions. It measured
147 feet at each base and 43 feet in height. The walls were of
limestone faced with red granite. It was in this building in a deep
pit that Mariette found the famous diorite statue of Chephren
(now in the Cairo Museum), one of many royal statues that
originally graced the hall. The Valley Temple, according to
Egyptologists, was used for the purificatory ritual and embalming.
It was customary to wash the body of the king before it was taken
into the Funerary Temple. The washing was the means of re-
generation and identified the god-king with the immortal Osiris.
In addition to the purification and embalming which took place

in the Valley Building, there was the ceremony called "The Opening of the Mouth", a ritual performed either with the royal statues or the mummy itself to symbolize the king's status as a living person.

The mummified body of the king was then transported across a causeway to the Mortuary Temple. This was a rectangular building about 370 feet by 160 feet, flanked on the north and south walls by five boat pits. The walls and columns resemble those of the Valley Building. At the western end in front of the sanctuary was an open court containing five statues of the king.[1] After the funeral ceremony the priestly procession made its way to the Pyramid over an enclosed ramp.

The chief exploration of the Third Pyramid was made by the expedition of Harvard University and the Boston Museum of Fine Arts (1905–27) under the direction of George A. Reisner. The Mycerinus Pyramid measures 356 feet at each base and originally it was 218 feet high. The casing was in limestone and granite. Situated parallel to the south base are three subsidiary pyramids each one of which was connected with a Mortuary Temple.

THE TWO MAIN FIELDS OF PYRAMIDS

With the Giza group, we have reached the climax in the development of the pyramidal form. There are two main fields of pyramids: the first (and more important) extends from Abu Roash, a few miles north of Giza, to Hawara, 60 miles south of Giza. The second field lies in the Sudan in the Meroë and Napata territory, the sites of the Ethiopian Pharaohs of the Twenty-fifth Dynasty (eighth century B.C. and later).

The pyramids in the northern field, following those at Giza, were built from the Fifth to the Thirteenth Dynasty (2560–1777 B.C.). The first was that of Userkaf at Sakkara, followed by those of Sahura, Neferirkara and Niussera at Abu Sir. These three are known for their sun-god temples. The Pyramids of Unas, Teti, Pepy I, Merenra, and Pepy II are important chiefly for their long inscriptions, which have provided us with valuable information about the early Egyptian religion, and for their coloured low

[1] For diagrams and descriptions of the architecture of the Mortuary Temple, see Kurt Lange and Max Hirmer, *op. cit.*, pp. 47, 48.

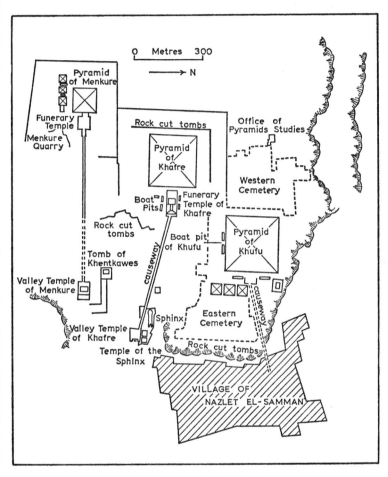

Fig. 5. The Giza Necropolis

reliefs illustrating various aspects of social and economic life. The hieroglyphic inscriptions connected with these pyramids are known as the Pyramid Texts. They were usually found in the Mortuary Temple and contain the ritual, prayers, hymns, and spells recited by the priests for the welfare of the king in the after-life. The Pyramid of Pepy II had an elaborate complex of buildings which were excavated by the Swiss archaeologist

Gustave Jéquier. The other important pyramid sites were those of the Amenemhets and the Senusrets at Lisht, Dashur, Hawara, and Illahun.

The Lisht area had been explored earlier by Maspero, Jéquier, and Gautier, but from 1906 to 1934 it was thoroughly excavated by Ambrose Lansing, Albert Lythgoe and Arthur Mace of the New York Metropolitan Museum of Art. The chief pyramids here are those of Amenemhet I and Senusret I. Amenemhet (1991–1962 B.C.) was a strong ruler and inaugurated a period of prosperity and stability. He was a Theban but removed the seat of government to the Fayum near the modern village of Lisht where he erected his pyramid. He departed from the standard form in building the complex on two levels, the Pyramid being on the upper terrace. It was made of crude brick and was covered with limestone. In the 1920 season the Metropolitan staff found, just outside the pyramid enclosure, a series of tombs of the royal family, all of which had been thoroughly plundered shortly after the burial. The Mortuary Temple was located east of the Pyramid and near it were tombs of prominent nobles. Owing to a rise in the level of the Nile bed, the water seepage in the Burial Chamber has made it impossible to explore the interior. Outside the enclosure wall were the mastaba tombs of other officials, princesses, and courtiers. Many blocks from the older tombs at Giza, Sakkara, and Dashur were used in the construction of the Amenemhet Pyramid and Mortuary Temple. As Edwards notes, the difference between the Old Kingdom reliefs preserved on these blocks and those of the Twelfth Dynasty is difficult to trace because Amenemhet deliberately imitated the style of the former temple decoration.[1]

In February 1907, Mace and Winlock of the Metropolitan staff discovered in the cemetery outside the *temenos* wall the almost intact tomb of the House Mistress Senebtisy, a wealthy lady of the court and probably related to the vizier under Amenemhet. The tomb consisted of a vertical shaft or entrance pit, an offering chamber, and a burial chamber. The body was encased in an anthropoid coffin of wood overlaid with gold foil and decorated with an inlay of carnelian and blue and green faience. The second

[1] For plan of the Amenemhet complex see James Baikie: *Egyptian Antiquities in the Nile Valley* (New York, Macmillan, 1932), p. 191.

coffin was undecorated except for the two magic eyes of Horus. The mummy was well wrapped in sheets and bandages which were soaked in resin. The heart had been removed, wrapped in linen and replaced in the body, but the other organs were found in alabaster canopic jars. On her head was a circlet of gold from which hung ninety-eight rosettes of beaten gold, and around her neck were three necklaces made of carnelian, feldspar, gold and ivory. The mummy was decorated with typical funeral jewellery: broad collars, wide bracelets, and wide anklets. One of the collars was made of sheet copper overlaid with gold foil and another consisted of nine strands of turquoise, carnelian, green faience, and gilded plaster, with a falcon head at each end. One of the most interesting pieces of funeral jewellery found on the mummy of Senebtisy was an apron of polychrome beadwork. Hanging from the faience belt were twenty-two long beadwork streamers. The belt clasp bears the name Senebtisy in painted blue hieroglyphics.

In the twentieth year of his reign Amenemhet appointed his son Senusret as co-regent. The dual reign continued for ten years during which period events were recorded by the year of their respective, overlapping reigns. This practice of co-regency between father and son was followed throughout the dynasty.

The Pyramid of Senusret I was first identified by Maspero in 1882. In 1894 Jéquier and Gautier found ten white limestone statues on the site, each one about 6 feet high. They had never been set up but were lying in the sand near the Mortuary Temple. The Metropolitan expedition cleared the Pyramid, the Enclosure Walls, the Cemetery, and the Mortuary Temple where six Osirian statues of the king were found. The Pyramid measured 343 feet at each base and was originally 200 feet high. It was constructed internally of walls of limestone blocks filled with rubble. On the outer surface was a revetment of heavy blocks of cut stone covered with a smooth limestone casing. Around the Pyramid was a great wall of limestone decorated with carved panels bearing the names of the king.[1]

The Funerary Temple was an elaborate structure consisting of

[1] For further details on the Pyramid Complex of Senusret see William C. Hayes: *The Sceptre of Egypt: Part I* (New York, Harper and Brother, 1953), pp. 182–95.

an entrance corridor, an open court containing a large granite altar, a transverse corridor, a serdab, a second vestibule, an ante-chamber, and finally the sanctuary, which was surrounded by storerooms. A causeway connected the Mortuary Temple with the Valley Temple. Between the inner wall, which enclosed the Pyramid and the Mortuary Temple, and the outer wall were nine small pyramids belonging to members of the royal family, each one with its own temple, chapel, and enclosure wall. In the burial chamber of one of these pyramids the excavators found a beautiful quartzite sarcophagus which had been plundered. A canopic chest, made of the same material, lay nearby. Also within the outer wall were many mastaba tombs of courtiers, officials, and priests. Just outside the enclosure was a large mastaba tomb which bore the plurastic title "The Hereditary Prince and Count, Treasurer, High Priest of Heliopolis, Priest of Horus, Priest of Min, Chief Scribe of Divine Records, Super-intendent of Land, Superintendent of all Works, the King's Favourite, Great in his Office, Imhotep". This namesake of Zoser's great architect must have been, among other things, the High Priest under Senusret. Near Imhotep's tomb were two funerary barques, each about 9 feet in length. Near the tomb were two statuettes of the king carved from cedar-wood. These figures, according to Lythgoe, "exhibit finer qualities in sculpture then anything previously known from this period of the Middle Kingdom."

No pyramids were built in Egypt proper after the Seventeenth Dynasty but during the Twenty-fifth (eighth century B.C.) the practice was resumed in the Sudan and continued for almost a thousand years. The chief excavations of the Sudanese or Meroë Pyramids were those of the American G. A. Reisner, whose work will be described later.

Chapter Five

FROM PETRIE TO GONEIM

PETRIE IN THE FAYUM

The three most important names in pyramidology are Petrie, Borchardt, and Reisner. Unlike present-day archaeologists who usually confine their investigations to one area, these three men took all Egypt as their province. In each case, however, they can be identified with one particular field that stands out above the others: Petrie at the Fayum, Borchardt at Abu Sir, and Reisner at Giza.

Flinders Petrie's first trip to Egypt was occasioned by his father's attraction to the theories of Charles Piazzi Smith, one of the many pious souls in the latter part of the nineteenth century who were working the esoteric interpretation of Egyptian antiquities for more than it was worth. Fantastic theories were being proposed maintaining that the measurements of the Great Pyramid proved the divine inspiration of the Bible, that it was built by Joseph for a storehouse, that it was meant to be an astronomical observatory, that it contained the divine revelation of standard weights and measures, and that it contained a prophecy of everything that would ever occur on earth. For one who had written a book on the inductive method, all these forced interpretations were sheer nonsense. Petrie set out first to make accurate measurements, which, incidentally, did not bear out the figures used by Smith and other fanatics to prove their theories. (It might be borne in mind that the numerologists who were "proving" this or that mystery by "exact" dimensions in the Pyramid must have forgotten that the Egyptians did not use centimetres or inches.)

Petrie continued in a more scientific fashion the investigations at Giza carried on previously by Caviglia, Vyse, Perring and Belzoni. Then he moved on to the Fayum where his excavation of the Pyramids of Dashur, Meidum, Hawara, and Lahun was pioneer work.

Typical of Petrie's tenacious and painstaking methods was his discovery and excavation of the Pyramid of Amenemhet III at Hawara. The period of Amenemhet's long reign (1840–1790 B.C.) was one of the most peaceful and prosperous eras in Egyptian history. Under him Egyptian unity was a reality and the country enjoyed freedom from foreign entanglements as well as domestic harmony. Projects that led to an increase in royal revenue, such as the Sinai Mines, were successfully completed. At the Second Cataract the king installed a Nilometer which recorded the level of the high water from year to year, thus enabling the vizier to estimate the extent of the crops for the ensuing season.[1] His most brilliant success, however, and his chief title to fame was his monumental work in the regulation of the water of the inundation. About 70 miles south-west of Cairo and 25 miles from the Nile is a depression in the Libyan Desert created by a river called the Bahr-el-Yussuf. This is known as the Fayum. The small canals irrigating this region have produced a fertile land luxuriant with fruit, corn, and cotton. Lake Moeris, which was formed by this depression, was once some 40 miles square but today it is only a fraction of that area and is known as the Birket el-Kurum. Diodorus, writing in the first century, credits the building of the lake to Amenemhet III, but there is reason to think that it existed before his time. It was he, however, who built vast retention walls inside the Fayum in order to reclaim the land for cultivation. It is estimated that the land so reclaimed measured 27,000 acres. It has been further calculated that enough water could have been accumulated behind the walls to double the volume of the river below the Fayum during the hundred days of the low Nile. Thus the enlightened Pharaoh by the use of locks anticipated the great present-day barrages of Aswan and Assiut.

Near the town of Arsinoe, just inside the depression, was a

[1] These records still stand and indicate that the level was 25 to 30 feet higher than the present level of high Nile.

vast rectangular building some 800 by 1,000 feet, which apparently served as an administrative centre for all of Egypt as well as a place of worship. It contained a series of separate halls for each nome. Among Greek travellers it was known as the Labyrinth and was still standing in Strabo's time. He describes it as follows:

We have here also the Labyrinth, a work equal to the Pyramids, and adjoining to it the tomb of the king who constructed the Labyrinth. After proceeding beyond the first entrance of the canal about 30 or 40 stadia, there is a table-shaped plain, with a village and a large palace composed of as many palaces as there were formerly nomes. There are an equal number of aulae, surrounded by pillars, and contiguous to one another, all in one line and forming one building, like a long wall having the aulae in front of it. The entrances into the aulae are opposite to the wall. In front of the entrances there are long and numerous covered ways, with winding passages communicating with each other, so that no stranger could find his way into the aulae or out of them without a guide. The (most) surprising circumstance is that the roofs of these dwellings consist of a single stone each, and that the covered ways through their whole range were roofed in the same manner with single slabs of stone of extraordinary size, without the intermixture of timber or of any other material. On ascending the roof,—which is not of great height, for it consists only of a single story, there may be seen a stone-field, thus composed of stones. Descending again and looking into the aulae, these may be seen in a line supported by twenty-seven pillars, each consisting of a single stone. The walls also are constructed of stones not inferior in size to these.

At the end of this building, which occupies more than a stadium, is the tomb, which is a quadrangular pyramid, each side of which is about four plethra in length, and of equal height. The name of the person buried there is Imandes. They built, it is said, this number of aulae, because it was the custom for all the nomes to assemble there together according to their rank, with their own priests and priestesses, for the purpose of performing sacrifices and making offerings to the gods, and of administering justice in matters of great importance. Each of the nomes was conducted to the aula appointed for it.[1]

Herodotus, somewhat more ecstatic and superlative, regarded

[1] *The Geography of Strabo.* Translation by H. C. Hamilton and W. Falconer. Vol. III (London, Bohn, 1857), pp. 255, 256.

the Labyrinth as one of the wonders of the ancient world: "This I have myself seen and found it greater than can be described. For if anyone should reckon up the buildings and public works of the Greeks, they would be found to have cost less labour and expense than this Labyrinth. It surpasses even the Pyramids."[1]

Petrie appeared on the scene in 1888. His investigations showed the Labyrinth was indeed the Mortuary Temple of Amenemhet III, but by Petrie's time little was left of the building. The nearby Pyramid at Hawara, at the entrance to the Fayum, proved to be one of the most intricate of all the pyramids. Conspicuous for the complexity of its interior which was designed to thwart the efforts of tomb robbers, it taxed the patience and determination of the archaeologist to the utmost in his efforts first to find the entrance and later to explore the interior passages.[2] Labouring under the fierce Egyptian sun, plagued with the usual labour troubles, and working with inadequate tools, Petrie spent two seasons trying to locate the entrance, which, unlike that of other pyramids, was on the south side. "Then, after a further search on all four sides for the entrance," he writes, "the masons attacked the sloping stone roof, and in two or three weeks' time a hole beneath it was reported. Anxiously I watched them enlarge it until I could squeeze through, and then I entered the chamber above the sepulchre. At one side I saw a lower hole and, going down, I found a broken way into the sandstone sepulchre, but too narrow for my shoulders. After sounding the water inside it, a boy was put down with a rope-ladder; and at last on looking through the hole, I could see by the light of his candle two sarcophagi, standing rifled and empty."[3]

How often this frustrating experience was to be repeated with exhausted but expectant archaeologists exclaiming: "The sarcophagus was empty." How ancient vandals could have found

[1] *The Histories of Herodotus.* Translation by Harry Carter (New York, Heritage, 1958), Vol. I, p. 149.

[2] Amenemhet III built a second pyramid at Dashur which may have been built first and then abandoned in favour of Hawara. It contained a sarcophagus. For a description of the black granite cap-stone of the Dashur Pyramid and its importance for the study of the solar system see my *The First Heretic* (Boston, Beacon, 1961), p. 76.

[3] *Ten Years' Digging in Egypt* (New York, Revell), p. 86.

their way into the burial chamber is beyond comprehension. A diagram of the interior passages—false doors, false pits, trap-doors, and dead ends—resembles a modern mystic maze arranged vertically as well as horizontally. A descending flight of steps led from the entrance to the first chamber from which a passage led to a dead end. A trap-door of stone opened on another chamber followed by more blind corridors that had been carefully sealed to appear like the real entrance to the tomb. Such passages continued to the right and then to the left for three turns, each containing false shafts filled with rubble and blocked with a stone slab. Reaching the antechamber, Petrie found one complete wall blocked as if to conceal the tomb.

As the above narrative of Petrie indicated, the entrance to the burial chamber was made through the roof. The construction of the death chamber resembled that of the Cheops Pyramid with its "relieving chambers" or roof-layers. Before the Pyramid was built, a rectangular cavity was cut out of the living rock. Into this pit was lowered a single block of yellow quartzite, 26 feet long and 12 feet wide. Out of this block was hewn a chamber measuring 22 by 8 feet and 6 feet high, and weighing over a hundred tons. The walls were 2 feet thick and were beautifully polished.[1] The roof of the chamber consisted of three blocks of quartzite, each weighing about 45 tons. Above this roof were two relieving chambers, one flat and the upper one pointed. Above the pointed roof of heavy limestone blocks was an arched roof of brick 3 feet thick.

In the Burial Chamber Petrie found an alabaster vessel containing a cartouche of Amenemhet III, thus revealing the ownership of the Pyramid. The presence of a second sarcophagus puzzled Petrie until he found nearby an alabaster altar with representations of various offerings, all dedicated to the king's daughter, Neferu-ptah. Bowls on the altar also bore her name. The wooden inner coffins of the king and his daughter had been burned.

The difficulty encountered by an expert like Petrie in finding the entrance and tracing the maze of passages—encountering trap-doors and blocked corridors and shafts that led to nothing—suggests that in all the instances of ancient vandalism the thieves

[1] The sarcophagus, made of the same material, was lowered into this room through the roof.

were not operating with their own knowledge and ingenuity but were merely following the instructions of priests, guards, and high officials. This is more than conjecture as will be shown in a later chapter.

BORCHARDT AT ABU SIR

Ludwig Borchardt (1863–1938) is the most prominent German name in Egyptian excavation. Along with Breasted, he studied Egyptology under Adolf Erman. One of the things for which he is known is his "ramp" theory. His detection of an inclined road in front of the Meidum Pyramid led to his belief that the construction ramp of stones, rubble, and sand was the means used for building the pyramids. He is also famous for his evolutionary theory of the pyramids, his discovery of the studio of Thutmose at el-Amarna with its bust of Nefertiti, and for his exploration of many sites in Egypt, the most prominent of which was Abu Sir.

Fifth-dynasty inscriptions indicate that six kings of that period built sun-temples to Ra, the sun-god. These were probably a priestly line of usurpers who claimed to be descended from Ra, a relationship which was continued by all subsequent kings and embodied in the royal title. One of the sun-temples—that of Niuserra—was excavated by Borchardt in 1898–1901 in an expedition sponsored by the Deutsche Orient-Gesellschaft. It was situated at Abu Gurab which is near the Abu Sir pyramids. A covered causeway connected the Temple with a pavilion outside the enclosure walls. The Temple itself, in the form of an obelisk, is at the western end of the enclosure on a raised platform, which in turn was built on a paved oblong court measuring 330 by 250 feet. The obelisk on its truncated pyramid was 120 feet high. Since the Pyramid-Temple was a sun-temple, it may have been a representation of the *benben*. In front of the Temple was an immense alabaster altar. Leading from the Temple were troughs in the pavement through which the blood of the sacrificial animals flowed into alabaster basins. The slaughter rooms were on the north side of the enclosure and behind them was a row of magazines for storage. A solar boat-pit was found outside the enclosure on the north side. Numerous excellent reliefs covered the walls of the Causeway, the Enclosure Walls, and the

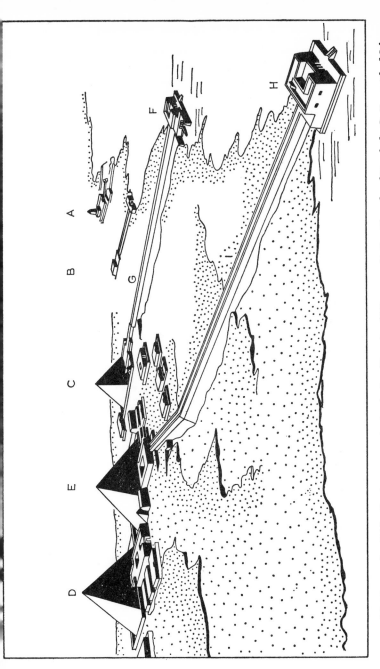

Fig. 6. The Pyramids of Abu Sir (reconstruction). A, Sun Temple of Niuserra. B, Sun Temple of Userkaf. C, Pyramid of Sahura. D, Pyramid of Neferirkara. E, Pyramid of Niuserra. F, Landing State. G, Causeway. H, Valley Building. I, Causeway. These pyramids were excavated by Ludwig Borchardt 1898–1908, and by C. M. Firth 1928–29.
(After I. E. S. Edwards, *The Pyramids of Egypt*.)

small Chapel at the east end of the Enclosure. Many of the sculptured reliefs, among the earliest examples of mural decoration in Egyptian temples, were removed to the Berlin and Cairo museums.

The Fifth-dynasty pyramids of Sahura, Neferirkara, and Niuserra, excavated by Borchardt in 1902–08, originally must have presented a more imposing sight than even the Giza Complex. Unfortunately the Pyramids and Enclosure Walls suffered much depredation from later builders and robbers. Of the three, the Sahura Pyramid and Complex was the most impressive. Originally it measured 257 feet at the bases and was 162 feet high. Only the inner core and some of the limestone casing remain. The entrance and corridors leading to the Burial Chamber follow the pattern of earlier pyramids, including the "relieving chambers" and pointed roof. The roof-blocks are 35 feet long, 9 feet wide and 12 inches thick and have remained intact.

The Sahura complex started at the river with two landing-stages and a portico. The latter had a polished basalt floor, a ceiling of beautifully painted limestone, and eight granite columns in the form of date palms. The king's name was incised in hieroglyph on each column. A Causeway led from the Valley Building to the Mortuary Temple which consisted of the usual entrance hall, an open court, and a sanctuary. It was surrounded by a cloister, the walls of which were covered with reliefs. In front of the sanctuary was a small chamber containing five niches for statues. The sanctuary floor was of alabaster. The drainage system used in connection with the Temple ritual was most elaborate and contained, according to Edwards, over a thousand feet of metal piping.[1]

The Neferirkara Complex was never completed. The Pyramid was one of the largest of the Old Kingdom, measuring 360 feet at the base and 228 feet in height. The Niuserra Complex closely resembles that of Sahura with Valley Building, Causeway, Funerary Temple, and Pyramid.

REISNER AT GIZA

The third great pyramidologist (along with Petrie and Bor-

[1] *Op. cit.*, pp. 143, 144.

chardt) was George A. Reisner (1867–1942). He was Curator of the Egyptian Department of the Boston Museum of Fine Arts (1910–42) and Professor at Harvard University (1905–42). His excavations in Egypt, sponsored by Harvard and the Boston Museum, extended over forty years. Part of that period was spent at the pyramid fields of Meroë, Napata, and Nuri. Almost a thousand years after the last pyramid was built in Egypt, the custom was revived in the Sudan, known by the ancient Egyptians as Ethiopia. The Ethiopian kings of Egypt, starting with the eighth century B.C., erected pyramids as their tombs, a method which was continued until about A.D. 350. Reisner's excavation of these pyramids made him the acknowledged authority in that field.[1] But he is known better perhaps as the discoverer of the tomb of Queen Hetep-heres, the wife of Seneferu and mother of Cheops. Reisner and his staff, starting in 1902, devoted a quarter of a century to the entire Giza Complex.[2] After adding much to the accumulating knowledge about the construction of the Pyramids, he confined his attention to the exploration of the Necropolis surrounding the Great Pyramid. This area was a veritable town of mastabas arranged in streets. These were the tombs of Cheops' family, prominent courtiers, priests, and nobles. Some twenty seasons were spent clearing the tombs, photographing, and recording reliefs and inscriptions. East of the Great Pyramid stand three small ones which belonged to the three queens of Cheops. On the north side of the middle pyramid, Reisner found a great rock-hewn pit, 60 feet in length, which once held the solar barque of the queen.[3]

[1] See his *Excavations at Napata*. Bulletin of the Museum of Fine Arts, Vol. 15, No. 89. Boston, 1917, and *Known and Unknown Kings of Ethiopia*. Bulletin, Vol. 16, No. 97.

[2] The following archaeologists served as chief assistants in the Giza Expedition: A. C. Mace (Oxford), 1902–03, 1905–06; A. M. Lythgoe (Harvard), 1905–06; C. M. Firth (Oxford), 1906–08; Oric Bates (Harvard), 1908; C. S. Fisher (Pennsylvania), 1909–15; Dows Dunham (Harvard), 1914–16, 1925–26; Alan Rowe, 1923–25; N. F. Wheeler (Lt.-Com. R.N.), 1925–33; W. Stevenson Smith (Harvard), 1930.

[3] For a complete report on Reisner's excavation of the mastaba tombs and the Giza Complex see his *A History of the Giza Necropolis*, Vol. I (Cambridge, Harvard University Press, 1942). This volume contains many valuable photographs of the entire region as it was at the beginning of the century before his excavation of the mastabas.

The appearance of a strip of gypsum plaster on a nearby rock led Reisner to conclude that a tomb might be underneath. This occurred in the 1924–25 season. The surmise proved to be correct when he found a stairway leading to a tunnel, which in turn ended in a vertical shaft filled with masonry. As the clearing of the shaft proceeded, there were niches at different levels containing the bones of a sacrificial bull, fragments of pottery, bowls, and copper objects. At a depth of 90 feet, Reisner's assistants broke through a sealed wall of masonry to the Burial Chamber and saw in the glow of the candle light a white alabaster sarcophagus with its lid in place and the viscera nearby in a canopic chest. On the lid of the coffin lay several gold-cased rods from the collapsible bed-canopy and an inlaid box for the bed-curtains. Much of the woodwork in the tomb had turned to ashes and rested between the layers of gold and inlays. Two armchairs inlaid with coloured faience stood near the entrance of the Chamber. Near the sarcophagus was an ornate inlaid chest containing jewellery. Other objects in the room were a palanquin with carrying poles, the ends of which were in the form of gold palm-capitals; a leather walking-stick holder; and a bed with inlaid foot-board and silver head-rest. The back of the carrying chair contained strips of ebony inscribed with solid-gold hieroglyphs. The bed-canopy was a tent-like structure, probably used as a protection against flies and mosquitoes as well as for privacy. When later assembled, the canopy had the appearance of a room with one side open and measured 10 feet in height. The outer framework consisted of beams and on the sides and top were wooden rods encased in gold.[1] Of course, much of the tomb furniture had to be reconstructed since most of the wooden parts had disintegrated.

Uppermost in the minds of the party was the identification of the owner of the tomb. On one of the gold sheets was an inscription: "Lord of the Two Crowns, Seneferu, the Horus, Nebmaat." This led some to think that it was Seneferu's tomb but it is quite unlikely that such an important king with two pyramids at Meidum and Dashur would have been buried in such a small tomb as this. Reisner, noticing that the Burial Chamber

[1] For a discussion of the artistry of the objects in Hetep-heres' tomb see W. Stevenson Smith: *op. cit.*, pp. 48–51 and Plates 30a and 30b.

and the shaft were unfinished and that the objects in the tomb had been hastily deposited, concluded that the sarcophagus and furniture had been brought hurriedly from another place. Obviously the tomb had not been plundered. Most of the objects were those of a woman.

Later in the season a close examination of the panelled hieroglyphs that formed the back of the carrying-chair revealed the inscription: "The mother of the King of Upper and Lower Egypt, follower of Horus, guide of the Ruler, favourite whose every word is done for her, daughter of the god of his body, Hetep-heres." Additional finds turned up further proof that the tomb was that of the mother of Cheops. A box of silver anklets inlaid with malachite, lapis lazuli, and carnelian, bore the inscription: "Mother of the King of Upper and Lower Egypt." Other personal possessions were gold vessels, a gold manicure set and a toilet-box containing eight small alabaster vases filled with unguents.

Having finally cleared the tomb, Reisner and his assistants made preparations for the opening of the sarcophagus. Suspense had been building up over the previous months and all were nervously awaiting the climax of the project. There could be no doubt in their minds that the coffin contained the body of the queen. The lid was slowly raised. The men leaned forward and peered within. The sarcophagus was empty.

The situation was all the more puzzling in view of the presence of the canopic chest containing the viscera and the intact condition of the tomb itself. Reisner concluded that Hetep-heres had been buried at Dashur near her husband's pyramid and that, shortly after the burial, robbers had entered the tomb, hurriedly prised open the lid of the sarcophagus and made off with the body. Their chief interest would be the gold and jewellery on the mummy; so they left the funerary equipment and quickly disappeared. Having taken the valuable objects, they burned or buried the body. When the news of the violation of the tomb was reported to Cheops, he ordered the contents (including, as he thought, the body of his mother) removed secretly to a safer place. A tomb with no superstructure was therefore hurriedly dug near the Great Pyramid which was being constructed at that time. When the shaft was dug and the Burial Chamber ready, the sarcophagus and equipment were rushed to the scene from Dashur and lowered into the tomb. The lid was replaced and the funerary equipment haphazardly deposited in the room. The workers even left their tools in the burial chamber. Then the masons blocked up the shaft and concealed the surface entrance. Within a few hours the drifting sand had obliterated all trace of the tomb and there it remained intact for 4,600 years.

Today the visitor to the Cairo Museum can see the restored furniture and jewellery of the queen as it looked when she was alive. This is possible only because of the careful planning of Reisner and the painstaking methods of those who restored the furniture. As W. Stevenson Smith writes,

> Every step was accompanied by a thorough photographic record in addition to thousands of drawings and sketches that were made day by day as each fragment, whether large or infinitesimal, was removed, sometimes only with the aid of tweezers and camel's-hair brushes. At almost any stage of the work an incautious decision or a clumsy movement could have irretrievably destroyed evidence. What might have remained an inextricable tangle of pieces of gold sheeting if carelessly handled can now be examined as unique pieces of complete furniture.[1]

Associated with Reisner in the excavation and the subsequent restoration of the funerary furniture were Alan Rowe, W. Stevenson Smith, R. D. R. Greenlees, Ahmed Said, Battiscombe Gunn, Dows Dunham, Miss Marion Thompson, Bernard Rise, and W. A. Stewart.

GONEIM AND THE LOST PYRAMID

Probably no region in the Near East has been more thoroughly combed over for antiquities than Sakkara. Certainly one could not reasonably expect to find a pyramid there! But that is what happened in 1954 and the discoverer was Zakariah Goneim, Chief Inspector of Antiquities at Sakkara. Aerial photos in 1951 had shown near the Step Pyramid of Zoser a faint rectangular

[1] W. Stevenson Smith and George A. Reisner: *A History of the Giza Necropolis*, Vol. 2 (Cambridge, Harvard University Press, 1955), Introduction, p. xxiv. A brief timetable of the steps in the discovery and clearance of the tomb (1925–27) is included in this volume (Introduction, p. xxv).

ground pattern with an elevation in the centre. Acting on that clue, Goneim began a search that was to last four years. He was convinced that the sands of the desert still held many secrets, even the groundwork of a Third-dynasty pyramid. Coming upon some chips of cut stone, he sank a trial shaft which struck a stone wall. This turned out to be the Enclosure Wall of a pyramid similar to that of Zoser. The limestone wall, measuring 1,700 by 600 feet, was a foundation platform for an upper-wall. There was also a complicated series of cross walls, one of which, extending for 138 feet, was faced with fine white limestone and was panelled. On this wall were rough scribblings made by the workers, signs or symbols of some kind, and levelling-lines used by the masons.

At the beginning of the 1953 season Goneim found the corners of a step pyramid, the base of which was 400 feet square. No trace of an outer casing was found. If the Pyramid had been finished, its height would have been 230 feet, but in its present unfinished state rose to a height of only 25 feet. The search for the entrance was begun in January 1954, and after two months it was found—a ramp on the north side sloping down to a doorway which was sealed with masonry. In the presence of government officials and representatives of the press, the entrance was made on 9th March 1954. Breaking through the stone blockage, Goneim and his helpers climbed over the stones into an open corridor and continued for about sixty feet. Two days later they located the burial shaft at the bottom of which was a blockage 15 feet deep. This was penetrated with great difficulty and with the loss of a worker who was caught under falling debris and was suffocated. Under the stones at the foot of the shaft they found hundreds of stone vessels and alabaster bowls used for funerary purposes, twenty-one golden bracelets and armlets, a small cosmetic box of embossed gold, beads, and many other golden ornaments. Goneim was surprised to find such a rich collection of gold jewellery in a Third-dynasty tomb (2780–2720 B.C.). Its presence was a guarantee that the tomb had been used. Also of importance was the discovery of pottery jars sealed with clay. Some of these seals bore the cartouche of Sekhem-Khet, an unknown king.

Towards the end of May, the workers had penetrated some

236 feet down the sloping corridor. Here they encountered
another wall of rock which had all the appearance of a dead-end
Was there anything beyond that huge obstruction? After several
days of drilling, a hole was made in the top of the 10 foot thick
wall. Crawling through this hole, Goneim dropped into a deep
vault—the Burial Chamber itself.

When we had picked ourselves up and the lamp was raised [he
writes], a wonderful sight greeted us. In the middle of a rough-cut
chamber lay a magnificent sarcophagus of pale, golden, translucent
alabaster. We moved toward it. My first thought was: "Is it intact?"
Hurriedly, with my electric torch, I examined the top for the lid.
But there was no lid; the top was of one piece with the rest.

This was unique in my experience as an Egyptologist. Normally
sarcophagi are closed by a lid which fits over the top. But this
sarcophagus was different. It had been carved out of a single block
of alabaster, and the entrance was not at the top but at one of the
ends facing the entrance to the chamber on its northern side. I knelt
down and carefully examined this end.

It was sealed by an alabaster panel, roughly T-shaped—with a very
broad vertical arm to the T and short projecting arms which had
been slid into position from the top, presumably along vertical
grooves cut in the side of the alabaster box. And to my amazement
and delight it appeared to be quite intact. . . .

Near the northern end, on the top, lay the decayed and carbonized
fragments of some plant or shrub, arranged roughly in the form of
a V. This would appear to be the remains of a funerary wreath, left
there, presumably, by those who placed the sarcophagus in the
chamber 4,700 years ago. . . .

Then, one by one, my other workmen clambered through the
hole in the blockage and scrambled down into the chamber. They
were mad with excitement and, catching their enthusiasm, I gave
way completely to my pent-up feelings, kept in check for so long.
We danced around the sarcophagus and wept. We embraced each
other. It was a very strange moment in that dark chamber, 130 feet
beneath the surface of the desert. As I have said, many of these
workmen had been employed by great archaeologists such as Reisner
and Junker and Petrie, and they told me that never in their whole
lives had they seen such a thing.[1]

After the first spontaneous outburst of joy had subsided,

[1] M. Zakariah Goneim: *The Lost Pyramid* (New York, Rinehart and Company,
1956), pp. 115–17.

Goneim set about the systematic measurement of the chamber and inspection of the surroundings. The hall had never been finished. The floor was covered with soft clay. Around the chamber were several large galleries used for funerary furniture. The next few weeks were spent building supports for the walls and roof, photographing, and studying the finds.

Finally on the morning of 26th June, senior officials of the Antiquities Department assembled for the opening of the sarcophagus. Over the north end of the coffin was a scaffolding from which hung a large pulley with a rope and hooks to raise the sliding panel. Goneim continues:

> At last all was ready, and I gave the order to begin the operation. Two of my workmen began to haul on the rope, while others applied crowbars to the crack between the lower part of the panel and the sarcophagus. The men heaved with all their might; there was a scraping of metal on stone. Nothing happened, the panel was wedged tightly in position. The men heaved again, but for a long time the heavy panel resisted all our efforts to move it.
>
> Then at last it began to move, a mere inch or so. Wedges were inserted in the aperture, and I carefully examined the panel to make sure that no damage had been done. I was right in my assumption that there were vertical ribs running down each side of the panel, sliding in grooves. I gave the order to continue. In all six men were at work on raising the panel, but such was its weight (about 500 pounds), and the tightness with which it was sealed with a mixture of gypsum plaster and glue, that nearly two hours had passed before at last it slowly began to go up. I went down on my knees and looked inside.
>
> The sarcophagus was empty.[1]

Was it ever filled? That was the question. The interior of the sarcophagus bore no evidence of ever having been occupied. Yet there was the funerary wreath on the lid. If there had been a burial, it seems incredible that the tomb could have been robbed, when the blocking wall ten feet thick was completely intact, the blockages at each end of the corridor in place, and the sarcophagus itself tightly sealed. Goneim concluded that the coffin had never contained the body of the king. That being the case, there must have been another pyramid or at least a tomb. Several kings are

[1] M. Zakariah Goneim: *ibid.*, pp. 143, 143.

known to have built a "dummy" tomb as well as the actual burial place. Goneim's experience was an exact duplicate of that of Reisner in the tomb of Hetep-heres at Giza.

The 1955 season was devoted to a deeper penetration of the shaft and exploration of other corridors in the hope that the real Burial Chamber might be found among the vaults under the Pyramid. This effort failed to uncover a burial chamber but did result in the discovery of an ivory plaque and several jar sealings bearing royal names. It is logical to assume that since the Pyramid was left unfinished, there must be in or near the Enclosure Walls a second tomb which may sometime be found.

After the shift of the capital of Egypt from Memphis to Thebes the kings were buried on the west side of the river opposite Karnak and Luxor. The pyramid continued here for a short period in an abbreviated form, but it gradually became obvious that the accompanying mortuary chapel too easily revealed the whereabouts of the tomb. Starting with the New Kingdom and the Eighteenth Dynasty (1570–1314 B.C.) the kings and nobles were buried in tombs cut deep into the rock in the Valley of the Kings. The first prominent king to be buried in the Royal Valley was Amenhotep I. From his time down through the Twentieth Dynasty, all the Pharaohs were buried in the Valley, the most famous royal burial area in the world—a place which the kings vainly thought would be more secure than the pyramids. The dramatic story of the tombs—their construction, their magnificence, and their desecration—is the subject of our next chapter.

Chapter Six

TOMBS

Visitors to museums have probably wondered why most of the Egyptian antiquities have come from tombs. The reason is twofold: the tombs were under ground and were made of solid rock and sealed; whereas, the houses and palaces were above ground and were made of wood and mud-brick. Little or nothing remains of the palaces and private homes of the two capitals, Memphis and Thebes. The reason why ancient Egyptians chose to build their homes of perishable material and their tombs of lasting material was their subordination of the present earthly life to the after-life. It was not that the Egyptians did not enjoy this life; on the contrary, their literature shows a healthy delight in the work and pleasures of daily life. It mattered little, however, where and how they lived in this life, but it was all-important that their "House of Eternity" be secure and permanent. "The Egyptians," wrote Diodorus, "call their homes 'hostelries' because of the short space of time during which they sojourn there; whilst they speak of their tombs as 'eternal abodes'." This is why, paradoxically, it is the west bank of the Nile—the City of the Dead—that has given us the treasures of Egypt, not the east bank where the people lived. Such a city as the Theban necropolis is conceivable only in the light of a triumphant belief in the future life—a belief expressed in a Valley tomb inscription: "Thou livest again after death; thy soul does not forsake thy body; thou becomest that which thou wast. All thy members regain their powers; thy heart is really thine. The varied activities of life are there for the departed just as they

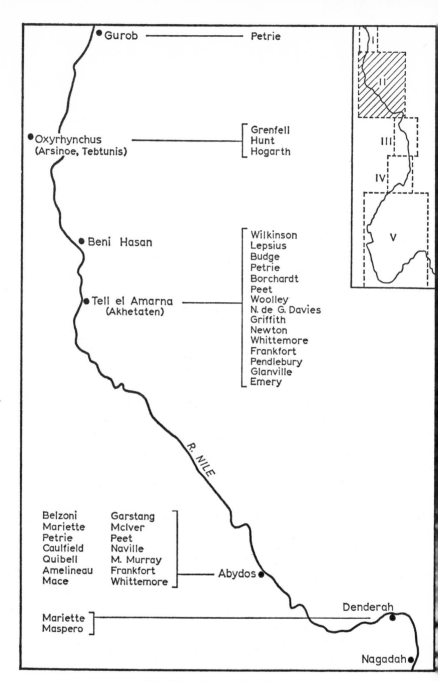

EGYPTIAN EXCAVATIONS Part II

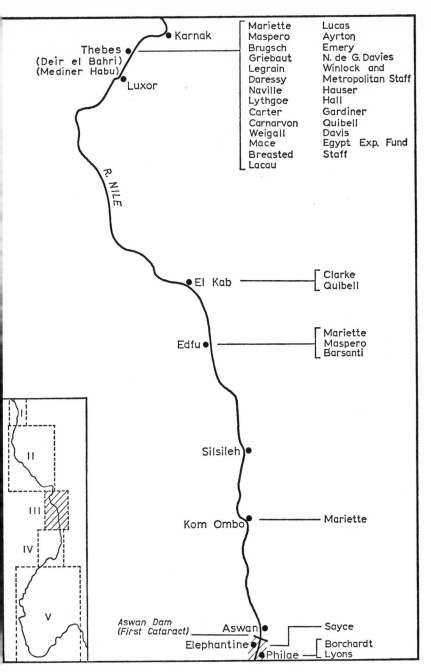

Karnak

Thebes
(Deir el Bahri)
(Mediner Habu)

Luxor

Mariette	Lucas
Maspero	Ayrton
Brugsch	Emery
Griebaut	N. de G. Davies
Legrain	Winlock and
Daressy	Metropolitan Staff
Naville	Hauser
Lythgoe	Hall
Carter	Gardiner
Carnarvon	Quibell
Weigall	Davis
Mace	Egypt Exp. Fund
Breasted	Staff
Lacau	

R. NILE

El Kab — Clarke
Quibell

Edfu — Mariette
Maspero
Barsanti

Silsileh

Kom Ombo — Mariette

Aswan Dam
(First Cataract) — Aswan — Sayce

Elephantine — Borchardt
Philae — Lyons

EGYPTIAN EXCAVATIONS Part III

were when he was on earth. The span of our earthly deeds is as a dream; but fair is the welcome that awaits him who has reached the hills of the West.''

Magnificent as the Thebes of the Living was—the temples of Karnak and Luxor testify to that—the Thebes of the Dead was probably even more imposing. The City of the Dead forms a large bay in the Libyan hills, which rise abruptly to a height of several hundred feet and are crowned with a pyramid-shaped peak called by the ancients ''the Horn'', or Kurna, from which the village below was named. The Thebaid extends from Kurna at the northern extremity to Medinet Habu on the south. Within the semicircle of the bow are Biban el-Muluk or the Valley of the Kings, Biban el-Harim or the Valley of the Queens, and, stretching like the string of the bow, facing the river, are the royal funerary temples. These chapels of the New Kingdom may be seen as continuations of the Valley Temples of the Giza Pyramid field and were built at some distance from the tombs in order not to reveal the location of the burial places. Amenhotep I, ascending the throne in 1557 B.C., was the first king to build his funerary temple apart from his tomb, in his case, about a mile distant. His decision to do this created considerable difficulty for the sustenance of his *ka*, the indispensable guarantee of the welfare of the king in the after-life, for it was in the mortuary chapel, near the body, that the offerings for the *ka* were made. But the security of the mummy finally outweighed all other considerations; hence the new secret tombs in the East Valley.

In the centre of this amphitheatre is the magnificent pink and white temple of Queen Hatshepsut at the base of the cliffs of Deir el Bahri. Guarding the southern approach to Thebes are the twin Colossi of Memnon, doorkeepers of the vanished temple of Amenhotep III, floating in the waters of the inundation or rising majestically out of the green fields of winter crops. Some of the funerary temples have partially survived; only the foundations of the palaces remain; and the houses of the citizens have completely disappeared. Tunnelled into the limestone cliffs on the western side of the bay are some seventy royal tombs. Nearer the river are the tombs of the nobles and the viziers.

The resident population of the Necropolis was large, consisting of labourers of all kinds, stone cutters, masons, builders,

sculptors, painters, scribes, metal workers, engineers, embalmers, politicians, mercenaries, and civil servants, not to
mention the most flourishing occupation of them all—the tomb
robbers.

THEBAN THIEVES

The irony of Egyptian excavation is that the most sacred thing
in that ancient culture—the preparation for, and security of, the
after-life—was blasphemed by the Theban priests themselves as
they betrayed their sacred trust by their participation in the
ghoulish trade of tomb-robbery, sometimes called "the world's
second oldest profession". Because of the corruption of city
officials and the priesthood, the City of the Dead, which should
have been the holiest of places, was from the first the unholy
scene of the highly organized business of tomb desecration, so
that not a single royal tomb (including, incidentally, that of
Tutankhamon) escaped this sacrilegious defilement. Perhaps if
the tombs of the Pharaohs had been less gorgeously furnished,
their security would have been more likely. As it was, human
greed was stronger than human piety and the repose of the kings,
who had taken such precaution to make sure of their happiness
in the realms of Osiris, was rudely disturbed by cunning and
skilful robbers. It was only a question of time until their tombs
would be excavated by archaeologists in a scientific and orderly
way. What a pity that they were anticipated by professional
thieves who for the sake of private gain ransacked the tombs
throughout the Royal Valley and sold their contents to any and
all buyers. The result was that half the treasures of Egypt disappeared long ago and the knowledge of that great civilization
that could have been gained from these tombs is lost for-
ever.

Startling evidence of the activity of the Theban thieves came
to light in the discovery of the Amherst-Leopold Papyrus which
has made it possible for us today to know more about the "goings
on" than most of the residents of Thebes at the time. The business of robbing tombs seems to have reached its peak in the
Twentieth Dynasty, particularly during the reign of Ramses IX
(1142–1123 B.C.). Following the strong rule of Seti I and his son,

Ramses II, the government of Egypt became more corrupt and undisciplined than ever.

At that time the capital city of Thebes had two mayors: one for the Eastern City and one for the City of the Dead. The leak which brought into the open the political intrigue connected with tomb robberies involved Pewero, the mayor of Western Thebes.

In 1935 Jean Capart found the second half of the Abbott Papyrus which had been in the British Museum since 1857.[1] Capart was examining a collection of Egyptian antiquities which had been brought to the Royal Museum in Brussels about 1860. One of the objects was a wooden statuette of a scribe inside of which was a long piece of papyrus. Carefully he unrolled it and read its date, "Year Sixteen of the Reign of Ramses IX", which was the precise date of the Abbott Papyrus! Capart sent for a photo facsimile of the piece in the British Museum and found that "the lower edge of the new papyrus fitted exactly the Abbott, and that where the latter only showed fragments of signs, the piece we were in the course of unrolling gave the missing portions". The two halves when pieced together told the realistic story of the Great Robbery Trial in Thebes.

Peser, the Mayor of Eastern Thebes, and apparently an honest man, had accused Pewero, the Mayor of Western Thebes, of being an accomplice in the robbery of ten tombs of kings and four of queens. The matter was reported to the vizier or governor of the Theban district, Khamwese, who sent a committee across the river to investigate. As Howard Carter, in his account of the proceedings, suggests, Khamwese and the members of the commission were all implicated and had probably written their report before they rowed across the Nile. The inspectors, after examination of the tombs, declared that only one royal tomb— the one that had been mentioned in the confession—and two of the queen's tombs had been rifled, but it was clearly evident that many more had been plundered. Accompanying the vizier and his inspection committee were the men who were accused of the

---

[1] Another roll of papyrus was in the possession of Lord Amherst of Hackney and some fragments are now in the Turin and Liverpool Museums. The Mayer Papyri (in Liverpool), consisting of two pieces, describe the prosecution of the tomb robbers.

robberies. One of them was a coppersmith who was commanded to point out the tomb he had robbed. The vizier left the other thieves in charge of some of his men, blindfolded the copper-smith, and then proceeded farther into the Valley. After the blindfold was taken off, he was asked to identify the tomb which he confessed to have entered some time ago. He pointed to an empty tomb in which no burial had taken place. He was "examined" by having his hands and feet beaten with the *bastinado* (a form of torture) and threatened with much worse punishment but replied that on pain of having his nose and ears cut off and of being impaled, he knew of "no place here among the tombs save this one which is open and the house I pointed out to you". Meanwhile the other prisoners had escaped from their guards and fled into the hills.

The whole episode turned out in favour of Pewero who became a hero. Following his exoneration, Pewero assembled the Necropolis workmen, administrators, and police and staged a victorious celebration in Eastern Thebes near Mayor Peser's residence. Their insults provoked Peser to anger and he shouted: "As for this deputation, it is no deputation at all. It is simply your jubilation at my expense. You exult over me at the very door of my house. Oh indeed! Remember I am a Mayor and I make my reports direct to the Pharaoh and thus you exult over him. You were there when the tombs were inspected, were you, and you found them uninjured? I tell you the tomb of Sebekemsaf and of his queen *was* broken into. I invoke the severity of Amon-Ra, King of the Gods, upon you in defence of these sacred tombs." Peser avowed that he had further proof of the robberies and concluded: "I am going to write about them to Pharaoh, so that he may send someone to take you all in charge."

The report that Peser intended to go over the Vizier's head was good news to Pewero who promptly informed the Vizier that Peser was about to go to the King. Khamwese convened the court and the hapless Mayor was forced to sit in judgement on himself and receive the condemnation of the vizier for his breach of protocol. Through this bit of misdirection the court by-passed the issue of the violated tombs, dealing only with the tombs which had *not* been robbed. Peser's mistake was that he had been too specific in saying that ten tombs had been robbed.

Peser's case, however, received some confirmation three years later, as the second part of the papyrus shows. Someone finally had the courage to report on the activities of the tomb robbers, eight of whom were arrested and tried for their desecration of the tomb of King Sebekemsaf. The papyrus contains the confession of Amenpnufer, the son of a stonemason. He told of stripping the Pharaoh and his queen of the gold, silver and costly stones and setting fire to the coffins. "We penetrated through the masonry and mortar of the tomb," ran the confession, "and we found the queen lying there. We opened the coffin and the coverings in which it was. Then we found the august mummy of the king. There were numerous amulets and golden ornaments at his throat, his head had a mask of gold upon it, and the mummy itself was overlaid with gold throughout. Its coverings were wrought with gold and silver within and without, and were inlaid with every splendid and costly stone. We stripped off the gold which we found on the august mummy of the king, and the amulets and ornaments, and the coverings in which it rested. We found the queen likewise, and we stripped off all that we found on her in the same manner. We then set fire to the coffins, and carried away the funeral-furniture which we found with them, consisting of gold, silver and bronze. We divided the booty, and made the gold, amulets, ornaments, and coverings into eight parts." After some time, he continued, he was arrested. He gave his share of the gold to the Clerk of Thebes who released him. "I joined my companions and they made up for me another share. And I, as well as the other robbers who are with me, have continued to this day in the practice of robbing the tombs of the nobles, and a large number of men rob them also." Such is the sordid record of bribery and corruption in high places.[1]

The court found the thieves guilty and meted out punishment, but the practice continued unabated. In the Twenty-first Dynasty the situation became much more serious as the tombs of the great Pharaohs of the Eighteenth Dynasty were pillaged and all the contents stolen. There was "gold in them thar hills" and the temptation was too strong to resist, as Howard Carter writes: "One can imagine the plotting beforehand, the secret rendezvous

[1] See James H. Breasted: *Ancient Records of Egypt* (Chicago, University of Chicago Press, 1906), Vol. 4, pp. 245–73.

on the cliff by night, the bribing or drugging of the cemetery guards, and then the desperate burrowing in the dark, the scramble through a small hole into the burial chamber, the hectic search by a glimmering light for treasure that was portable, and the return home at dawn laden with booty. We can imagine these things, and at the same time we can realize how inevitable it all was. By providing his mummy with the elaborate and costly outfit which he thought essential to its dignity, the king was himself encompassing its destruction. The temptation was too great. Wealth beyond the dreams of avarice lay there at the disposal of whoever should find the means to reach it, and sooner or later the tomb-robber was bound to win through."[1]

But the systematic tomb robbing was not carried on without opposition. There were some honest city officials and priests who tried to thwart the thieves in their nefarious work. They moved the bodies of the kings from tomb to tomb, keeping just ahead of the robbers as they heard of their plans. Sometimes the priests would rewrap the mummies and place them in new coffins. The bodies of Ramses II, Amenhotep I, Seti I, and Thutmose II were reburied in new hiding-places. Finally, the priests decided upon a new scheme and, under strict military protection, they gathered all the known royal mummies and divided them into two lots, one of which they put in a tomb in the Valley and the other larger group they transported to a secret tomb over the Valley ridge. This time they were successful and the bodies of the Pharaohs lay unmolested for 3,000 years.

A CACHE OF FORTY PHARAOHS

In the late 1870s some articles bearing royal insignia began to appear on the black market in Luxor. It was reported that a few Americans and Europeans, who frequented the bazaars of Luxor, were known to have bought these objects and hurriedly smuggled them out of Egypt. One man purchased a rare and valuable papyrus; another, a mortuary gift from a royal tomb; and still others bought the leg or an arm of a mummy.

These illegal proceedings came to the attention of Gaston

[1] Howard Carter: *The Tomb of Tutankhamen* (New York, Doran, 1923), Vol. I, p. 92.

Maspero, the Director of Egyptian Antiquities. This was in 1881. It appeared to him that the articles had come from the tombs of several different kings which suggested the possibility that the thieves had come upon a mass burial. Not trusting the police and deciding to operate secretly, he sent an assistant to Luxor to investigate. The young man, disguised as a tourist with money, spent his time at the bazaars, buying a few things and gaining the confidence of some of the dealers. On one occasion, after several weeks, he was invited into the shop of a dealer who placed in his hand a statuette. He pretended ignorance but he recognized it to be a genuine funerary gift from a royal tomb of the Twenty-first Dynasty. After some extended haggling he bought the piece. At the same time he was introduced to an Arab named Ahmed Abd-el-Rasul who showed him several mortuary objects from Nineteenth- and Twentieth-dynasty tombs.

Maspero's assistant had Abd-el-Rasul arrested. At a hearing conducted by the local Mudir, Abd-el-Rasul was declared not guilty of tomb robbery. The trial produced a flood of testimony from villagers, family, and officials to the effect that Abd-el-Rasul "never had excavated and never would excavate, that he was incapable of misappropriating the smallest antiquity, to say nothing of violating a royal tomb". A month later, however, the brother of the man in question confessed to the Mudir that Rasul was the leader of a gang of thieves and that the whole village of Kurna was made up of tomb robbers, a profession handed down from generation to generation. The leaders, in addition to Abd-el-Rasul, were his brother Mohammed and the consular agent of Great Britain, Belgium, and Russia, stationed at Luxor. Guaranteed protection by the consul, who himself enjoyed diplomatic immunity, Rasul denied everything. After holding out for two months, during which time he was given the third degree, Rasul returned to the consul and demanded half of the treasures as his share or "he would disclose the whole matter to the police". Mohammed, the brother, realizing that the game was up, confessed to the Mudir and promised to take him to the tomb.

On 5th July 1881 Emil Brugsch, Assistant Keeper of the Cairo Museum, was conducted to the tomb. Maspero at the time was not in Egypt. The party was taken to Deir el Bahri. Rasul led the way up the side of the steep cliff and, after climbing some

180 feet, came to a hidden opening in the rock. He dropped a coil of rope down the hole and told Brugsch to let himself down. This took some courage on the part of Brugsch in view of the fact that his prisoner was holding the rope. The shaft was 35 feet deep. At the bottom was a corridor that ran for 150 feet and after two or three turns opened upon a large burial chamber. What Brugsch saw is reported by Maspero:

> The first thing Monsieur Emile Brugsch saw when he reached the bottom of the shaft was a white and yellow coffin bearing the name of Neskhonsu. It was in the corridor, some 60 centimeters from the entrance; a little farther on was a coffin whose shape suggested the style of the XVIIth Dynasty, then Queen Tiuhathor Henttaui, then Seti I. Beside the coffins and scattered over the ground were boxes with funerary statuettes, canopic jars, libation vessels of bronze, and, farther on, in the angle formed by the corridor where it turns northward, the funeral tent of Queen Isimkheb, folded and crumpled, like something of no value that a priest in a hurry to get out had carelessly thrown into a corner. All along the main corridor were the same profusion of objects and the same disorder; he was forced to crawl, never knowing upon what hand or foot might be set. The coffins and mummies, fleetingly glimpsed by the light of a candle, bore historic names, Amenophis I, Thutmose II, in the niche near the stairway, Ahmose I and his son Siamun, Soqnunrî, Queen Ahhotpu, Ahmose Nefertari, and others. The confusion reached its height in the chamber at the end, but no more than a glance sufficed to reveal that the style of the XXth Dynasty was predominant. Mohammed Ahmed Abd-el-Rassul's report, which at first seemed exaggerated, was actually far short of the truth. Where I had expected to find one or two obscure kinglets, the Arabs had disinterred a whole vault of Pharaohs. And what Pharaohs! perhaps the most illustrious in the history of Egypt, Thutmose III and Seti I, Ahmose the Liberator and Ramses II the Conqueror. Monsieur Emile Brugsch, coming so suddenly into such an assemblage, thought that he must be the victim of a dream, and like him, I still wonder if I am not dreaming when I see and touch what were the bodies of so many famous personages of whom we never expected to know more than the names.[1]

The removal of the coffins and funerary equipment and their transportation to the river and across to Luxor was a good week's

---

[1] *Rapport sur la trouvaille de Deir el-Bahari.* Institut Egyptien Bulletin Ser. 2, No. 2 (1881). Translation by W. R. Trask, p. 42.

work for Brugsch, his assistants and three hundred Arabs. When later, the steamboat and its cargo of forty kings started back to Cairo, on both banks of the river, as Maspero relates, the women, with their hair hanging down, followed the boat wailing, and the men fired shots in honour of the dead kings.

These were the greatest Pharaohs of Egypt. Thutmose III, Ramses II, Seti I, Ahmose I, and Amenhotep I. It was several years before the findings of the Deir el Bahri cache were sorted and classified and the mummies unwrapped. The body of Ramses II, of course, aroused the greatest interest. It was un- wrapped in the presence of high officials including the Khedive of Egypt. It is to this day one of the best preserved mummies in Egypt. "The figure," writes Maspero, "is still tall and of perfect proportions. Even after the coalescence of the vertebrae and the shrinkage produced by mummification, his mummy still measures over 5 feet 8 inches." Even better preserved was the mummy of Seti I. "The fine kingly head was exposed to view," continues Maspero. "It was a masterpiece of the art of the embalmer, and the expression of the face was that of one who had only a few hours previously breathed his last. A calm and gentle smile still played over his mouth, and the half-open eyelids allowed a glimpse to be seen from under the lashes of an apparently moist and glistening line, the reflection from the white porcelain eyes let into the orbit at the time of burial." Surely in the case of Seti I we are seeing a king as he was when alive, a noble and dignified ruler.

The second group, consisting of thirteen royal mummies, was found in 1898 by Loret in the tomb of Amenhotep II. He was the first Pharaoh who had ever been found lying in the tomb where he had originally been buried. Lying beside him was his famous bow. Along with Amenhotep II were the mummies of Thut- mose IV, Merenptah and Amenhotep III, the father of Ikhnaton. The priests who had rescued the royal mummies 3,000 years before and reburied them finally succeeded in their effort to foil the tomb robbers. According to Howard Carter, it was thought proper to leave the body of Amenhotep II in his tomb. This was done. Two years later an armed band of robbers overpowered the night guards, entered the burial chamber, unwrapped the mummy, and made off with all the treasures!

THE VALLEY OF THE KINGS

For a thousand years the Pharaohs of Egypt were buried in Biban el-Muluk or Valley of the Kings, one of the most barren spots in the world—a sun-scorched wilderness of rock and parched land, lonely and desolate. But it was for that very reason that the kings, starting with Amenhotep I and Thutmose I, chose this region as their resting-place, vainly thinking that such an uninhabitable place would guarantee their eternal security.

The many-chambered tomb of Seti I, penetrating deep into the limestone hills of the Valley, is the most beautiful of all royal tombs. The discovery and partial excavation of this tomb by Belzoni has been described earlier. Fortunately for posterity, perhaps, Belzoni did not find the mummy but the transparent alabaster sarcophagus, which he found and shipped to England, is one of the most magnificent in Egyptian history.

The most important modern expedition to the Valley was begun in 1902 by Howard Carter, Arthur Weigall, and Edward Ayrton for the Service of Antiquities. Edward J. Quibell and Gaston Maspero also participated in this series of excavations financed by the American, Theodore M. Davis.[1] In 1903 Carter found the tomb of Thutmose IV, whose mummy was among those discovered in the burial-chamber of his father, Amenhotep II. Between 1903 and 1912 the Davis expedition also discovered the tombs of Queen Hatshepsut, Horemheb, and Queen Tiy. But more interesting than these royal tombs, at least from the standpoint of artistry and workmanship, was the tomb of two individuals who were not of royal blood but had much to do with the making of royalty. On 5th February 1905 Davis's workmen came upon a neatly cut stone block which proved to be the first step in a staircase that descended to a tomb corridor. When, a week later, Davis, Maspero, and Weigall opened the tomb door and made their way to the burial chamber, they found themselves in the presence of Yuaa and Tuaa, the parents of Queen Tiy. It is

[1] Davis's contract with the Egyptian government stated that he was to continue the concession as long as he wished as the sole excavator in the Valley. He was to pay all bills and the objects found were to be held by the Egyptian government.

interesting to speculate on the profound influence these two persons had on the thinking of Queen Tiy whose ill-fated son produced the one great artistic and religious revolution in ancient Egypt. Already in the reign of Amenhotep III the emerging solar faith of Atonism was beginning to make itself felt. There can be no doubt that Yuaa and Tuaa had something to do with the beginning of that reform. Yuaa's mummy is one of the three best preserved in existence. Davis describes the entrance of the party into the tomb:

> The chamber was as dark as dark could be and extremely hot. Our first quest was the name of the owner of the tomb, as to which we had not the slightest knowledge or suspicion. We held up our candles, but they gave so little light and so dazzled our eyes that we could see nothing except the glitter of gold. In a moment or two, however, I made out a very large wooden coffin, known as a funeral sled, which was used to contain all the coffins of the dead person and his mummy, and to convey them to his tomb. It was about six feet high and eight feet long, made of wood covered with bitumen, which was as bright as the day it was put on. Around the upper part of the coffin was a stripe of gold foil, about six inches wide, covered with hieroglyphs. On calling Maspero's attention to it, he immediately handed me his candle, which, together with my own, I held before my eyes, close to the inscriptions, so that he could read them. In an instant he said: "Yuaa." Naturally, excited by the announcement, and blinded by the glare of the candles, I involuntarily advanced them very near the coffin; whereupon Maspero cried out: "Be careful!" and pulled my hands back. In a moment we realized that, had my candles touched the bitumen, which I came dangerously near doing, the coffin would have been in a blaze. As the entire contents of the tomb were inflammable, and directly opposite the coffin was a corridor leading to the open air and making a draft, we undoubtedly would have lost our lives, as the only escape was by the corridor which would have necessitated climbing over the stone wall barring the doorway. This would have retarded our exit for at least ten minutes.[1]

The attention of the excited discoverers was now torn between the two lidless gilded coffins containing the sleeping couple and

[1] Jean Capart: Lectures on Egyptian Art (Chapel Hill: University of North Carolina Press, 1928), pp. 275–80.

the resplendent funerary furniture which rivalled that of Hetep-heres. The funeral equipment consisted of three carved and inlaid armchairs decorated with gold, alabaster vases, wooden chests, inlaid and enamelled in blue, jewel boxes, ushabti figures, wicker baskets, couches, and heavily-gilded chariots. For the physical sustenance of the dead there was a great supply of meat and other kinds of food; and for their spiritual welfare, there were figures from the Book of the Dead and a roll of papyrus 22 yards long, containing the magical formula that would assist the departed on their journey through the realm of Osiris. Quibell recorded and catalogued the articles and was assisted by the artist, Joseph Lindon Smith, who made sketches of the furniture and the faces of the old couple. The tomb of Yuaa and Tuaa yielded the richest treasures found in the Valley up to that time. The tomb had been robbed but the mummies and furniture were intact. The latter was of the finest design and workmanship, making this one of the most rewarding finds of modern times.

The next discovery of the Davis party precipitated a controversy which has not died down yet. The importance of the tomb they discovered had to do, not with valuable funerary furniture, but with the identity of the mummy. The site of this find in 1907 was near the tomb of Seti I. Davis and Ayrton, who had been drilling through a hill covered with debris from the excavation of other tombs, suddenly came upon a walled-up doorway. The seal of the door was found intact which indicated that the tomb apparently had not been opened. Weigall and Maspero arrived to assist in the excavation. The entrance corridor was filled with rubble almost to the ceiling. Joseph Smith, the artist, crawled along the passage and hurriedly sketched the relief of a queen, worshipping the sun disk, and the accompanying cartouche. When he emerged from the corridor and showed it to Maspero, the latter exclaimed: "This is the tomb of Queen Tiy!" Entering the burial chamber with great difficulty they found what seemed to be at first glance a room filled with gold. This turned out to be merely gold-foil. The coffin had fallen or had been knocked over, exposing the head and feet of the mummy. The body was wrapped in sheets of gold-foil and the coffin bore the inscription: "Ikhnaton, the beautiful child of the sun." This was a surprising development, for the heretic Pharaoh had presumably been buried in his own tomb at el-Amarna. Further search, however, disclosed on the funerary canopy an inscription stating that this tomb had been made for the queen mother Tiy. The skeleton—the body had not been mummified—was sent to Elliot Smith, an anatomical expert at the University of Cairo, for examination. He reported that it was the body of a young man not more than twenty-six years of age when he died. It seemed, therefore, that the body was that of Ikhnaton, who, it was thought, had died in his late twenties. Ikhnaton was no doubt buried originally at el-Amarna. When Tutankhamon and his wife, Ankhsenamon, moved to Thebes as king and queen, they reburied the great reformer in the tomb of the queen mother. Later, the orthodox priests of Thebes, learning of this secret action of Tutankhamon, and resenting the pollution of the queen's tomb by the presence of the "criminal of Akhataton", removed the body of the queen, erased Ikhnaton's name from all inscriptions except the one on the coffin, blocked the entrance and sealed it with the seal of Tutankhamon. Such was the view of authorities at the time. Maspero himself was satisfied that the body was that of Ikhnaton, arguing that when the bodies of the royal family had been brought from el-Amarna at night and secretly buried, the men in charge had interchanged the coffins of Tiy and her son. Joseph Lindon Smith suggested that the exchange was deliberate and that faithful adherents of Ikhnaton had "brought the son's mummy to a place where no desecration need be feared—his mother's reburial chamber; and that these followers of the hated Ikhnaton must have had sufficient influence with the priests of Amon to secure the placing of the seal of the priestly college of Amon on the entrance door!"[1] More recently the identity of the body in Queen Tiy's tomb as that of Ikhnaton has again been brought into question. For what it is worth, Rex Engelbach of the Cairo Museum staff and Dr. Douglas Derry, professor of anatomy at the University of Cairo, produced evidence, inscriptional and physiological, that rules out the probability that the body is that of Ikhnaton. It is now believed that Ikhnaton acceded to the throne about fifteen years later than formerly thought and therefore died in his forties. We cannot

[1] *Tombs, Temples and Ancient Art* (Norman, University of Oklahoma Press, 1956), p. 68.

go into the details of the inscriptional argument, but most authorities now hold that the body of the young man was that of Smenkhkare, whose reign, following Ikhnaton, was very short, and who was buried by Tutankhamon.

Crowning the series of successful finds of the Davis expedition was the discovery in 1908 of the tomb of Horemheb, who had seized the throne after the brief reigns of Tutankhamon and Ay. He had been the general of the army under Ikhnaton, had supported his religious reform up to a point, but continually warned the king of the imminent disintegration of the empire. After Ikhnaton's death, the general capitulated to the reactionary Amon priesthood, initiated an aggressive foreign policy, and restored order in Egypt. His tomb, located between those of Tutankhamon and Amenhotep II, had been thoroughly plundered and the mummy was missing, but the magnificent pink granite sarcophagus was unharmed. It is 9 feet in length, 3 feet 10 inches wide, and 4 feet high and is exquisitely carved. The bones of four persons were found in the six-pillared burial chamber, which may or may not indicate that the members of his family were buried with him. The walls of the corridors and chambers were decorated with scenes from the Book of the Dead, some of which were sculptured in relief. These funerary scenes depict the journey of the sun and the king in the presence of the gods.

The Horemheb paintings provide a good illustration of the procedure followed by the decorators of the tomb. The draftsman first traced long vertical and horizontal lines on the wall to indicate the position of the figures and their proportions. He also made preliminary sketches of the principal objects and figures in the mural. He was followed by a foreman who traced over the figures with a firmer line. On the west wall of the Horemheb tomb is a preliminary drawing of the solar boat being drawn by four genii. The horizontal lines have determined the exact position of the top of the heads, the neck, hands, thighs, knees, and bottom of the feet. On the south wall is a funerary scene the top register of which is a complete blank, the middle register is drawn and painted, and the bottom is completed in coloured relief. This shows how the artists abruptly stopped their work at the death of the king. In the second register gaps appear in the hieroglyphic text with the notation "found empty".

The artists used a papyrus copy-book with models of scenes from the Book of the Dead. Sometimes the papyrus roll developed holes in it made by long use. The artists did not always know the text of the religious books; so they left a space in order to draw the attention of the final decorator to the omission. These final artists were sometimes known as "scribes of the gaps". They restored the missing sections and made sure that the mural was complete. As the tomb of Horemheb was never finished, these gaps remained. The scenes of the after-life were sketched first by the draftsmen and then coloured. Later the sculptor chiselled the painted drawings in relief, after which the painter had to put the colours on again. In the Horemheb burial-chamber Ayrton and Davis found, at the base of the wall, fragments of stone chipped out by the sculptor as he carved the relief. The fact that the fragments were not removed is a further indication that work on the tomb was suddenly discontinued. This recalls the same situation in the tomb of Seti I where the preliminary sketching on one wall ceased when the king died. The finished adoration scene in the chamber of the well is one of the best examples of Eighteenth-dynasty tomb paintings. Equally excellent decoration is found in the Memphite tomb of Horemheb.

It is entirely fitting that the tomb of Hatshepsut, who called herself King and reigned as such, should be in the Valley of the Kings. This tomb, cleared by Carter and Davis, in 1903, is noteworthy from the standpoint of sheer size, being 700 feet in length and reaching a vertical depth of 320 feet, but it has no decoration. It was evidently designed to run underground towards Hatshepsut's great funerary temple at Deir el Bahri so that the burial-chamber should be directly below the temple, or at least near it. This plan was abandoned when the builders of the tomb encountered difficulties in the rock formation and were forced to cut the tomb in a curve, making a semicircle. It is a crude tomb and was never finished, although the queen was undoubtedly buried there. In the burial chamber Carter and Davis found Hatshepsut's red sandstone sarcophagus, the canopic chest of the same material, and the sarcophagus of her father, Thutmose I,

Festival scene (Eighteenth Dynasty) from the tomb of Nakht, Thebes.
(*Courtesy, Hirmer Verlag, Munich*)

Throne of Tutankhamon. (*Courtesy*, *Metropolitan Museum of Art*, *New York*)

Burial mask of Tutankhamon, made of polished gold and inlaid with lapis lazuli, carnelian, alabaster and obsidian. On his forehead are the royal insignia of vulture and serpent.
(*Courtesy*, *Metropolitan Museum of Art*, *New York*)

all of which are now in the Cairo Museum. The tomb had been completely ransacked. The mummy of Thutmose I, of course, was among those in the great cache at Deir el Bahri.

In 1916 Carter found another tomb of Hatshepsut high in the face of the cliff and in it was an unfinished sarcophagus of the queen. This tomb was 130 feet below the top of the cliff and 220 feet from the floor of the Valley. At the time of the discovery an armed band of robbers had dropped a rope from the plateau above and were about to enter the tomb. Carter slid down the rope and entered the corridor which ran straight into the cliff for 55 feet, then made a right-angle turn and led down a slope into the burial chamber which was 17 feet square. Hatshepsut had apparently changed her plans before the tomb was finished and had the other tomb built. "How the Egyptians raised the sarcophagus," writes Carter, "weighing much more than a ton up 220 feet of cliff and then turned it down the passage, is quite beyond all that we have seen of their engineering."

Burial in the Valley of the Queens on the south wall of the Theban necropolis began, as far as we can ascertain, with Ramses I, who buried his queen there. Whether Seti I, his son, followed his example is unknown, but Seti's son, Ramses II, buried his queen, Nefertari, in that place. Although Ramses II was a much married man, Nefertari was his favourite wife from the first year of his reign until her death. Her influence on Ramses is eloquently attested in her rock-cut temple at Abu Simbel and the frequent appearance of her figure on the colossi of the king. Her distinction as queen is also suggested in her tomb, which was discovered and cleared by an Italian expedition in 1904. The decorations have suffered greatly but the painted reliefs that remain are noteworthy for their freedom and naturalism. The burial-hall has four square decorated pillars and a sunken space in the centre where the sarcophagus stood. The walls of the first room are covered with painted reliefs of Nefertari making offerings to Osiris, Atum, and Hathor. The ceiling is painted to represent the night-sky with stars. One of these wall-paintings shows the queen being led by Isis, who wears a head-dress of cow's horns containing the sun's disk and uraeus. Another one shows Nefertari offering a pair of vases to the goddess Hathor. A third pictures the god Re-Harakhti and Amentit, goddess of the West, sitting side by side. For clarity, warmth and realism, these tomb paintings are unexcelled.[1]

The tomb of Merneptah, whose mummy was found in the Amenhotep II cache along with a dozen other kings, is a good example of tomb construction and relief decoration in the late Empire, as are the Ramesside tombs of the Royal Valley, especially those of Ramses I, V, and IX.

VIZIERS, SCRIBES, AND PRIESTS

The tombs—or mortuary chapels, as they should be called—of the Theban nobles, who made up the aristocracy and court circle of the capital in its golden age, have an importance of their own. Their wall-paintings and reliefs vividly portray Egyptian life in all its varied aspects during the days of the Empire. In this connection it is necessary to call attention to the difference between the scenes in the royal mortuary temples and those in the tomb chapels of the nobility. The king, being a god, did not have to remind the deities of the activities of earthly life which he desired to continue in the next world, for they were inherent in his divine nature. The tomb paintings, therefore, recorded the king's great deeds and pictured his relationship with the gods. The nobles, on the other hand, in order to secure the continuation of all earthly pursuits had their artists paint scenes of daily life, showing them at work and at play. Consequently the walls of the tomb-chapel are given over to a faithful portrayal of actual life as the ancient Egyptians lived it—something unique in the history of art. These painted reliefs run the gamut of agricultural life from the sowing of the seed to the harvesting. A tomb properly decorated also contained scenes of hunting for fowl among papyrus thickets, fishing, pottery-making, games and sports of all kinds, banquets and domestic life, and funeral processions. These scenes were meant to be both retroactive and prospective, but it was the concern for the future life that was really important.

[1] For superior photographs in colour see Kurt Lange and Max Hirmer: *Aegypten* (Munich, Hirmer Verlag, 1955), pp. 246, 247, and *Egypt: Paintings from Tombs and Temples* (New York Graphic Society by arrangement with UNESCO. Paris, 1954), plates 13–16.

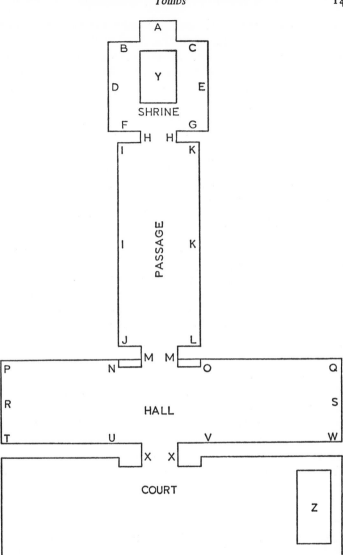

Fig. 7. Diagram of a typical Theban official's tomb. (After Davies.)
A, Niche for small statue of X. B, C, False doors (Middle Kingdom);
figures of deities (later). Sometimes full-size rock-cut statues of X and
family. D, E, List of offerings. Consecration of food to the service of X.

continued on next page

The tombs of the nobles are scattered throughout the Theban plain from the road leading to the Royal Valley in the north to Medinet Habu in the south. They are rock-cut, but in many instances the stone was of a poor quality and crumbled. In such cases the masons used mud-plaster to fill out the defects in the wall. On top of this they placed a finer lime plaster which was made smooth for painting. The artists who painted on plaster quickly reached a high level of quality in the Eighteenth Dynasty. It is interesting to note that among the painters of the tombs of the nobles not a single name is known. The artist worked anonymously as a member of the school. The tomb paintings invariably follow a set pattern with conventional group-ings and postures that were determined by tradition. Here and there a peculiarity of the artist may have asserted itself but generally each one followed the traditional themes and designs. These painters were indispensable, for it was their work that immortalized the piety of the king and noble and won for them the favour of the gods. The tomb murals must have been greatly admired by their owners but in spite of all this the artist did not rank high. We know the names of scribes, sculptors, priests, and viziers from the period but the painter is the forgotten man of ancient Egypt.

The tombs of the nobles were modelled not after the city house but the country bungalow which called for an elongated ground plan with narrow frontage, the rooms lying one behind the other. The rooms are decorated with bright colours and happy scenes. No earthly pleasures were alien to the realm of the dead and generally there was no place for gloom.

The artistic technique of the Eighteenth Dynasty was charac-

Funerary feast. F, G, Rites for welfare of X. H, H, Figures of X entering and leaving. I, Consecration of food. List of offerings. I, Series of burial rites. K, Consecration of food. List of offerings. K, Rites of opening the mouth. J, The pilgrimage to Abydos. L, Hunting scene. M, M, Figures of X entering and leaving. N, O, King sitting enthroned. P, Q, Tribute being brought to the king from foreign lands or some act of official life. R, S, Stelae. T, Family banquet presided over by X. U, V, Sacrifice performed by X. W, Craftsmen at work, reception of offerings, or produce of crafts-men. X, X, Figure of X adoring the light. Y, Z, Shafts to burial vaults.

terized by a careful preparation of surfaces, harmonious and brilliant colouring, delicacy and precision of detail. One of the interesting developments of this period was the showing of flesh colour through a transparent garment. Beginning with the Nineteenth Dynasty a decadence set in and the art lost many of the above qualities.[1]

The catalogue prepared by Gardiner and Weigall and supplemented by Engelbach lists 344 tombs of the nobles. Outstanding among these are the tomb-chapels of the viziers which, from the standpoint of art, are unexcelled. It must be held in mind that the vizier, as prime minister, stood next to the Pharaoh in importance. It follows that great skill and artistry would be called upon in the preparation of his tomb.

Foremost in this group is the tomb of Ramose who was governor of Thebes and Vizier during the reign of Ikhnaton. This tomb was restored by Walter B. Emery who installed windows in the roof, thus providing a "top light" for the matchless reliefs. As head of the religious, judicial and administrative organization, Ramose wielded great influence in court circles. He had been Vizier under Amenhotep III. When Ikhnaton acceded to the throne and announced his defection from Amonism, the Vizier joined him in the new religion.

Ramose's importance derives from the fact that his régime occurred during the outbreak of the religious revolution and the consequent transfer of the court from Thebes to el-Amarna. For that reason the tomb was never finished. The fact that Ramose was High Priest as well as Vizier made his conversion to Atonism strategically important for Ikhnaton and provides the key to the success of the reform in the face of the opposition of the Amon priesthood. The tomb reliefs therefore have both artistic and historical significance, exhibiting, as they do, both the delicate style of the earlier Eighteenth-dynasty artists as well as the free and bolder style of the Amarna reform. The religious transition

---

[1] For a definitive treatment of the technique and character of tomb-painting —mode of drawing, materials and implements, outlining, combination of relief and painting—see Nina M. Davies: *Ancient Egyptian Paintings* (with the editorial assistance of Alan Gardiner), Vols. I and II: Plates; Vol. III: Description. (Chicago, University of Chicago Press, 1936.) Special publication of the Oriental Institute of the University of Chicago, James H. Breasted, editor.

is likewise documented in the use of the traditional royal name of Amenhotep along with representations of the worship of the new god Aton. The reliefs of the royal couple—standing under the rays of the sun-disk in the Aton temple, showing the king with the unmistakable features of Ikhnaton, worshipping Aton, and appearing in public with his queen, as only Ikhnaton did— bear the name Amenhotep. This is conclusive proof that Amenhotep IV and Ikhnaton are one and the same person. The chiselled-out figures of the king and his wife may be the work of someone in the later period of Amon resurgence.

The unpainted reliefs on the east wall of the large-columned hall are well known for their delicacy and clarity of definition. They show in four groups Ramose and his wife, his brother and his wife, and their friends. The funeral scene on the south wall shows mourning women bearing funerary furniture and flowers, the funeral barque and its canopy being dragged on a sledge. Joseph L. Smith, the artist, gave his impression of this scene in his diary notes: "The composition and expressiveness of the funeral scene was the most dramatic I have seen on a painted wall of an Egyptian tomb. The mourners appeared actually to be wailing, and the illusion of real tears was an incredible creation through the medium of pigments on a stone surface."[1]

In 1907 the Metropolitan Museum of Art in New York appointed Norman de Garis Davies as director of an expedition to Thebes, the purpose of which was to make further excavations in the Necropolis but more particularly to record, before greater damage occurred, the paintings in the tombs of the Theban officials.[2] The work of this expedition was carried on from 1907 until 1910. The first tomb to be studied was that of Nakht, High Priest under Amenhotep II and Thutmose IV.[3] The chapel of Nakht is not the best example of the rock-hewn tomb. The transverse hall, the only room that is decorated, is noticeably askew to the main axis of the tomb and is not a perfect rectangle. Such things however are negligible in view of the vivacious,

---

[1] *Op. cit.*, p. 102.

[2] See Report in the Bulletin of the Metropolitan Museum of Art, March 1911.

[3] Not to be confused with the Nakht who succeeded Ramose as Vizier under Ikhnaton.

highly coloured scenes encountered here. As the visitor enters the tomb and admires the painted reliefs, he is forcefully reminded of the various groups of people whom he saw in the fields on his way to the Valley. Here in small compass are charming vignettes of ancient Egyptian life, painted in brilliant colours, which are remarkably well preserved. The subjects were so well executed that they became models for later murals in other tombs. The undamaged condition of the tomb indicates that it was unknown to earlier explorers. It was first cleared by M. Grébaut in 1889. When Davies commenced his copying of the tomb for the Metropolitan Museum in 1908–09, he assumed that the burial shaft and chamber had been cleared.[1] Later, finding that this was not the case, he proceeded with the excavation and was rewarded on the first day of work with the discovery in the mummy chamber of a fine white limestone statuette of Nakht himself. The High Priest, or Scribe, is shown in the act of presenting a stele to the sun-god. This unusual piece is still resting at the bottom of the Irish Sea, having gone down with the *Arabic*, which was torpedoed in the First World War. Some twenty pieces of funerary furniture were found in the burial vault but the importance of the tomb lies in its beautiful paintings. Chief among them are the festival or banquet scenes which are on the left end-wall of the transverse hall. These scenes are in several pictorial strips. Here the artist, departing completely from the religious theme, has given us a charming picture of a social gathering. The upper strip shows a blind harpist behind whom are six ladies in festival dress. They hold water-lilies in their hands and one holds a mandrake, or love-apple, for her neighbour to smell. A nude maid adjusts the ear-ring of one of the ladies. At such feasts the guests were provided not only with wine and fruit but also with "favours" such as ornaments and trinkets. All are smartly attired with a crown-like fillet binding the hair which falls down behind, a lotus bud on top of the head, a broad collar of coloured beads, bracelets, and a long mantle. The lower strip shows three female guests, all holding lotus-flowers to their noses. In front of them are three girl-musicians, an attractive composi-

[1] For plates in colour and description of the Nakht tomb painting, see Norman de Garis Davies: *The Tomb of Nakht at Thebes* (New York, Metropolitan Museum of Art, 1917).

tion often reproduced in prints today. One girl plays the double flute; another, the great harp; and a third, the lute. Their head attire is the same as the guests, but the two on the left are nude, while the harpist wears a transparent gown. Following the unbroken tradition, the artist has represented all three with legs in profile but the upper part of the body in full face. Nakht and his wife sit side by side facing the guests. Their son is shown presenting the royal pair with flowers and food. The pet cat sits under the royal chair eagerly devouring a fish which has been tossed to her.

The Egyptian love of outdoor life is seen in the decoration of the south side of the east wall where the Vizier overlooks the labour in the fields. Here we see the preparation of the soil after the inundation. Men are breaking up the clods with hoes and mallets, while others plough the ground with teams of water-buffaloes. Food and drink for the workers are kept under a tree. The main scene shows the harvest and ingathering of the grain; girls pull up flax by the roots, reapers cut corn with sickles, and binders secure the stalks with rope. The next scene depicts the winnowing of the grain and the storage.

Another well-preserved scene shows Nakht and his family hunting birds and spearing fish in the marshlands, a favourite theme among Theban artists even in royal tombs. This picture is accompanied by the following inscription: "The serving priest of Amon, the scribe Nakht and his beloved sister, the Chantress of Amon, Tawi, amusing themselves by looking at the good things, the products of the open lands and the papyrus beds." The remaining scenes have to do with the consecration of provisions for the dead with Nakht and his wife sitting before the table of offerings. Altogether, the wall-paintings in the tomb of Nakht are delightful, possessing real verve and dash.

The tomb of Senmut, the builder of the famous Hatshepsut temple at Deir el Bahri and her two obelisks at Karnak, is historically, if not artistically, important. Circumstance and intelligence combined to send him to the top in political life, and when Hatshepsut took the throne, she linked her destiny with him. Senmut was well known as the favourite and chief supporter of the queen. It is not surprising, therefore, that his tomb was severely mutilated by the agents of Thutmose III, the successor

of Hatshepsut. But in spite of its wrecked condition, a few fragments of decoration have survived, showing Minoan envoys bearing Cretan vases. Knowing the danger inherent in his conspicuous support of the queen, Senmut had the corridor inscriptions that bore his name covered with plaster. On top of the
plaster he had additional inscriptions bearing his name carved so
that his enemies, in destroying the outer inscription, would not
know that his name remained underneath. The plaster later fell
off and the concealed inscriptions can now be seen, minus
Senmut's name! His name and figure were also ruthlessly chiselled
away from the relief-scenes in the temple at Deir el Bahri.

Senmut's position as Prime Minister and intimate companion
of the queen inspired him to build a second tomb which he
tunnelled under the court of the great temple itself. With the
death of Hatshepsut and the quick take-over of Thutmose III, the
tomb was suddenly abandoned. It was discovered by the Expedition of the Metropolitan Museum of New York.[1]

After being held down for seventeen years by Hatshepsut and
her clique, Thutmose III, ascending the throne, initiated extensive military expeditions abroad and before he was through had
waged seventeen successful campaigns. These triumphs—Gaza,
Megiddo, Carchemish, Kadesh, Tunip—resulted in the first real
empire in history and established Thutmose as the first world con-
queror. Through these campaigns Egypt rose to world supremacy
with a vast suzerainty extending to the upper reaches of Mesopotamia. Thebes became the world capital, recipient of a continuous flow of wealth from a dozen provinces. Each year the
armies of Thutmose returned home borne down with the spoils
of Asia. The treasuries were bursting with gold. After the capture
of Megiddo, we are told, Thutmose brought back 924 chariots,
2,238 horses, 2,400 head of cattle, 200 suits of armour and vast
quantities of gold and silver. The islands of the Mediterranean
and the Aegean paid their yearly tribute. Envoys from north and
south were continually presenting themselves at court. From
Phoenician galleys, docked at the quays of Thebes, came gold and
silver vessels from Tyre, products of the craftsmen of Asia Minor,
Crete, and Cyprus; furniture of ebony and ivory and bronze

[1] See Bulletin of the Museum, Section II, 1928.

implements of war. Asiatics came to Thebes bringing tribute o gold to the office of the vizier.

The vizier under Thutmose III was the second most importan person in Egypt. His name was Rekhmire and his tomb, describe by Breasted as "the most important private monument of th Empire", is a storehouse of information, describing in great detai the conquests of the king, the tribute from foreign states, Asiati prisoners and Nubian slaves being brought to Thebes, the dutie of the vizier, methods of administration, and the constitution o the state. The tomb is not typical in shape but consists of transverse hall from which a long corridor penetrates the rock the roof gradually increasing in height as it goes. At the end o the corridor, high up in the wall, is a niche which once held th statue of the vizier. The importance of this tomb lies both ii painted scenes and hieroglyphic inscriptions, which depict an narrate the illustrious career of Rekhmire, starting with hi appointment to the office by the king. The Pharaoh gives hin instructions regarding the attitude of a vizier in the administra tion of his office, instructions which show a fine regard for justic and humane treatment.[1] This is followed by a detailed accoun of the office itself, a most valuable document for our knowledg of the organization of the Egyptian government. Other inscrip tions deal with the tabulation of tax lists and the administratio of works.

Coming next to the paintings, one of the most important ii the transverse hall shows Rekhmire receiving tribute from th representatives of foreign lands. The bearers of gifts are arrange in five rows: envoys from Punt, princes of Keftiu and the Aegea Isles, Nubians and Syrians. The Nubians bring a panther, elephant tusks, gold, giraffes, and monkeys. The chief of Keftiu and hi followers carry typical Minoan vessels similar to those found b Sir Arthur Evans on the island of Crete. The Aegean representa tives appear to be carefully drawn portraits of the actual envoys The Syrians are presenting horses and chariots and costly vases Another interesting scene represents the interior of the Cour presided over by Rekhmire. Prisoners or suppliants are conducte up the central aisle of the courtroom by officials and take thei

[1] For the text of this inscription and for all other inscriptions in this tom see James H. Breasted: *op. cit.*, Vol. II, pp. 266–94.

stand before the Vizier. Attendants stand on either side of the
dais, ready to carry out orders. Messengers wait at the door and
others bow as they enter the room. The walls of the long hall are
covered with strips showing festival scenes reminiscent of Nakht's
tomb: ladies kneeling in pairs, with water-lilies in their hands
and heads anointed with myrrh, receive from their maids per-
fumes and trinkets. Girl-musicians play on the harp, lute and
drum while others clap their hands. Agricultural and funerary
scenes complete the paintings in the long hall.

Among the many tombs of officials there is one more that
merits our attention—that of Menna, Scribe of the Fields of the
Lord of the Two Lands of Upper and Lower Egypt in the reign
of Thutmose IV. Menna apparently had enemies, for we notice
that the funerary scenes depicting the pleasures awaiting him in
the after-life were deliberately damaged. These scenes had portrayed the deceased enjoying perfect fishing and fowling, fine
harvests and vintages, banquets and festivals. It was believed that
damage done to such scenes would serve to deprive the owner of
these pleasures in the next world. Only a personal enemy could
have perpetrated such a malicious defacing which included the
obliteration of Menna's head so that he could not behold the
pleasures of the Elysian Fields. His boomerang is cut off close to
his hand, making it impossible for him ever again to hunt fowl
in the marshes. His spear is broken off at the hand, thus prohibit-
ing all future fishing. The disfigurement continues in the agricultural scenes where the eyeless Menna is kept from observing
the harvesting of the crops. Even the labourers are incapacitated
so that they are unable to work for their master. This post-
mortem revenge was not uncommon, a good example being the
treatment given the monuments of Hatshepsut by Thutmose III.
The deliberate mutilation of tomb-paintings belonging to kings
and officials, who had either fallen into disgrace or had incited
the enmity of their successors, is one of the chief causes of tomb
deterioration. There were other reasons such as the obliteration of female figures found distasteful by the early Christian
monastics, the damage caused by the fires of robbers and other
natives who lived in the tombs, and the removal of pieces from
walls by natives who sold them to collectors.

The colouring of the Menna tomb has remained brilliant; the

drawings are vigorous and vivacious to the point of humorous details. In the harvest scene, for instance, two girls are quarrelling and tearing each other's hair. A girl is seen taking a thorn out of another girl's foot. The agricultural scenes are done in four long registers, occupying the full height of the wall. Menna sits under a shelter observing the harvest operation. A servant with a napkin and a jar offers him refreshment. Nearby are trees with birds' nests and clamouring nestlings. A foreman supervises the reaping. One of the workers has put his sickle under his arm while he drinks from a jar. Women gleaners are at work. A peasant woman, sitting under a tree and eating fruit from a bowl, has taken off her dress and wrapped it around her baby, who is trying to grasp the mother's hair. The next register shows the workers bringing home the harvest of corn which they empty on the ground. Two men are resting under a tree; one is asleep and the other plays on a reed instrument. Further along, we see the corn being winnowed. Scribes register the harvest on their writing palettes as labourers measure the corn. Menna's chariot and horses, in charge of a groom, stand ready to take him home.

In another scene Menna and his wife are making the morning sacrifice to the gods. Girls, probably daughters, bring fruit and flowers. Their elaborate jewellery indicates their high station. The first girl carries a sistrum, the instrument used by all priestesses. The other section of this register shows two daughters of Menna entertaining him with music. Their head-dresses are the kind worn only by princesses or ladies honoured by the king.[1]

[1] For coloured plates and description of officials' tomb see Nina M. Davies: *op. cit.*

Chapter Seven

TUTANKHAMON

In the summer of 1922 Howard Carter was visiting Lord Carnarvon at Highclere Castle, the latter's home in England. They discussed their campaigns together starting in 1907. Carter's career as an Egyptologist received its impetus from his association with P. E. Newberry, in an expedition sponsored by the Egypt Exploration Fund, and later with Petrie. In 1899 Maspero appointed Carter Chief Inspector of Antiquities in Upper Egypt. In this capacity he collaborated with Theodore Davis in the discovery of the tomb of Thutmose IV. Lord Carnarvon went to Egypt in 1907 and after one season joined Carter. In 1914 they took over the Davis concession in the Royal Valley and the hunt for Tutankhamon's tomb was begun. For eight years they combed the Valley but in the end had nothing to show for their labours. Now Carnarvon was ready to call it quits, concluding that Maspero and Davis were correct in declaring that "the site was exhausted". He decided to abandon the Valley excavations and announced his inability to subsidize any further expeditions.

Carter was convinced that the Valley held at least one more undiscovered tomb, probably that of Tutankhamon. He called Carnarvon's attention to the small triangular area just below the entrance to the tomb of Ramses VI, virtually the only spot that had not been cleared. He was determined to investigate that site before finally giving up and was willing to do it at his own expense if Carnarvon would permit him to operate under his concession. He also assured his colleague that if a tomb should be found it would be credited, according to their previous arrangements, to

Carnarvon. The latter was impressed by this determination and agreed to support a final season in the Valley of the Kings.

In the 1907–08 season Davis had found a cache of baked clay jars containing funerary equipment. Herbert E. Winlock of the New York Metropolitan Museum of Art discovered that the seals of these jars bore the name of Tutankhamon. Later Davis found a faience cup bearing the same name and a fragment of gold foil containing the names and figures of the king and his wife. These three finds were enough to convince Carter that the tomb of the boy-king was in the vicinity of the Ramses VI tomb. More than once Davis had come within a few feet of discovering the tomb of Tutankhamon. But it remained for Howard Carter to stumble across the first of those famous "sixteen steps" that led him and Tutankhamon to world fame. That incident, however, cannot be called an accident. It should be clear from the foregoing that the discovery was a direct result of years of systematic search carried on in the face of continued disappointments but always with the deep conviction on Carter's part that the tomb was there, waiting to be discovered.

It is somewhat ironic that the most famous tomb in Egyptian history was one of the smallest and most inconspicuous of them all. The reason for this is well known: it is the only royal tomb that was not ransacked by ancient robbers and, when discovered, was practically intact. It was for that reason that Tutankhamon's name became in 1922 a household word the world over.

THE SIXTEEN STEPS

Carter, accompanied by Callendar, his assistant, arrived in Luxor 28th October 1922, immediately enrolled workmen and organized the expedition. Digging was begun at the north-east corner of the entrance to the tomb of Ramses VI, which was covered by the remains of the huts of workmen who made the Ramses tomb. On the morning of 4th November, upon his arrival at the site, Carter was told that "a step-cut in the rock had been discovered underneath the very first hut to be attacked". Carter continues:

> This seemed too good to be true, but a short amount of extra clearing revealed the fact that we were actually in the entrance of a

steep cut in the rock, some thirteen feet below the entrance to the tomb of Rameses VI, and a similar depth from the present bed level of The Valley. The manner of cutting was that of the sunken stairway entrance so common in The Valley, and I almost dared to hope that we had found our tomb at last. Work continued feverishly throughout the whole of that day and the morning of the next, but it was not until the afternoon of November 5th that we succeeded in clearing away the masses of rubbish that overlay the cut, and were able to demarcate the upper edges of the stairway on all its four sides.[1]

Clearly this was the entrance to a tomb. But previous experience had prepared the excavator for disappointments. It could be an unfinished and abandoned tomb, or a finished tomb that had been completely plundered in ancient times, or perhaps just a royal cache. The work proceeded feverishly but carefully. At the twelfth step, Carter saw the upper part of a plastered and sealed door. Since the doorway was under ancient (Nineteenth Dynasty) huts of workmen, it would appear that the tomb had never been opened. Making a small hole through the top of the door, Carter peered through and saw a passage completely filled with stones—another evidence that the tomb was intact. What lay beyond that rubble-filled passage? The entrance hall seemed almost too narrow for a royal tomb. The seal impressions on the upper part of the door were the usual ones of the royal necropolis. Carter did not know that a few inches lower, covered by the rubble, were the seals of Tutankhamon himself. Since it was the end of the day, he refilled most of the stairway and went to his house on the hill near the Valley. In deference to Lord Carnarvon, who was in England, he decided to discontinue the operation until his colleague could be present. The next morning he cabled Carnarvon the announcement of his "wonderful discovery". The stairway was filled to surface level and covered with huge boulders.

The news of the discovery spread fast. The two weeks of waiting for Carnarvon were devoted to securing additional help and conferring with other archaeologists. Meanwhile towards the end of the interval the workmen had cleared the staircase, completely revealing the true seals of Tutankhamon. But it was also

[1] *The Tomb of Tutankhamen* (New York, Doran, 1923), Vol. I, pp. 132, 133.

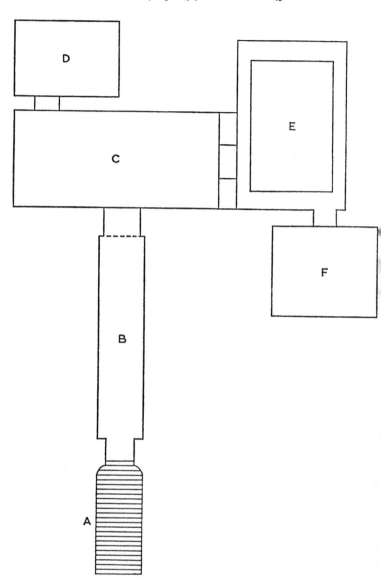

Fig. 8. Tomb of Tutankhamon. A, Entrance staircase. B, Passage. C, Antechamber. D, Annexe to Antechamber. E, Burial Chamber with Shrines. F, Store Chamber.

Howard Carter at Tutankhamon's tomb in March 1923. (*Courtesy, Radio Times Hulton Picture Library*)

Sir Flinders Petrie arranging pottery he found in Southern Palestine. (*Courtesy, Radio Times Hulton Picture Library*)

Amon-Mut-Chon's Temple at Luxor. Queen Nefertari at the side of the statue of Ramses II in the forecourt. (*Courtesy, Hirmer Verlag, Munich*)

clear that the door had been opened before, probably not later than the reign of Horemheb, and resealed. This indicated that the tomb might not be intact. Further, in the rubble that filled the stairway, the workers found numerous potsherds and boxes bearing the names of Ikhnaton, Smenkhkare, and Amenhotep III, as well as that of Tutankhamon. It might turn out, thought Carter, that the tomb was a cache containing objects brought from el-Amarna by Tutankhamon and buried there.

On the twenty-fifth, Carnarvon having arrived, they commenced the removal of the rubbish from the long inclined corridor behind the first door. Carter and Carnarvon were now joined by Lady Evelyn Herbert, Carnarvon's daughter, Harry Burton and A. C. Mace, photographer and field archaeologist respectively from the Metropolitan Museum in New York, Arthur Weigall, Inspector General of Antiquities in Cairo, and the American Egyptologist, James H. Breasted. Among the stones and debris in the passage were many alabaster jars, potsherds and vases. In the afternoon of the next day, 30 feet down from the entrance, the party came upon a second doorway containing the seal of Tutankhamon. This door likewise showed evidence of having been opened and re-sealed. It looked more than ever like a cache. Carter describes the clearing of the door and his first glimpse of the Antechamber:

> Slowly, desperately slowly it seemed to us as we watched, the remains of passage debris that encumbered the lower part of the doorway were removed, until at last we had the whole door clear before us. The decisive moment had arrived. With trembling hands I made a tiny breach in the upper left hand corner. Darkness and blank space, as far as an iron testing-rod could reach, showed that whatever lay beyond was empty, and not filled like the passage we had just cleared. Candle tests were applied as a precaution against possible foul gases, and then, widening the hole a little, I inserted the candle and peered in, Lord Carnarvon, Lady Evelyn and Callendar standing anxiously beside me to hear the verdict. At first I could see nothing, the hot air escaping from the chamber causing the candle flame to flicker, but presently, as my eyes grew accustomed to the light, details of the room within emerged slowly from the mist, strange animals, statues, and gold—everywhere the glint of gold. For the moment—an eternity it must have seemed to the others standing by—I was struck dumb with amazement, and when Lord

Carnarvon, unable to stand the suspense any longer, inquired anxiously, "Can you see anything?" it was all I could do to get out the words, "Yes, wonderful things." Then widening the hole a little further, so that we both could see, we inserted an electric torch.[1]

Later Carter, enlarging the hole at the top of the door, squeezed through the aperture and, with his companions looking on breathlessly, dropped out of sight and hearing; dropped back, one might say, 3,000 years in time. With understandable awe and a certain consciousness of trespassing, perhaps, he cautiously made his way, stepping on footprints made by priests of the Eighteenth Dynasty. He noticed finger marks on the wall, left by the artist as he finished his work and left the tomb. He almost stepped on the funerary bouquet which had been dropped at the threshold. He was overwhelmed by the thought that he was breathing the same sealed-up air breathed by those who last left the tomb and sealed it. After an unbearably long time Carter emerged from the Antechamber and announced that the tomb was that of Tutankhamon! What he had seen was bewildering, an endless profusion of "riches, an incredible vision". Many days would pass before the waiting world would learn what lay beyond that chamber.

The scene gradually grew clearer as Carter and Carnarvon stood in the doorway of the Antechamber and cast their beam of light from one object to another. First to catch their attention were three gilt couches, their sides carved in the form of monstrous animals with fearsome heads. Then there loomed into view two great statues of the Pharaoh in bituminized wood, with golden head-dresses. There were gold-plated chariots, many alabaster vessels, inlaid caskets, beds, beautifully carved chairs, a golden inlaid throne, walking-sticks and bows of every kind, decorated with gold and inlay, and countless other precious objects such as never before greeted the eye of an excavator. Finally, Carter noticed that between the two statues of the king was another sealed door. This confirmed his surmise that what he had been looking at was merely the Antechamber. But this was enough for one day. They refilled the doorway, left a guard at the tomb entrance and retired to the Valley rest-house.

[1] *Ibid.*, pp. 141, 142.

After a sleepless night spent in speculating about the rooms beyond the Antechamber, the excavators returned to the scene. With the aid of electric lights installed by Callendar, they were able to make a more accurate appraisal of what they had seen the day before. The temptation was overwhelming to break down the second door and learn what lay beyond but more sober judgement demanded that they proceed deliberately, photographing, cataloguing, and preparing the fragile objects for removal from the Antechamber. Several weeks more were required for this task in the process of which another sealed door was discovered beneath one of the couches. An unrepaired hole in the doorway, large enough for a person to crawl through, indicated that some ancient thief had visited the room. Carter peered through the hole and saw a collection of funerary equipment even greater than that of the Antechamber. The Annex, as they called it, looked as if a tornado had struck it. As they surveyed the vast contents of this store-room with its wealth of material of exquisite craftsmanship, it became evident to the two excavators that they were on the verge of an unprecedented find that could not be handled in one season. It was now clear that they must proceed slowly and carefully with the work of packing and preserving. A dark-room and laboratory were set up, stores of preservative materials were ordered, and measures were taken for making the tomb safe against robbery.

Meanwhile, the outside world was seething with all kinds of rumours and fantastic reports. Carter decided to have an "official" opening of the tomb. Attending the opening on 29th November 1922 were Lady Allenby, Egyptian officials, M. Pierre Lacau, General Director of the Service of Antiquities, and a reporter of the London *Times*. Following this event, the tomb was closed for a period to give time for Carter to arrange for more specialized assistance and the purchase of materials for preservation and packing. The most pressing need was for an expert photographer and Harry Burton of the Metropolitan Museum of New York was considered the logical man. With him were four members of the Metropolitan staff who were lent by A. M. Lythgoe, Director of the Egyptian Department: H. E. Winlock, Director of the New York excavations in the Valley; A. C. Mace, W. Hauser, and L. F. Hall. Alfred Lucas, Director of the

Chemical Department of the Egyptian Government, completed the working staff. Alan Gardiner and James H. Breasted, the two most noted epigraphists, assisted in the deciphering of inscriptions.

THE GOLDEN THRONE

The tomb was reopened on 16th December and the process of removal was begun. The most artistic treasure of the Antechamber—and the entire tomb for that matter—was the throne which was completely overlaid with gold and adorned with multicoloured inlays of faience, glass, and stone. The panel on the back of the throne was described by Carter as "the most beautiful thing that has yet been found in Egypt". The legs are those of a lion and on the front legs at the top are lion-heads of chased gold. The arm-rests are goddesses in the form of winged serpents, wearing on their heads the double crown of the Egyptian kings and protecting the names of the Pharaoh with their wings. The name shown here is Tutankhaton but elsewhere on the throne it is Tutankhamon. Supporting the arm-rests are six serpents, carved in wood, gilded and decorated with inlays.

On the back of the throne the king is seen seated with his legs crossed, one arm casually resting on the back of the chair and the other on his knee. He is talking to his queen, who leans forward in the act of adjusting his broad collar or perhaps spreading some perfume on it, since she holds in the other hand a jar of scent or ointment. It is a most intimate and informal scene, recalling the Berlin relief in which Ikhnaton is seen leaning on his staff in a very unkingly manner and Nefertiti holds a lotus blossom for him to sniff. Both pieces are typical of the unconventional naturalistic Amarna style. The king wears a wig adorned with a diadem and threefold cluster-crown entwined with serpents. The faces and other exposed parts are in red glaze and the headdresses are done in turquoise-coloured faience. The clothing is inlaid with coloured glass, faience, carnelian, and calcite. On a nearby table stands a bouquet made of semi-precious stones. The seat of the throne is patterned with coloured mosaic squares.

The importance attached to this throne derives as much from

the light it sheds on the religious and political situation of the time as from its intrinsic artistry. Above the royal couple is the sun-disk with uraeus and rays, ending in human hands, extended towards the royal couple in blessing. This, of course, represents the strong continuance of Atonism which Tutankhamon supposedly had repudiated upon his arrival in Thebes. Furthermore the inconsistency of the cartouches provides a revealing evidence of Tutankhamon's reluctant acceptance of Amonism. As we have pointed out, some of the royal names contain the original Aton sign while others were changed to Amon. The cartouche wrought in gold plate was comparatively easy to alter while those done in inlay were left intact. The wonder is—with such obvious signs of the Amarna heresy decorating the throne—that the Amon priests gave their approval to the royal burial.

The Antechamber also contained royal robes, chests, beds and couches of ebony and ivory, chairs, a golden sceptre, two sistra of wood and bronze, ushabti figures, and four chariots.[1] The work of clearing and removal, which took two months, was followed by the even longer task of restoration in the laboratory. In the course of this work Carter gained some evidence in regard to the tomb robbery. Entrance had been made shortly after the burial but the hole made by the thieves was too small to permit the theft of any sizeable objects. The Annex was found in a state of confusion just as the robbers had left it, whereas they had evidently tried to restore some semblance of order in the Antechamber and re-sealed the door after them. In any case, they could not have taken any great quantity of valuable objects. Carter found a gilded pedestal minus the statuette which had stood on it. The figure must have been of solid gold, similar to those found in other royal tombs. A handful of solid gold rings tied up in a fold of cloth—in the same way the *fellahin* today secure coins in their head-shawls—indicated that the thieves had been detected and had to leave in a hurry. Little or no damage was done to the chambers.

---

[1] Obviously the mere listing of the objects found in the tomb would result in a disproportionately long chapter. For a complete description of the contents of the tomb—all of which are on display in the Cairo Museum—see Howard Carter: *The Tomb of Tutankhamen.* 3 vols. (New York, Doran, 1923–33).

A NEST OF SHRINES

At last the day arrived for the opening of the sealed door to the Burial Chamber. On 16th February 1923, in the presence of Egyptian officials, the rest of the staff, and the government press, Carter broke the seal and made a hole in the doorway large enough to insert an electric light. Facing him stood what appeared to be a solid wall of gold. After breaking away more of the doorway, he was able to enter the Burial Chamber and found that the wall of gold was "the side of an immense gilt shrine built to cover and protect the sarcophagus". The shrine was 17 feet long, 11 feet wide and 9 feet high. It was completely overlaid with gold and on its sides were inlaid panels of brilliant blue faience. Opening the swinging doors of the shrine, the excavators found a second one with bolted doors and an intact seal. It was at this point that Carter decided to discontinue operations for the time. The guests were permitted to enter and gaze at the shrine and the surrounding statues of the protecting goddesses, caskets of ivory and ebony, boat models, and chariots. On 17th February, the Queen of the Belgian and her son Prince Alexander inspected the Sepulchral Chamber. The tomb was then closed, resealed and reburied. The season's work was finished. How Carter and Carnarvon could leave the premises without satisfying their curiosity as to what lay within the nest of shrines seems humanly impossible. The only explanation that can be thought of is that it was a scientific job which demanded the slow and deliberate examination, photographing, cataloguing, and preservation of each article in turn.

The work of the next two seasons was slowed up by complications over the contractual arrangements for excavation and the problem of the press. Permission to excavate on a given site was granted by the Department of Antiquities to accredited individuals or institutions by the issuing of an annual concession. The following stipulations in Carnarvon's agreement were normal for practically all expeditions in Egypt:

> Mummies of the Kings, of Princes, and of High Priests, together with their coffins and sarcophagi, shall remain the property of the Antiquities Service.

Tombs which are discovered intact, together with all objects they may contain, shall be handed over to the Museum whole and without division.

In the case of tombs which have already been searched, the Antiquities Service shall, over and above the mummies and sarcophagi, reserve for themselves all objects of capital importance from the point of view of history and archaeology, and shall share the remainder with the Permittee.

As it is probable that the majority of such tombs as may be discovered will fall within the category of the present article, it is agreed that the Permittee's share will sufficiently recompense him for the pains and labour of the undertaking.

Whether the Antiquities Service concluded that the tomb had *not* been searched earlier in the intended meaning of the term or, if it had been entered, contended that everything in the tomb was of "capital importance", it ruled, in any case, that everything found would be retained in Cairo. Carter agreed with the decision but Carnarvon insisted that the expedition was entitled to certain objects over and above mummies, coffins, and materials highly important for the Cairo Museum.

The other altercation that brought about strained relations between the two colleagues at this time was Carnarvon's arrangement from the outset that the London *Times* would have world copyright on the news and pictures and the privilege of selling the news to all other newspapers. This could only appear to other English-speaking papers as an unjustified monopoly on something that belonged to the world and resulted in widespread editorial criticism. Carter again went against Carnarvon and, in this instance, also the Egyptian government. The strain of the expedition had brought Carter close to a nervous breakdown, a condition which did not ease their strained relationship. Carnarvon at this time was stung by a mosquito and became infected when, after he had scraped the welt open in shaving, a fly poisoned the area. His previous illness had left him with little reserve strength and his condition grew steadily worse. Pneumonia set in and he died on 5th April 1923. Before his death a reconciliation was reached between the two men. It was arranged that Carter should continue the operations under the patronage of the Countess of Carnarvon and work was resumed in October 1923. The problem of tourists and guests became a highly troublesome one. In three months over 12,300 visitors entered the tomb and 270 parties visited the laboratory. Obviously this congestion did not make the work of the staff any easier.

The Burial Chamber, as we have said, contained four golden shrines tightly fitted into each other like a nest of enormous magic boxes, which filled the entire chamber. One immediately began mentally to reconstruct the seemingly impossible task of carrying the sides of the outer shrine into the room. Apparently they proved to be too large, for the doorway shows signs of having been suddenly enlarged. All four shrines were covered, inside and out, with hieroglyphic texts.[1]

Another exciting moment arrived when Carter was ready to open the door of the fourth and innermost shrine. Removing the seal and swinging back the doors, he saw "an immense yellow sarcophagus intact with the lid still firmly fixed in its place, just as the pious hands had left it". The outstretched wings and arm of the goddess, sculptured on the end of the sarcophagus seemed to be protecting the king from any intrusion. Before proceeding farther, it was now necessary to remove all four shrines, a project which consumed a month. The difficulty of doing this may be appreciated from the fact that the sides of the outermost shrine alone weighed one-quarter to three-quarters of a ton. With the removal of the shrines, the wall-paintings of the tomb came into full view for the first time.

The magnificent quartzite sarcophagus measured 9 feet in length, 4 feet 10 inches in width and 4 feet 10 inches in height. No finer specimen had ever been found. Its most impressive features were the guardian goddesses Isis, Nephthys, Neith, and Selkit, carved in high relief on each of the four corners, so placed that their full-spread wings and outstretched arms formed a protecting circle around the whole sarcophagus. It was noticed

---

[1] Strangely enough, with all the material that was published about the Tutankhamon tomb in the thirty years that followed, no attempt was made to edit and translate the inscriptions on the shrines. The project may have been considered not worth the time and effort involved. The exacting task was finally undertaken by Alexandre Piankoff who brought out the first translation of the texts in English: *The Shrines of Tutankhamon* (New York, Bollingen Foundation, 1955; Harper, Torchbook, 1962).

immediately that the lid was not of the same material as the body. This may have come about, as Carter suggests, because the intended lid was not ready in time for the burial and the rose-red granite slab was substituted. The lid was cracked in the middle which might indicate an accident in its transportation to the tomb.

The excavators now came to the last dramatic ceremony. Many dignitaries were invited to the occasion. It is only fitting that the description of this moment in history be described by the man who made it possible.

Many strange scenes must have happened in the Valley of the Tombs of the Kings since it became the royal burial ground of the Theban New Empire, but one may be pardoned for thinking that the present scene was not the least interesting or dramatic. For ourselves it was the one supreme and culminating moment—a moment looked forward to ever since it became evident that the chambers discovered, in November, 1922, must be the tomb of Tut-ankh-Amen, and not a cache of his furniture as had been claimed. None of us but felt the solemnity of the occasion, none of us but was affected by the prospect of what we were about to see—the burial custom of a king of ancient Egypt of thirty-three centuries ago. How would the king be found? Such were the anticipatory speculations running in our minds during the silence maintained.

The tackle for raising the lid was in position. I gave the word. Amid intense silence the huge slab, broken in two, weighing over a ton and a quarter, rose from its bed. The light shone into the sarcophagus. A sight met our eyes that at first puzzled us. It was a little disappointing. The contents were completely covered by fine linen shrouds. The lid being suspended in mid-air, we rolled back those covering shrouds, one by one, and as the last was removed a gasp of wonderment escaped our lips, so gorgeous was the sight that met our eyes: a golden effigy of the young boy king, of most magnificent workmanship, filled the whole of the interior of the sarcophagus. This was the lid of a wonderful anthropoid coffin, some 7 feet in length, resting upon a low bier in the form of a lion, and no doubt the outermost coffin of a series of coffins, nested one within the other, enclosing the mortal remains of the king. . . .

Among all that regal splendour, that royal magnificence—everywhere the glint of gold—there was nothing so beautiful as those few withered flowers, still retaining their tinge of colour. They told us what a short period three thousand three hundred years really was—

but Yesterday and the Morrow. In fact, that little touch of nature made that ancient and our modern civilization kin.[1]

THE MUMMY OF TUTANKHAMON

The coffins were opened in the 1925–26 season. The removal of the lid of the first coffin revealed another shroud which, when rolled back, disclosed another magnificent gold-sheathed coffin with a second likeness of the king on the lid. But these two coffins were but a prelude to greater splendour. The workers raised the third casket free of the second. It was a coffin of solid gold, 6 feet long, beautifully engraved inside and outside, and embellished with cloisonné work of gold and semi-precious stones.

Here in the gold coffin lay the neatly wrapped mummy of Tutankhamon, the quarry of a ten-year search, the kernel of which all the rest of the trappings were the husk. Three thousand years had passed since human eyes had gazed on this form. In striking contrast to the sombre linen wrappings, which had turned from white to black, was the magnificent gold mask or similitude of the king, covering the head and shoulders. The exterior of the mummy wrappings was covered with jewellery and emblems of royalty. The mummy itself had been soaked in unguents of a fatty resinous type. These had decomposed and formed a pitch-like coating which stuck to the mummy and the bottom of the coffin. The wrappings therefore had to be cut rather than unravelled. In order to extricate the mummy from the coffin it had to be subjected to a heat of 932° Fahrenheit.

One last process remained—the examination of the mummy itself. For this specialized job Carter was able to call upon Dr. Douglas Derry, Professor of Anatomy at the School of Medicine, University of Cairo, and Dr. Saleh Bey Hamdi. The bandaging had followed the conventional system including the depositing of all kinds of gold objects in the folds of the wrappings. The king's head was encircled by a richly ornamented gold diadem inlaid with contiguous circles of carnelian. With great care the final wrappings were removed from the head and face to reveal the refined, serene countenance of the youthful king. Carter and others have made much of the resemblance of Tutankhamon's

[1] Howard Carter: *op. cit.*, Vol. II, pp. 100–02.

facial features to those of Ikhnaton, an observation which leads
to the problem of their exact relationship, a question which
cannot be entered into here. Amulets and sacred symbols adorned
the neck as well as four gold collars and several pectorals which
hung down to the chest. The arms were covered with bracelets
and the rest of the body was literally smothered with precious
ornaments too numerous to mention. The arms and legs were
separately wrapped before being enclosed by the bandages which
covered the body as a whole. The fingers and toes were bandaged
individually, after which gold sheaths were placed over each
prior to wrapping the whole hand or foot. Owing to the carboni-
zation the mummy was not as well preserved as those of Seti I
and Ramses II. The body and limbs were found in a cracked or
brittle state.[1]

Not the least extraordinary aspect of the excavation was the
discovery of the mummies of two still-born children in the inner
treasury of the tomb. They were found intact in two miniature
anthropoid coffins. Each of the two gilded coffins was encased in
an outer coffin of a similar design and shape. The mummies were
exceptionally well preserved—one of a still-born child and the
other of premature birth. Who were these two nameless babies
that died before they were born? Derry concluded from the
length of the foetus, the absence of eyebrows and eyelashes, the
state of the eyelids and other indications that the age of the
premature child was five months and that the more advanced one
was seven months. Both were girls. There could be no doubt,
according to Carter, that they were the issue of Ankhsenamon,
either the outcome of an abnormality in the young queen or the
result of deliberate injury to the expectant mother. The latter
possibility, remote perhaps, if true, would have left the throne
vacant for ambitious usurpers. At any rate, as Carter speculates,
"it may be inferred that had one of those babes lived, there might
never have been a Ramses".

The last room to be cleared was the Treasury, a hall leading
off from the Burial Chamber. In contrast to the chaotic jumble
of the Annex, the Treasury presented a more orderly scene.

[1] For a detailed anatomical report see Howard Carter. *Ibid.*, Vol. II. Appendix I by D. E. Derry.

This room contained boat models, caskets filled with treasures, chariots, jewellery and twenty-two shrine-shaped chests each one containing a statuette of the king. One object, however, dominated the room. Standing against the east wall, almost reaching the ceiling, was a large gilded canopy. Around the top were two rows of dazzling inlaid solar cobras. Inside the canopy was a chest on the sides of which stood statuettes of the four goddesses, Isis, Nephthys, Neith, and Selkit. This was a square alabaster box containing the four canopic jars which held the viscera of the king. On the four corners of the chest were the same guardian goddesses with outstretched arms. The idea of the canopic chest was a deep-seated mystical conception and served along with ushabtis and other funerary equipment to facilitate the king's passage through the Underworld. The human-headed lids are highly interesting as an over-refinement of style—the eyes, eyebrows, nostrils, and mouth being heavily outlined in colour. The effect is somewhat startling, having the appearance of a modern lady with too much make-up.

How are we to explain this stupendous mass of treasure, stored in the tomb of a young and unimportant king, a mere ''stop-gap'', as Baikie wrote, in Pharaonic history? How explain the splendours of a tomb which, when discovered, transformed an obscure youth, whose ephemeral reign took place 3,000 years ago, into a world-renowned figure? Could it be that Tutankhamon symbolized the successful resurgence of Amonism, causing the Theban priests to celebrate by burying the king with such lavish funerary equipment? Or was it the design of Ankhsenamon to honour her husband as the last of the great Eighteenth-dynasty royal line by burying with him all the palace treasures that might otherwise fall into the hands of the vulture-like usurpers of the throne? A more plausible explanation is implicit in the fact that the tomb of Tutankhamon is the only one in the history of Egyptian archaeology that was found intact. This could imply that this tomb was not exceptional and also that the tombs of Seti I, Ramses II, Amenhotep III, and Thutmose III contained riches that would put Tutankhamon's tomb to shame. What the ancient robbers took from these more magnificent tombs simply staggers the imagination. The answer to this question we shall probably never know.

As one contemplates in retrospect the event that fascinated the world, something very human remains in the mind, something more profoundly significant than all the riches and Pharaonic pomp: the finding of the ivory-handled, ostrich-feather fan in perfect condition, just as it was when the boy-king last used it, his sandals, and the funeral bouquet—pathetic tokens of the tender regard in which the king was held by those who buried him and of their sure conviction that life did not end with the physical death.

Chapter Eight

TEMPLES

We have observed the originality of the Egyptians in the pyramids, remarkable for their vastness and symmetry, and in the tombs, noted for their ingenious construction and beautiful decoration. No less original and equally impressive are the temples. Extending from the Delta to the Sudan, they have a grandeur of their own. It is in their fluted columns, external colonnades, and flowering capitals that we recognize the nature of the Egyptian genius. And it is here that we are impressed with the originality of those master builders of the Nile Valley, for there were no precedents for them to follow. What the architects of Karnak and Deir el Bahri created was something new under the sun.

The story of the excavation of the Egyptian temples presents a different picture from that of the tombs—and, for that matter, the temples in ancient Mesopotamia. In the latter case, the temples, like everything else, were buried in tells or mounds and were unknown quantities until they were discovered in the strata of antiquity and uncovered by the archaeologist. The Theban tombs likewise had to be found and then excavated from their hiding-places in the hills. The Egyptian temples, on the other hand, had never been completely lost to view. In some cases they were half-buried by the shifting sands which had accumulated around their columns over the centuries. Some had been partially destroyed by man and nature. In other instances, Arab villages had grown up on top of them. But Karnak, Luxor, Dendera, Philae, and Abu Simbel were always known and seen, at least in part. Even at Deir el Bahri, the terraces of the Mentuhotep and Hatshepsut temples protruded far enough to be recognized by early explorers. In connection with the temples, therefore, the element of discovery is absent. Instead of experiencing the thrill of finding something whose existence was unknown, the archaeologist is here engaged in the less romantic but important task of rescuing buildings from the grip of time, recovering what was partially hidden, clearing away debris, and finally, restoring and preserving the wall-paintings and inscriptions. Not the least important job of the excavator has been the attempt to determine when and by whom the temples were built. Thus in the case of a vast complex like Karnak, the excavator has enabled us to trace the successive stages by which the whole enclosure came to completion.

KARNAK: THE GLORY OF THEBES

The great temple of Karnak was almost two millenniums in the making. It can therefore be considered not only as an architectural wonder but, what is more important, as a historical repository in which the course of ancient Egyptian history can be traced from 2000 B.C. to A.D. 100. Covering such a long span of time, the Karnak complex obviously does not present an architectural unity; rather it is a bewildering accumulation of sacred buildings erected by one Pharaoh after another, century after century.

The history of the Karnak temple coincided with the rise and fall of Thebes. By 1600 B.C. Thebes had emerged as the queen city of Egypt and for five centuries remained the chief power in Egypt. The only remains today of that city of splendour is the temple itself, for, as we have previously explained, the administrative buildings, the palaces, and the houses were made of mud brick and rapidly disintegrated. The wooden furniture in those buildings, however elegant, was made only for the lifetime of the occupants. The religious architecture, like the tombs across the river, was a different matter. Crude brick was good enough for Pharaoh's residence but Pharaoh's temple required lasting granite, sandstone, and limestone. Strangely enough, the master builders of Egypt were not too concerned about the foundations of the temples so that it is a wonder that they have survived at all. In spite of earthquake and erosion, enough of Karnak remains to suggest to the modern visitor the magnitude and splendour of this megalithic structure, the sight of which caused Belzoni in 1817 to exclaim: "These ruins had such an effect upon my soul as to separate me in imagination from the rest of mortals and cause me to forget entirely the trifles and follies of life."

To approach the complex from the western or river side, as most visitors do, and proceed eastwards, is to reverse the chronological order of its building, for the successive additions were made from east to west. Consequently, the first structure to be encountered, as one passes through the avenue of sphinxes, is the last one that was built—the gigantic pylon erected by Ptolemaic Pharaohs, the last native rulers of ancient Egypt. This mighty portal of the Amon temple is 49 feet thick, 143 feet high, and 370 feet wide. Passing through the pylon the visitor finds himself in an open court which measures 275 by 338 feet, an area exceeding that of St. Paul's in London by 8,000 square feet. It was built by Libyan Pharaohs of the Twenty-second Dynasty and is often called the Court of the Bubastites because these Pharaohs held their court at Bubastis. It was cleared by Georges Legrain, the French Egyptologist, in 1896–97. Lining the north and south walls of the court is a colonnade of single pillars. In the northwest corner stands the small temple of Seti II which is divided into three chapels, dedicated to Amon, Mut, and Khonsu. Jutting out from the southern wall is the temple of Ramses III, a perfect example of the typical Egyptian temple and which, having been built by one monarch, presents a homogeneous and unified whole, consisting of the usual forecourt, pillared hall, and sanctuary. In the centre of the court stands the "Unfinished Symphony" of the Pharaoh Taharqua—one surviving column from the ten which had been planned as a part of a hypostyle hall.

Rising at the eastern end of the Great Court is the Second Pylon, built by Ramses I. The stone blocks that went into this gateway have an interesting history for they were brought from Amarna where they had served another god and they bear the names of Ikhnaton, Tutankhamon, and Ay. The vestibule leading to the pylon is flanked with statues of Ramses II and on the doorway itself are the cartouches of Ramses I and Seti II.

Next comes the Hypostyle Hall, to which Karnak owes its fame and which from ancient days has been considered "one of the wonders of the world". This hall with its 134 pillars measures 335 by 169 feet. It was planned by Horemheb, begun by Ramses I, and completed by Seti I, who was responsible for the most imposing feature of the huge hall—the nave with its double row of gigantic open-flower columns, the largest ever known. Each of the twelve columns of the nave is 33 feet in circumference and 69 feet in height, added to which are the 12-feet-high open-papyrus capitals. The columns in the other fourteen rows, each 48 feet high, have papyrus-bud capitals. The nave was lighted by clerestory windows. The rows adjoining the central pillars support rectangular blocks which compensate for the difference in height and hold up the roof of the nave. Whatever one might say of the architecture of the Hypostyle Hall, one cannot fail to be impressed by its sheer vastness. The nave with its towering columns and grated side windows above, is a prefiguration of the later basilica and Gothic cathedral.

The reliefs on the inner walls, depicting scenes from the lives of Seti I and Ramses II, give us an insight into the ritual of the Amon temple. On the outer walls are vivid reliefs showing victories of the two kings over the armies of Libya and Palestine, as well as Ramses' campaign against the Hittites. Abandoned by most of his troops and confronted by the Hittite combined armies, the warrior-king prays to Amon for help:

> What then, my father Amon? Can it be that a father has forgotten his son? I call to thee, my father Amon. I am in the midst of strangers whom I know not. All the nations have banded together against me. I am alone and no one is with me. My soldiers have abandoned me and not one of my charioteers turned his head to seek me. If I cry after them, no one hears me. But I call and see that Amon is better for me than millions of footsoldiers and hundreds of thousands of charioteers. The work of many men is as nothing; Amon is better than they. I have come here obedient to the thoughts of thy mouth, Amon. And I have not departed from thy thoughts.[1]

Facing the eastern end of the Hypostyle Hall is the Third Pylon which was built by Amenhotep III, whose reign climaxed the glories of the Thutmosid empire. Into this portal went frag-

---

[1] K. Lange and M. Hirmer: *Egypt: Architecture, Sculpture, Painting in Three Thousand Years*. Translation by R. H. Boothroyd (London, Phaidon Press, 1956), p. 347.

ments of the temples of Senusret I and Amenhotep I. On the northern tower one can discern the remains of a scene portraying a procession on the Nile in honour of Amon. Amenhotep built an adjoining temple to Mentu which was embellished by later kings.

The work of preservation of Karnak continues under the auspices of the Egyptian Service of Antiquities. Now and then in the course of this work the archaeologist makes some rewarding finds, the most sensational of which was a series of incredible discoveries in the *Karnak Cachette* by Legrain. From December 1903 to July 1904 he found 456 stone statues, seven sphinxes, and 8,000 bronzes. In the 1904–05 season, he recovered 200 stone statues and an additional 8,000 bronzes. All of these were drawn out of the water of the *Cachette*. Maspero, reporting on Legrain's finds, wrote: "For a year and eight months we have been fishing for statues in the Temple of Karnak. Seven hundred stone monuments have already come out of the water and we are not yet at the end—statues of Pharaohs enthroned, queens, priests of Amon and individuals . . . found in all the attitudes of their profession or rank, in limestone, in black or pink granite, in yellow or red sandstone, in schist, in alabaster—indeed, a whole population returns to the upper air and demands shelter in the galleries of the Museum."

By far the finest statues to come out of the *Cachette* were the pink granite head of Senusret III, a brilliant example of Twelfth-dynasty sculpture, and the green schist statue of Thutmose III, now in Cairo.

How can we account for this incredible collection of discarded works of art? Apparently in the course of their clearing the area for new buildings, the Ptolemies came upon these statues and since the persons associated with them were of no great importance in their minds—although this does not seem too plausible—they buried them in a great pit which had to be within the sacred enclosure because they had been dedicated to Amon. Consequently, the figures of great kings and nobles were consigned to a watery grave to be rescued 2,000 years later by a French engineer.

Mariette, after excavating at Karnak for several years, made the statement, so often uttered in connection with other sites, "Nothing more will be found here; Karnak is finished." Legrain came upon the scene in 1902 and inaugurated his great project of restoration and preservation. He was of the opinion that the present level of the Nile at Karnak is higher than it was in the period of the Eighteenth Dynasty and felt that there might be a cache of valuable objects under the Ptolemaic buildings to the south of the Hypostyle Hall. Day after day he drained water off the area by means of *shadoofs* so that his workers could walk about in the mud feeling for hidden objects. In 1903 he found his first statue much below the present level of the Nile—the first of a long list of sculptures in the round. Joseph Lindon Smith, the artist, tells of a humorous incident in which Legrain "discovered" a beautiful black granite statue "on order".

One afternoon he [Legrain] sent for me when the head and shoulders of a large black granite statue were brought far enough out of the mud to be clearly seen. Large wooden beams were thrust beneath the statue for support. Legrain was jubilant. We spent much time down in the mud examining the fine head and face. Meanwhile a boy came with a telegram for Legrain, who read it and handed it to me. It was from Cromer saying that Lord and Lady X—— would be arriving at Luxor the following day and to show them something "particularly interesting".

We clambered out of the hole, and Legrain screamed to his workmen, "Pull out the beams and let the statue sink down." The men looked puzzled and hesitant about obeying such an unexpected order. Legrain screamed at them again louder. And down into the mud disappeared the head that had taken so much effort to raise. He said to me with a broad grin, "I intend to 'discover' a statue for Cromer's distinguished guests. You must help me in creating an atmosphere of expectancy."

The next morning I found, commanding a view of the spot where we had seen the statue, two gilt, upholstered armchairs and over them a large sunshade. And a bit of red carpet had been spread to the chairs from the nearest point of entry. I was on hand to take part in the reception of the distinguished couple, who appeared towards the late afternoon with a dragoman, maid, and other attendants.

Legrain, looking doubtfully at her Ladyship's very high narrow heels, asked how much walking they wished to do.

"Not much," she said. "Haven't you something unusual quite near at hand?"

I had my cue in Legrain's nod and asked, "How about your new excavations, Legrain?"

She took fire at once, and we all walked together through the Hypostyle Hall, while Legrain talked briefly about Karnak. Beyond the third pylon she caught sight of the red carpet and the armchairs beyond. In obvious relief, the visitors settled themselves comfortably. And Legrain explained, again briefly, what he was doing.

"Do you mean to say in that muddy water in which those half naked men are splashing about some object of value may be found?" she asked.

Legrain shrugged his shoulders, winked surreptitiously at me, and said, "One never knows."

"It's in the lap of the gods," I added, "and a wonderful moment when it happens."

"It must be," remarked his Lordship with the first spark of enthusiasm he had shown.

Legrain's timing was perfect. There was some desultory conversation before he gave a signal to his workmen submerged almost to their armpits. They at once redoubled their efforts, and louder and louder came their song, until it reached a crescendo, and their muscles strained as the head of a statue became visible. The visitors jumped from their chairs, their excited shouts mingling with the triumphant cries of the workmen as, leaning forward, they almost lost their balance and fell into the pit. Higher and higher the head was lifted until the shoulders and breast appeared out of the muddy depths.

Legrain gave orders to have the planks shoved beneath the statue to hold it in place. When he explained that unfortunately there was not time to get the statue up before dark, her Ladyship leaped down into the pit, followed by her husband.

Workmen emerged from the mud, their naked backs dripping, and stood about cheering the guests.

Legrain interpreted the rapid flow of words that accompanied the splashing of mud over the immaculate garments of the thrilled visitors.

"They are thanking you both for bringing good luck," he said.

Lord and Lady X—— were delighted, and she exclaimed exultantly, "To think I was actually present at a great discovery—weren't you surprised, Monsieur Legrain?"

He replied gallantly, "I was pleased to have Lord Cromer's guests see something particularly interesting."[1]

---

[1] *Tombs, Temples, and Ancient Art* (Norman, University of Oklahoma Press, 1956), pp. 44–6.

THE LUXOR COLUMNS

The most advantageous view of the temple at Luxor is from a boat in the river in the late afternoon when the lights and shadows play upon the papyrus columns and one can take in the temple as a whole—unless it be to approach it by night when the colonnades are bathed in the light of the full moon.

In contrast to Karnak, the Luxor temple is simple and uncomplicated, consisting chiefly of a pylon, forecourt, colonnade, another forecourt, hypostyle hall, and sanctuary, all on one straight axis parallel to the river. Karnak, as we saw, is not so much a temple as an aggregate of buildings, representing an accumulation of almost 2,000 years; whereas Luxor is a comparatively unified structure and in its main features was built within a period of 200 years. "Thus while Karnak," writes Baikie, "so much vaster than its sister temple, bewilders and overwhelms almost as much as it impresses us, Luxor charms us by the clarity and intelligibility of its lay-out." Also unlike Karnak, the Luxor temple was almost lost to view before modern excavation rescued it. In the course of the centuries, in addition to the natural deterioration of the temple, the village of Luxor encroached upon it and houses were built within it. When the hovels fell into decay, new houses were built on top of the rising mound of debris until only the tops of the colonnades protruded above the rubbish. At the beginning of our century the whole temple area was buried under the modern village. At that time the sinking of a drainage-shaft from a house situated on the top of a column revealed the existence of a building below. When this was reported to the Department of Antiquities, Maspero was appointed to continue excavations which he had started in the 1880s. In two years most of the temple was cleared.

There is still another difference between the two great temples. Whereas Karnak represents an accumulation of structures, Luxor was conceived as a whole. As an architectural unity, the Luxor temple is much the finer of the two. It is 853 feet long and 181 feet wide. The chief builders were Amenhotep III and Ramses II. The appearance of the name of the Pharaoh Sebekhotep III provides some evidence, although slight, that the temple was built on the site of a Thirteenth-dynasty shrine but no other trace of the existence of such a sanctuary remains. Thutmose III also built a shrine at the northern extremity of the site.

Amenhotep III really owed his position as the Pharaoh of Egypt in its greatest period of prestige to Thutmose III who established the empire. Amenhotep's claim to the throne was at best a tenuous one, being neither the son of a royal couple nor married to the eldest daughter of a pharaoh. His mother was the daughter of a Mitannian king. His wife Tiy was not of royal blood. It seemed imperative, therefore, to remedy this defect in his qualifications. Following the example of Hatshepsut, he attributed his birth, not to human parentage, but to the great god Amon. He erected the Luxor Temple and on its walls were recorded in relief the details of his divine birth. The gift of the temple in itself would have been enough to forestall any questions about the story.

Unfortunately Amenhotep did not live to see the completion of his designs. His son, Ikhnaton, cancelled all work, erased the name of Amon wherever found, and built a shrine within the precincts to Aton. With the restoration of Amonism, Tutankhamon and Horemheb made some slight contributions but it was Ramses II who completed the complex with the addition of the forecourt and pylon at the north end.

The present entrance to the temple is from the river road at the north-west corner of the Forecourt of Amenhotep III. For our description, however, we shall start with the northern end, which was the entrance in the Ramesside period. Such an approach is architecturally logical but not chronological. The entrance is through the stately pylon of Ramses II. An avenue of sphinxes once led from this spot to the south or tenth pylon of Horemheb at Karnak, two miles away. The presence of sphinxes at the entrance of the two sites led modern archaeologists to believe that the complete royal avenue would be found under the houses of Luxor. In 1949 Goneim unearthed a few of them and in the early 1960s Abdel Elrazik organized a mass excavation. Removing 60 feet of dust and debris, his three hundred workmen have succeeded in unearthing the famous "Avenue", a stone road 20 feet wide and lined with perfectly preserved sphinxes. It is expected that when the task is completed a total of 1,400 sphinxes will be uncovered. They are uniform in size—10 feet long, 4 feet high, and are mounted on inscribed pedestals that are 5 feet tall.

The pylon consists of two towers of stone in front of which stood two fine obelisks, one of which remains standing. The other has from 1836 adorned the well-known Place de la Concorde in Paris. The gateway was originally flanked by six granite colossi of Ramses II. Of these three remain. On the façade of the pylon are reliefs of the Battle of Kadesh, Ramses' favourite but questionable boast.

Behind the pylon is the Forecourt of Ramses II. Its double row of columns form a colonnade around the court, broken only in the north-west corner by a small chapel of Thutmose III. In the north-east corner is the modern mosque of Abul Haggag, the patron saint of Luxor. The columns of the court are of the papyrus-bud type but show the decadence of the Ramesside period. On the west side are six royal statues, presumably of Ramses II. At the foot of each is the small figure of the queen, Nefertari. This court is slightly askew to the rest of the temple axis, made so perhaps to conform to the river bank.

From the court of Ramses II we enter the Colonnade of Horemheb, composed of seven pairs of 52-foot-high columns with capitals in the form of open papyrus umbels. Originally this vestibule was roofed over, making a dark passage between the two open-air courts. It was designed by Amenhotep's architects but was added to by Tutankhamon and Horemheb both of whom decorated the walls with reliefs of the annual religious festivals.

The Horemheb Colonnade leads to the beginning of the temple proper—the Forecourt of Amenhotep III, undoubtedly the best example of Eighteenth-dynasty architectural style. This peristyle court, measuring 148 by 184 feet, is surrounded on three sides by double rows of clustered papyrus-bud columns. "The effective balance," writes W. Stevenson Smith, "between the broad open spaces and the architectural mass of the huge columns, with their wonderful play of light and shade, makes this perhaps the most beautiful employment of the plant column anywhere in Egypt."[1] The centre of the court was originally open to the sky, thus

[1] *The Art and Architecture of Ancient Egypt* (Baltimore, Penguin Books, 1958), p. 152.

affording a striking contrast of deep shadow with brilliant sun
shine.

Adjoining the Forecourt of Amenhotep III is the Hypostyle
Hall which has thirty-two columns arranged in four rows of eight
each. On the left side is a Roman altar dedicated to the Emperor
Constantine. The Hypostyle Hall leads to a vestibule which was
converted into a Christian church in the fourth century. The
reliefs of Amenhotep III were covered with a coat of whitewash
upon which Christian scenes were painted. Needless to say, the
under-side of this palimpsest is more important, from a historical
as well as from a religious point of view, than the upper side.

Adjoining the vestibule is the Birth Room with its reliefs
depicting the divine origin of the king. Completing the temple
to the south are two sanctuaries. One was rebuilt by Alexander
the Great and the other, the original chapel, contains reliefs
showing Amenhotep in the presence of the god Amon-Ra.

THE TEMPLE OF SETI I

Abydos was the holy city of Egypt, home of the cult of Osiris
and site of the royal tombs of the early kings. The excavations
here of the Egypt Exploration Society under the direction of
Flinders Petrie contributed more to our knowledge of early
dynastic history than any other expedition in Egypt. The clearing
of the Necropolis, inaugurated by Amélineau in 1897, resulted
in the discovery of royal tombs of the First and Second Dynasty.
This somewhat haphazard project was continued in more scientific
fashion in 1899 by Petrie with the assistance of Mace, Garstang,
and MacIver. No royal mummies were found in these tombs for
they had been rifled at an early date. The significance of the Petrie
excavation lies in the knowledge gained regarding the nature of the
early Egyptian culture and the construction of the archaic tombs.

Work on the Necropolis was continued by T. Eric Peet and
Edouard Naville. In the 1912–13 season of the Egyptian Exploration Society, Peet found an ibis cemetery. The birds were mummified as carefully as royal personages and were placed in large
clay jars. Only members of a professional guild connected with
the bird-cult could have achieved such perfection in weaving the
fabrics and wrapping the mummies of the sacred birds. The ibis

cemetery was only one of the many witnesses to the prominence
of the cult of Thoth.[1] The expedition found hundreds of thousands
of mummified jackals, cats, and other animals—all killed as sacrifices to Osiris, the god of immortality.

The importance of the necropolis of Abydos derives from its
connection with Osiris, the god who had been murdered and
dismembered. Abydos was supposed to be his burial-place and
here the god was miraculously restored to life. An annual Passion
Play was held to celebrate his death and resurrection. This gave
rise to the mystery religion of Osiris which flourished down into
the Christian era. It became the wish of every devout Egyptian
to be buried at this holy place near the tomb of the god of
immortality. That being impossible, many caused memorial stelae
to be erected here; others brought votive pots and dedicated
them to the god. One of those who wished to honour Osiris was
the great Pharaoh Seti I whose mortuary temple is our chief
interest in Abydos.

Margaret Murray called the Temple of Seti I "the most beautiful temple in all Egypt", an opinion which had support from no
less an authority than James H. Breasted, at least as far as decorative reliefs were concerned. Be that as it may, the temple, at any
rate, has the distinction of being the most complete of all
Egyptian temples. Its existence was discovered by Mariette who
partly cleared it. In 1901–02 Petrie assigned St. G. Caulfield to
survey the site. The Temple area, including the Cenotaph, was
excavated from 1900 to 1930 by the Egypt Exploration Society
staff which included Petrie, Quibell, Margaret Murray, Frankfort, Naville, and Whittemore.

The two outstanding features of Seti's temple are its wall-
decorations and its unusual shape. The low relief on white limestone, found throughout the temple, is reminiscent of Ramose's
tomb at Thebes and is unexcelled in its technique and artistry.
No other temple or tomb contains such a profusion of ritualistic
scenes, all of which are masterfully executed in the utmost
delicacy of detail. The decoration of the outer courts is clearly
inferior to the rest of the rooms and was done undoubtedly during
the reign of Ramses II who obviously employed less competent

---

[1] See Thomas Whittemore: *The Ibis Cemetery at Abydos: 1914*. Article in
Journal of Egyptian Archaeology. Vol. I, Part IV, October 1914.

artists. The similarity of Seti's decorative style to that in the
Ramose tomb is seen best in two classic reliefs. One is on the
north wall of the Second Hypostyle Hall and pictures two god
desses standing before Osiris. The other, nearby, shows the god
Khonsu offering the king the *ankh* or emblem of life. Another
beautiful relief, found in the rear of the temple, shows the king
with outstretched wings protecting his people. These are only
three of hundreds of scenes adorning the walls of the sanctuaries
and halls.

The Seti Temple departs radically from the architectural
scheme of the typical Egyptian temple. In many instances, of
course, an original temple was continually added to until there
was no clear design left; yet there was a set pattern to which
most temples in their original state conformed; namely, pylon,
forecourt or peristyle court, colonnade or hypostyle court, and
sanctuary, flanked by store-rooms—all on a single axis in a
straight line. The Abydos temple, on the other hand, is L-shaped
and instead of a single sanctuary, has seven.

The approach to the temple is from the north. The pylon and
first court are destroyed. Behind the half-ruined second court is
a terrace on which stand twelve square pillars of Ramses II. Next
are two hypostyle halls; the first, a magnificent room, 171 by
36 feet, contains twenty-four clustered papyrus-bud columns.
The second hypostyle hall contains the first series of beautiful
Seti reliefs. They represent the king performing various acts of
worship in the presence of Osiris, Isis, and Horus. Here is the
famous sculpture of Seti before the goddesses, the artistic gem of
the whole temple, and representing the best work of the Nineteenth Dynasty. "The relief," writes Maspero, "is at once
flexible and precise, a surface over which the chisel lingered
lovingly, giving a kind of colour to the epidermis by a multitude
of almost imperceptible strokes. To have seen the Pharaoh and
the three goddesses is to understand to what a degree Egyptian
art, so mournful superficially, may kindle with life and exquisite
tenderness."

Behind the Second Hypostyle Hall are the seven sanctuaries
which are completely covered with reliefs of the highest quality,
the contents of which it is impossible to describe here. Behind
the seven shrines are the Osiris Halls which are also decorated

with reliefs in colour. Now the building turns westwards with more shrines, in one of which is the well-known king-list, bearing the cartouches of all the Pharaohs from Menes to Seti himself. This list has been of considerable importance in establishing Egyptian chronology. The western section of the temple consists of a chamber where the mysteries of Osiris were performed, halls for the offering of sacrifices, and slaughter-rooms.[1]

Some thirty feet to the south of the temple wall is the *Osireion* or Cenotaph of Seti I. This peculiar underground sanctuary was discovered by Margaret Murray in 1903 and was later excavated by Naville and Frankfort for the Egypt Exploration Society. The main feature of the *Osireion* is the Great Hall, a three-aisled chamber, 100 by 65 feet, surrounded by seventeen small cells. The room is one enormous sarcophagus and the ceiling is decorated with figures of Nut, goddess of the sky. In the centre is an island, cut off from the rest of the hall by a trench or moat, bearing ten red granite pillars 9 feet thick. These columns originally supported architraves and roofing blocks each of which was 6 feet thick. The pillared island is approached by a double flight of steps. In its centre are two pits which probably housed a symbolic coffin and canopic chest. A passage leads from the Great Hall to the sarcophagus chamber which is filled with more beautiful sculpture.

The *Osireion*, made of fine lime-stone, hard red-stone, and red granite, must certainly have been a most imposing structure, gigantic but simple. The central hall with its island served presumably as a symbol of the mythological "Primeval Hill" where Osiris was buried and rose again. The "Primeval Hill" in the Nile was considered to be the site of creation. The hillock arose out of the receding waters and became the source of all life. The moat surrounding the island was fed from the sub-soil sheet of water underlying the desert and may represent Strabo's "well" or spring.[2]

---

[1] For coloured plates of Seti's reliefs see Kurt Lange and Max Hirmer: *Aegypten* (Munich, Hirmer Verlag, 1955), pp. 216–25.
[2] For an official report on the excavation of the *Osireion* see Henri Frankfort: *The Cenotaph of Seti I at Abydos*. 2 vols. (London, Egypt Exploration Society, 1933); also Edouard Naville: *Excavations at Abydos*. Article in *Journal of Egyptian Archaeology*. Vol. I, Part III, July 1914.

THE RAMESSEUM

Many of the monuments upon which the reputation of Ramses II rests were really not built by him but were usurped by the simple act of substituting his cartouche for that of a predecessor; yet, excluding such instances, enough authentic temples remain to justify his position as the most universally known name in Egypt and its greatest builder. His building enterprises extended from the splendid temple at Tanis in the Delta to Abu Simbel in Nubia. Dwarfing the pylons of the Tanis temple, the colossus of Ramses towered 90 feet and weighed 900 tons. He built the "store-city" of Pithom and another near Heliopolis called Per-Ramses. He erected temples at Memphis, Abydos, Karnak, Luxor, and throughout Nubia.

The mortuary temple known as the Ramesseum stands at the edge of the cultivated fields not far from the Colossi of Memnon on the Theban Plain. The Greeks called it the Memnonium or Tomb of Osymandias, a name made famous by an ancient Greek explorer and a modern English poet. In the first century B.C. Diodorus described the temple at great length and quoted the inscription on the colossal statue of Ramses: "I am Osymandias, king of kings; if any would know how great I am and where I lie, let him excel me in any of my works." Shelley's sonnet is equally famous:

> I met a traveller from an antique land
> Who said: Two vast and trunkless legs of stone
> Stand in the desert. Near them, on the sand,
> Half sunk, a shattered visage lies, whose frown,
> And wrinkled lip, and sneer of cold command,
> Tell that the sculptor well those passions read
> Which yet survive, stamped on these lifeless things,
> The hand that mocked them and the heart that fed;
> And on the pedestal these words appear:
> "My name is Osymandias, King of Kings,
> Look on my works, ye mighty, and despair!"
> Nothing beside remains. Round the decay
> Of that colossal wreck, boundless and bare
> The long and level sands stretch far away.

The Ramesseum covers an area of 130,000 square feet. The approach was from the east through an enormous twin-towered pylon upon which was sculptured the ever-present Battle of Kadesh. Some of these reliefs are extremely fine, requiring a magnifying glass to catch the detail. The first court is completely in ruins. Here lie the remains of the colossal statue of Ramses, probably, as Baikie suggests, "the largest block of stone ever handled by man". The upper part of the granite statue has fallen to the ground and is broken into many pieces. Originally it stood 58 feet high, and measured 24 feet across the breast. The forefinger was almost 4 feet long and the face between the ears was 7 feet. The weight of the statue was computed to be 1,000 tons. The thought of cutting this single block of granite from the quarry at Aswan, carving it in proper proportions, floating it 135 miles down the Nile, dragging it across the fields to the temple and placing it in position leaves one with a keen admiration for these ancient Egyptians who worked without benefit of modern machinery, having only the inclined plane and man-power.

The second court has been better preserved than the first. It has double rows of columns on the north and south sides, a row of square pillars on the east, and on the west side, a raised terrace with a row of Osiride pillars. Here also are more Kadesh battle-scenes. Colossal black granite statues of Ramses once stood in this court. The removal of the head of one of these was the memorable achievement of Belzoni who had it sent to the British Museum.

The glory of the Ramesseum is the Hypostyle Hall which reminds one of Karnak with its stately nave of great papyrus columns and clerestory windows. The pillars are profusely decorated with battle scenes. Three smaller hypostyle halls follow in succession on a straight axis, each one having eight pillars. The first of the three halls has a roof which is decorated with a map of the sky showing the position of the various constellations at the time of Ramses' coronation.

The rest of the temple enclosure contains the remains of brick buildings from the same period, the priests' houses, the royal library, servants' quarters, and storehouses. In the ruins of the library Petrie found papyri of the Twelfth Dynasty containing early narratives and dramas. Just outside the enclosure wall to the south are the ruined chapel of Prince Wazmose of the Eighteenth Dynasty and the mortuary temple of Thutmose IV. These were cleared by Petrie in 1896.

MEDINET HABU

At the southern extremity of the Theban necropolis is a group of buildings known as Medinet Habu, the most important of which is the mortuary temple of Ramses III. The towers on the south-east side commemorate the Syrian campaigns of the king and his forebears. This is the best preserved temple of the Ramesside period. It represents the decline of the classic style of architecture but it is none the less impressive because of its massiveness. One might say that Medinet Habu—inferior though it may be—is the last extant example of the greatest period of Egyptian architecture. It has a most majestic appearance, conveying to the visitor an idea of its former glory.

The general plan is almost an exact copy of the Ramesseum. Entrance is made by way of a pavilion which consists of two towers with a gateway between them. The towers are decorated with sumptuous harem scenes. The gateway leads to an open area containing several temples beyond which stands the first pylon. In the masonry of the pylon towers are four holes or slots for the great flagpoles which were also kept in place by wooden and copper clamps. One can easily conjure up in his mind a festive day and its pageantry, with the banners fluttering from the towers and the royal procession entering the portals below. Chariot wheels have worn grooves in the triumphal gateway, adding a touch of realism to the scene.

The noteworthy thing about the First Court is the different styles of its columns. On the left side are graceful pillars with calyx capitals while on the right side they are square, fronted by large figures of Osiris. Attention must be called to the unusually deep relief carvings which portray the military exploits of the king. The Second Court contains five columns on each side and a row of eight figures of Osiris at each end. The Hypostyle Hall has been destroyed almost to ground level due to the fact that a Coptic village was built on top of it. The hall has twenty-four pillars and a high nave with clerestory windows like the Ramesseum. The rest of the temple consisted of treasuries, chapels, and storerooms.

The girdle wall of Medinet Habu encloses a group of independent temples, including those of Thutmose III, Amenhotep I, and Hatshepsut. A short distance to the south lie the ruins of the palace of Amenhotep III, one of the few examples of the survival of royal palaces. It was successively excavated by Grébaut, Daressy, and the Metropolitan Museum of Art. Here was the mile-square lake where Queen Tiy sailed in the royal barque *Aton Gleams*.

PTOLEMAIC TEMPLES

Following the Ramesside era of the Twentieth Dynasty (1197–1085 B.C.), the period of Medinet Habu, there was a considerable number of Egyptian temples but we jump over 700 years of history to the Ptolemaic period (332–330 B.C.). The two outstanding temples from this period are Dendera and Edfu, the best preserved in all Egypt.

The city of Dendera and the temple itself were sacred to Hathor the goddess of love. "Hathor, Lady of the Pillar", was a mother-goddess, similar to Isis and Aphrodite. She was usually represented as a cow or as a woman with a cow's head. The presence of secret chambers in the temple of Dendera indicates that the worship of Hathor took the form of a mystery-religion or sacramental cult. The completeness and attractiveness of the temple as a whole offset the fact that, coming from Graeco-Roman times, it is not characteristically Egyptian and represents a greater decline in artistic detail. Thus, while it is admirable for its lavish decoration and abundance of relief work, yet compared with the architecture and reliefs of Seti's temple at Abydos, the Ptolemaic structure suffers under close inspection. But each temple has its intrinsic merits and to all but the professional critic of architecture the Dendera temple is a magnificent specimen.

There is some evidence of previous building on the site but the present edifice was begun during the reign of Ptolemy VIII, Soter II, about 116 B.C., and work was continued on it by Ptolemy X, Ptolemy XI and into the reign of Tiberius (A.D. 34).

Later Roman emperors made some additions. The names of Domitian and Trojan appear on the gateway.

Many early explorers visited the temple. Mariette inaugurated the clearing which was later continued by the Service of Antiquities under the direction of Maspero.

Sharing honours with Dendera as a Ptolemaic specimen is the beautiful temple of Edfu, half-way between Luxor and Aswan. Edfu was dedicated to Horus, the consort of Hathor. The present structure was begun by Ptolemy III, Energetes I (237 B.C.), and was completed by 212 B.C., although additions were made as late as 57 B.C. For symmetry, consistency of design and completeness it is unsurpassed and, although a product of the Greek period, it is none the less typically Egyptian. From the standpoint of beauty, Edfu can be considered the climax of our story of Egyptian temples.

Again Mariette was the first to excavate. Beginning the work of clearing in 1860, he wrote: "The modern village had invaded the temple, its very terraces being covered with dwellings, stables, and storehouses of every kind. In the interior the chambers were filled with rubbish almost to the ceiling." Mariette suddenly abandoned the work, leaving it half-done, but the project was continued later by the Service of Antiquities. It was no small undertaking, for some forty houses had to be bought and pulled down and much debris had to be cleared away. Excavation was continued in the early part of our century by Barsanti under the supervision of Maspero. Columns had to be taken down and set up again; architraves had to be supported and foundations strengthened—a long and dangerous operation. The villagers could not have lived in the temple halls with their cattle and chickens for a thousand years without causing terrible damage to walls and ceilings. Maspero, reviewing the work of Barsanti, wrote: "The Pharaohs would have been immensely proud of so well executed an enterprise; they would have recorded it in big hieroglyphics on a stele with much emphasis and prolixity, extravagant in praise of themselves and prayers to the gods. Such panegyrics on stone are out of fashion. M. Alexandre Barsanti will think himself fortunate if the four years of hard work and anxiety which Edfu cost him obtain a couple of lines in the next edition of some tourists' Guide to Egypt."

Amon-Mut-Chon's Temple at Luxor. Great Court of Amenhotep III.
(*Courtesy, Hirmer Verlag, Munich*)

Wall relief in tomb of Seti I at Abydos showing Ramses and prince
capturing a bull. (*Courtesy, Hirmer Verlag, Munich*)

Temple of Queen Hatshepsut in Thebes. (*Courtesy, Hirmer Verlag, Munich*)

Hatshepsut Temple: aerial view of the Eleventh- and Eighteenth-Dynasty temples. (*Courtesy, Metropolitan Museum of Art, New York*)

A third fine example of Ptolemaic architecture is the well-preserved temple of Kom Ombo. Mariette in 1869 wrote that the temple "sooner or later is doomed to become the prey to the Nile, however carefully it may be protected". Towards the end of the century the Department of Antiquities cleared it of sand and erected an embankment to check the encroachment of the river.

Kom Ombo was built for the worship of the gods Sobk and Haroeris, a circumstance which produced something altogether unique in Egypt. These two deities being equally honoured, the temple was built in duplex form; that is, there were actually two temples side by side within one building of the usual shape. Each court, vestibule, chamber, hall, corridor, and sanctuary on the west or Haroeris side of the temple was duplicated exactly on the east or Sobk side. From Forecourt to Sanctuary this exact correspondence was meticulously maintained.

Space does not permit inclusion of the other temples of ancient Egypt but we have dealt with the most important ones.[1] Rescued by excavators from the encroaching sand and river, these magnificent sanctuaries are mute but eloquent evidence of a religious people whose reverence for the gods cannot be shrugged off by us as merely primitive polytheism or a commercialized priestly system. Behind their outward forms and symbols was an experience of a spiritual presence which brought comfort and courage to rich and poor. Their temples demonstrated the beauty of holiness and the holiness of beauty. And their gods were just as real to them as the later gods of the West were to Jews, Christians, and Moslems.

[1] For the temples of Philae, Abu Simbel, and others in Nubia see Ch. 12.

Chapter Nine

DEIR EL BAHRI

THE TERRACED TEMPLE OF HATSHEPSUT

On the western bank of the Nile, directly opposite Karnak, the Libyan range forms a great semicircle containing the funerary chapels of the Eighteenth and Nineteenth Dynasty kings. Behind these chapels and tombs, clinging firmly to the base of the salmon-red cliffs, stands the most beautiful of all Egyptian buildings—the temple of Queen Hatshepsut at Deir el Bahri. The appeal of this structure derives from beauty of line, unity and coherence rather than massiveness. To build this temple at the base of a mountainous wall of rock required nothing short of genius, for the magnificent background of the awesome cliffs could easily have been the architect's downfall. Such a backdrop could well have dwarfed the temple into insignificance and the attempt to compete with the beautiful natural setting was an invitation to disaster. The Giza pyramids compel our admiration because of their contrast to the flat desert, stretching endlessly at their base. But at Deir el Bahri the builder saw that pylons, obelisks, and gigantic papyrus columns could only have the effect of a dog barking at a lion. He wisely avoided any attempt at height and erected a structure which emphasized horizontal lines, knowing that only such an arrangement could survive on the background of the overwhelming cliff. Every visitor who has ever stopped long enough to ponder the matter has been convinced that Senmut, the architect, confronted with an almost insurmountable problem, made the only wise solution.

W. Stevenson Smith describes the temple thus:

Approaching from the valley up a processional way lined with
sandstone sphinxes, the visitor would have been conscious from far
away of the great painted limestone Osiride statues of the queen
fronting the colonnade of the upper terrace. They stood against
square pillars, being carved from built-up masonry courses forming
an integral part of the architecture. A few have been re-erected
from the fragments found with the other broken statues and sphinxes
of the queen. The outwardly simple treatment of the two lower
colonnades forms an effective base for this line of statues above. The
rhythmical repetition of light and shadow is broken only by the broad
central ramps which give access to the two terraces. The lowest
colonnade was given weight at each end by a large Osiride statue.
The glare from the intense sunlight striking the amphitheatre of
cliffs behind must always have tended to nullify the surface decoration and to emphasize the simple shapes. The colonnades offered
their shade, while the darkness of the inner rooms of the shrines
intensified in characteristic Egyptian fashion the solemn feeling of
awe as one approached the deity.[1]

Some scholars have questioned the originality of Senmut by
citing the adjacent Mentuhotep temple as his inspiration. It is
true that Senmut adopted the idea of the terrace from the
Eleventh-dynasty architect but that is as far as the indebtedness
goes. Senmut must be credited with making the terrace-form his
own and bringing it to fruition in a building that stands in perfect
harmony with its surroundings. The earlier temple with its
incongruous combination of designs and its squatty undersized
pyramid protruding from the middle of the central court cannot
compare with its graceful neighbour. The earlier architect's real
gift to Senmut was the opportunity to profit from a mistake.

The name of Deir el Bahri is a comparatively recent appellation
given to the site by some Egyptian Christians who, in the seventh
century A.D., built a monastery on the ruins of the temple.
Hatshepsut called it *Zoser-zosru* or "Holy of Holies". It was also
known as "Paradise for Amon", to whom it was dedicated,
although it contained chapels for other deities. It was originally
designed to be a mortuary temple for the queen and her parents.
As mentioned earlier, the queen had planned to have the burial
chamber of her tomb located directly under the temple but, in
tunnelling under the mountain from the Valley of the Kings, the

[1] *The Art and Architecture of Ancient Egypt* (Baltimore, Penguin, 1958), p. 133.

engineers ran into poor rock and were forced to veer off into another direction. Hatshepsut had a further design in erecting the temple and that was to establish beyond any doubt her claim to the throne. This she accomplished by inscribing in detailed hieroglyphic scenes the story of her divine birth from the union of her mother with Amon-Ra, an idea used by many later religions.

The inscriptions on the temple walls reflect the political conflict and family dissension which raged throughout her lifetime. The "Thutmosid Feud" was an involved one which we can relate only in bold outline. The duration of the individual reigns being uncertain, the three Thutmose periods and that of Hatshepsut are usually grouped together and dated roughly 1525–1436 B.C. The relationship of Hatshepsut to the three kings is equally dubious. Thutmose III is variously referred to as Hatshepsut's half-brother, nephew, husband, and stepson.

Hatshepsut might well be called the first great woman of history. She was the first woman to rule a nation, maintaining the throne for twenty-one years against tough opposition. About a century before her birth, a powerful prince named Ahmose united the Egyptian forces and expelled the Hyksos invaders. Thus ended the Dark Ages of Egyptian history and thus began the Renaissance with the establishment of the Eighteenth Dynasty. Ahmose was succeeded by Amenhotep I and he was followed by Thutmose I, who, in order to make secure his kingship (his mother was not of royal birth), married one of his half-sisters, a royal princess named Ahmose. From here the Thutmosid succession has always been a confusing problem due to the mutilation of the monuments of Hatshepsut by Thutmose III. The earlier solutions of Naville, Sethe, Meyer, and Breasted were highly involved, with the rule changing hands repeatedly, the Thutmose III-Hatshepsut reign being interrupted by the resurgence of Thutmose I and II. The most probable sequence is the simplest one; namely, that Thutmose I was succeeded by Thutmose II, who married his half-sister, Hatshepsut. She served as co-regent and, after his death, was appointed co-regent for the young Thutmose III. Rejecting this title, Hatshepsut proclaimed herself "king" and for the rest of her life ruled as such. She thrust Thutmose III into the background and took the title "Chief

Spouse of Amon, the Mighty One, the Lord of East and West, the Good Goddess, the Pious Lady, the Golden Falcon in her Risings, the King of Upper and Lower Egypt, the Daughter of Ra, Khnumit-Amon-Hatshepsut". Thutmose III was reduced to the rank of a courtier. At her death, he took the throne.[1]

As king, Hatshepsut launched several major projects, the first of which was her mortuary temple. After some five years, surprisingly enough, Thutmose II and the old king seized the throne and reigned as co-regents, a reign which ended shortly with the death of both. Thutmose III had hopes of regaining power but he was again relegated to a subordinate position by the powerful queen and her partisans.

Closest to Hatshepsut was Senmut, her architect and chief supporter. Her coterie also included Hapuseneb, who was both Grand Vizier and High Priest of Amon and also head of the entire Egyptian priesthood; Thutiy, who had succeeded Ineni as treasurer; and Nehsi, her chief steward and administrative officer. With the backing of such powerful nobles, nothing could stand in the way of Hatshepsut's success. The union of the administrative government and the priestly party in the person of Hapuseneb was enough to ensure her position.

Hatshepsut's reign came as a peaceful interlude between the aggressive wars of Thutmose I and Thutmose III. With tribute money flowing into the capital and little or no military expenditure, the queen's government became rich. One of her peaceful enterprises was the expedition in the ninth year of the reign of the legendary land of Punt. Under the command of Nehsi the fleet returned with spices, ebony, ivory, apes, hides of panthers, 3,300 cattle, some specimens of that distant land's inhabitants, and incense-bearing trees which were set out along the terraces of the temple. The most interesting reliefs in the temple are those which picture the departure of the flotilla, the landing in Punt and the return.

[1] For political details on this period see John A. Wilson: *The Culture of Ancient Egypt* (Chicago, University of Chicago Press, Phoenix Books, 1951), pp. 174–7; James H. Breasted: *A History of Egypt* (New York, Scribners, 1912), pp. 266–83. For a recent and authoritative discussion of the Hatshepsut problem, see Barbara Mertz: *Temples, Tombs and Hieroglyphics* (New York, Coward, McCann Inc., 1964), pp. 186–91.

Hatshepsut's next project was the erection at Karnak of two obelisks that would be "taller and statelier than any in Egypt", a memorial for the jubilee celebration of her appointment as "king". She wrote thus: "I sat in the palace; I remembered him who fashioned me; my heart led me to make for him two obelisks of electrum, whose points mingled with heaven." For this task she appointed her favourite, Senmut. We are told that he began work at Aswan in February of the fifteenth year of the reign and seven months later the huge blocks were cut free from the quarry. He was thus enabled to use the high water to float them on barges to Thebes. They were erected in the colonnaded hall of the Karnak temple where Thutmose III had been named king by the Amon oracle. Senmut had the roof of the temple removed in order to accommodate the obelisks. They were of rose granite and their tops were encased in white burnished electrum, a metal more valuable than gold. One of them still stands squarely and firmly on its foundation perpendicular to the hundredth of an inch, 98 feet high and weighing 350 tons, without doubt one of the most exquisite objects of all Egyptian antiquities. The clean-cut hieroglyphic inscriptions appear to have been incised only yesterday.

In the same year Hatshepsut sent an expedition to the Sinai mines to resume the work which had been discontinued during the Hyksos occupation. This project lasted five years.

The circumstances of Hatshepsut's death in the twenty-first year of her reign are obscure. The first act of the outraged Thutmose upon ascending the throne was to take vengeance upon the dead queen. He obliterated her portraits wherever found, chiselled out her cartouches from the temples of Karnak and Deir el Bahri, built a wall of masonry around the obelisks, and hacked out the names of Nehsi, Senmut, Hapuseneb and Thutiy from all monuments. But today the masonry around the obelisks has disappeared, leaving the beautiful monolith standing erect among the ruins; and three miles across the river Deir el Bahri joins with Karnak to testify to the greatness of the queen.

We now turn to our main concern—the story of the excavation of this most graceful temple in Egypt, a story which takes us back a century and a half. The attention of the outside world was first called to Deir el Bahri by the scientists attached to

Napoleon's expedition in 1798, although Pococke had visited the site sixty years earlier. The French explorers saw traces of the avenue of sphinxes leading up to the temple and part of the enclosure wall. Most of the temple lay buried in the sand. A few years later Champollion copied some of the portal inscriptions which were exposed and noted that "all the nouns referring to the unknown king were in the feminine" and that the ruler was referred to as "the daughter of Amon-Ra". He concluded that the ruler and builder of the temple must have been a woman who was "related somehow to an unknown Thutmose". The colonnades that he could see led to his theory that Greek art and architecture had their origin in Egypt. In both theories he anticipated the conclusions of archaeologists a century later. Wilkinson visited the temple shortly after Champollion but contributed no further information. He was followed by Lepsius who confirmed the name Khnum-Amen as the title of Hatshepsut.

The first archaeologist to do any significant work on the temple was Mariette who excavated in 1858, 1862, and 1866. As a result of his expedition the general form of the temple was revealed for the first time and some of the sculpture and reliefs were cleared, chiefly those of the Punt Expedition, which are on the retaining wall of the second platform. Unfortunately, as with most of his excavations, the work was too hurried and clearances were not methodical with the result that instead of removing the debris to a point outside the probable limits of the temple area, he dumped it nearby within the temple complex so that later excavators had first to clear away his dumpings before they could begin their work.

THE EGYPT EXPLORATION FUND

The clearing of Deir el Bahri took on a more scientific complexion with the expedition of the Egypt Exploration Fund which lasted from 1893 to 1903. Under the expert direction of Edouard Naville, the Swiss Egyptologist, the long ramps, terraces and courts were cleared. The coloured reliefs were roofed over but the excavator wisely confined his work to preservation rather than restoration. The work of the expedition was summarized in several excellent volumes which were published from 1894 to 1908.

In 1879 Mariette expressed his belief that a smaller temple of the Eleventh Dynasty had once existed near the Hatshepsut temple. This belief was based on his discovery of a block of stone

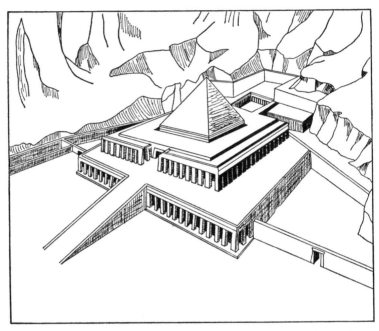

Fig. 9. The Temple of Mentuhotep (reconstruction). The tomb of Mentuhotep (Eleventh Dynasty) was cut out of the rock cliff at Deir el Bahri, adjacent to the Temple of Hatshepsut. This funerary temple surmounted by a pyramid was the inspiration for Senmut's design of the Hatshepsut temple. It was excavated by Naville (Egypt Exploration Fund) and Winlock (Metropolitan Museum of Art, New York).

bearing the name of the Eleventh-dynasty king, Mentuhotep. With this in mind, Naville and H. R. Hall in 1903 began digging in the mounds just south of the Hatshepsut temple and continued for four years. Naville's original idea was to clear the Eleventh-dynasty cemetery which he thought lay beneath the mounds, but he soon came upon a ramp which ran parallel to the enclosure wall of the Hatshepsut temple. This ramp led him to the remains of a temple which was buried under twenty feet of sand—a building unique in history, being the first of its kind and the inspiration for Senmut's terraced temple of Hatshepsut. As Mariette had guessed, it turned out to be the temple of Mentuhotep Neb-hepet-Ra.[1]

It appears that the temple was torn down during the Nineteenth Dynasty by contractors who used the stone for other buildings. What remains today of the superstructure is only a few feet in height but it is enough to provide a fairly accurate idea of the original appearance of the temple. The first court was approached by a causeway on the right hand of which lies the entrance to an underground passage discovered by Howard Carter in 1900 and which led under the pyramid in the centre of the court. A ramp joined the lower court and the square colonnaded terrace. From the terrace a narrow corridor ran to the pyramid which was surrounded by 140 octagonal pillars. The pyramid was 60 feet square at the base and was originally encased in fine limestone. Behind the pyramid in the rear of the temple were the shrines of six ladies of the royal harem whose shaft-tombs were in the adjoining court. From the centre of this court an underground passage 500 feet long led to the granite-lined tomb of Mentu-hotep III. To the west of the pyramid court stood a hypostyle hall with eighty octagonal pillars and beyond this a niche was hewn into the living rock and here the temple ends. In the time of Thutmose III a chapel to Hathor was added near the pyramid court. It was here that Naville and Hall discovered the beautiful Hathor shrine containing the statue of the goddess in the form of a cow. The statue, now in the Cairo Museum, represents the best example of Egyptian animal sculpture. The circumstances under which the shrine and statue came to light were somewhat dramatic. Naville was clearing a steep hill of debris. Stopping suddenly, he advised his foreman to discontinue digging because of the danger that a loosened boulder might cause a small avalanche. As they started to leave the spot, they heard the roar of falling rocks and, after the dust had cleared, they turned and saw the entrance to the shrine and in it was the undamaged statue of Hathor.

[1] See Edouard Naville: *The Eleventh-Dynasty Temple at Deir el-Bahri*; 3 vols. (London, 1907–13).

THE METROPOLITAN EXPEDITION

The climax of our story of the Deir el Bahri excavation is reached with the expedition of the New York Metropolitan Museum of Art (1911–31).[1] The first few seasons of this twenty-year dig were spent in the completion of the work of the Egypt Exploration Society on the Mentuhotep temple. Among the accomplishments in this period were the clearing of the great causeway leading to the temple and the discovery of the unfinished mortuary temples of Ramses V and VI. With the resumption of work immediately after the First World War, the Expedition was rewarded with the discovery of several important royal tombs in the cliffs overlooking the Deir el Bahri temples. One of these was the tomb of Meket-Re, Chancellor and Steward of the Royal Palace under Mentuhotep. In the secret room or *serdab* of this tomb Winlock and his associates were given the most charming picture imaginable of ancient Egyptian life and work. After several days of digging through rock, following a path of chipped stone, the party suddenly came upon an untouched chamber filled with brightly painted models of every description. In the Middle Kingdom it was the custom to supply the deceased with models of himself and his servants doing everything he had done in life. The purpose of this was to secure the welfare of the king in the future life, but the value of such models for our knowledge of the social and economic life of that period is inestimable. All tombs contained such a display but it happened that Meket-Re was a wealthy person and was able to supply himself with the most elaborate collection of models ever seen. In accordance with the agreement, half of the collection remained

[1] For a complete official report of the expedition see H. E. Winlock: *Excavations at Deir el-Bahri: 1911–1931* (New York, Macmillan, 1942). The Metropolitan staff at Deir el Bahri was as follows: Albert M. Lythgoe, Curator of the Egyptian Department until 1929; James Brewster, 1926–29; Donald F. Brown, 1929–30; Harry Burton, 1919–31; Charlotte R. Clark, 1928–31; Walter Cline, 1924–25; Spencer Foster, 1930–31; Lindsey F. Hall, 1919–23, 1930–31; Walter Hauser, 1919–31; William C. Hayes, 1927–31; Ambrose Lansing, 1919–20; Albert Nixon, 1920–22; Gouverneur M. Peek, 1924–25; Edward M. Weyer, Jr., 1925–26; H. G. Evelyn White, 1919–20; C. K. Wilkinson, 1920–31; H. E. Winlock, 1911–14, 1919–31.

in Cairo and the other half went to the Metropolitan Museum.[1] On either side of the chamber stood the statues of two girls, elegantly dressed, carrying wine jugs and food to the tomb. Each one had a live duck in one hand. All the rest of the models show Meket-Re in his various activities, foremost of which is one showing the king seated in a pavilion checking his cattle which are being driven past by a herdsman. His secretary makes a record on a papyrus roll. Also on the reviewing stand are stewards and butlers. Altogether it is a realistic and colourful scene.

Other scenes portray the process of fattening and slaughtering the cattle. Still others picture the baking process from granary to oven, brewing, spinning and weaving, and gardening. Half of the models are of ships, exact replicas of the king's vessels that plied up and down the river four thousand years ago. One of the travelling boats has a square sail and the sailors are making fast the back-stays and hauling on the halyards. Another, apparently going downstream, has the sail lowered and the sailors are at the oars. Among the other boats are a yacht being paddled by its crew, a travelling boat with its kitchen tender, and a fishing vessel.

In the burial-chamber of Meket-Re's tomb were found an immense sarcophagus, a gilded coffin, and some 1,200 weapons and tools such as chisels, axes, adzes, squares, drill shafts, bows, arrows, and shields. In the course of the excavation, Winlock found the untouched tomb of Wah, the estate manager of Meket-Re. The tomb was located at the end of a tunnel about 26 feet long. Clearing the entrance, which was still intact, the excavators saw the coffin lying undisturbed in the rear of the chamber.

The mummy of Wah, having been untouched, provided an excellent study of embalming. It was one of the most carefully wrapped mummies ever found. The bandaging was, in fact, such an artistic job that, at the time, Winlock gave no thought to dismantling it. In 1936, however, X-ray photographs were taken and they showed that the neck, chest, and wrists were covered with fine jewellery. This discovery led Winlock and Hayes to

[1] For pictures and descriptions of the models see H. E. Winlock: *ibid.*, Plates 24–29, and William C. Hayes: *The Scepter of Egypt*, Part I (New York, Harper and Brothers and the Metropolitan Museum of Art, 1953), pp. 167, 262–74.

the decision to unwrap the mummy. In all they unwrapped 375 square metres of linen from the mummy itself and a total of 845 square metres from the coffin and tomb. At different levels in the layers of bandages and pads they found many necklaces of gold, silver, faience, and lapis-lazuli, a broad collar, and brace-lets.

Naville's clearing of the temple complex disclosed the location of six shrines belonging to the king's wives. The 1920–21 season was devoted to this area. The chief finds were the coffins and mummies of princesses Ashayet and Mayet which were practically intact. Each tomb had a limestone sarcophagus carved with elaborate hieroglyphic reliefs. In one of the tombs was the mummy of a five-year-old child lying within two nested coffins. On the body of the girl were five beautiful necklaces. On the coffins of the child and the two ladies of the harem were painted the large magical Horus eyes.

The seasons of 1921 to 1923 were given largely to the removal of Naville's dump south of the Mentuhotep temple and clearing the grove in front of it. The outstanding finds here were the tombs of the Viziers Ipi and Nesy-pe-ka-shuti, and the Hekanakhte Papyri from the tomb of Hesem.

From 1924 to 1931 the Metropolitan Expedition concentrated on the Hatshepsut complex, commencing with the clearing of the tomb of Queen Neferu which Mariette had previously located under the temple. In the same year Winlock found the tomb of Hent-towy, a Theban lady, with coffins and mummy untouched, and the coffins of three princesses. The temple was explored from its foundations to the neighbouring cliffs. It was in this period that Senmut's tomb was cleared. We have previously called attention to Senmut's hillside tomb and mortuary chapel near the tomb of El-Sheikh Abd el-Qurna.[1] Like Hatshepsut, he also built this secret tomb which tunnelled under the queen's temple. The chambers were a hundred yards from the entrance, down stairs all the way. Only one room was decorated. Here and there in the vertical columns of the hieroglyphic carvings the sculptor had written the date at the spot where he had stopped work each day. On another wall where the white stone had been prepared for a stele, a draftsman or scribe had hurriedly sketched the head

[1] See pp. 152, 153.

of the architect and labelled it "The Steward of Amon, Senmut". The outstanding feature of the decorated room is the ceiling which was done in the form of an astronomical chart by a highly skilled draftsman. This map of the heavens shows the position of Orion, the Great Bear, and the stars of the northern and southern skies. "We have here an earlier and a finer celestial chart," writes Winlock, "even than that in the tomb of King Seti, and one which no future study of Egyptian astronomy can neglect."

Another tomb which was tunnelled from the outside area to a point under the temple was that of Queen Meryet-Amun. It started just north of the temple and ran underneath the portico. The long corridor leading to this tomb was clogged with boxes, baskets, carved figures, and rubbish. Almost at the end of the passage Winlock came suddenly upon an intact coffin containing a mummy. The lid and outer coffin were propped up on the side of the passage. The name appearing on the ushabti figures and the coffin was Entiu-ny, who died in a much later period and was hastily buried in the tomb passage. The mummy of Entiu-ny was later unwrapped and in the layers of linen Winlock found a papyrus of the Book of the Dead, which may now be seen at the Metropolitan Museum. It was done by a skilled calligrapher and the colouring is brilliant. After removing the coffins and statues of Entiu-ny, the excavators proceeded farther into the tomb. The coffin of Entiu-ny had been dropped at the edge of a deep well which blocked further ingress. They placed boards across the well and Winlock crawled on hands and knees to the other side. Here he found himself in a long, dark passage which led to another chamber. Winlock continues:

> I took eight or ten strides across the empty chamber and came to a standstill just within the doorway beside three little empty saucers and a dried and shriveled bundle of leaves lying at the foot of an enormous recumbent figure. My light flickered along it and came to rest on a great placid face staring fixedly upward in the deathly silence of the dark crypt. Then it flickered back and followed down a column of hieroglyphics announcing that "the King gives a boon to Osiris, the Great God, Lord of Abydos, that he may cause to come forth at the call bread and beer, beef and fowl, bandages, incense and unguents and all things good and pure on which a god

lives, and the sweet north wind; for the spirit of the King's Daughter and Sister, the God's Wife, the King's Great Wife, joined to the Crown of Upper Egypt, the Mistress of the Two Lands, Meryet-Amun, true of voice with Osiris.'' The silence, the dark, and the realization of the ages that the coffin had lain there—for it was a coffin—all combined in creating an eerie effect; and whatever one may expect, that does not happen so very often in digging.[1]

Meryet-Amun was the daughter of Thutmose III and his wife Meryet-Re and probably the wife of her brother Amenhotep II. The outer coffin was over 10 feet high. Within it was the disproportionately small inner coffin containing the queen's mummy which was decorated with flowers. The outer coffin was the work of a superior craftsman and has been compared with that of Tutankhamon. Both inner and outer coffins show signs of ancient vandalism. During the Twenty-first Dynasty the tomb was reopened and repaired. Curiously enough, the date upon which the coffins were repaired, repainted, and the mummy rewrapped is carefully recorded on the breast of the mummy itself —"Year 19, Month 3 of Akhet, Day 28 (25th November, 1049 B.C.). The mummy had been stripped to the body and the original wrappings were found thrown aside by the thieves. One of them was marked with the queen's name. A third or intermediate coffin had been completely destroyed. The mummy is now in the Cairo Museum.

The tomb of Queen Meryet-Amun was discovered in the 1928–29 season. The next two seasons were spent in assembling the statues of Hatshepsut previously found. Starting with 1926–27 season the expedition had turned up, in the quarry on the north side of the causeway, sculptures of all shapes and sizes: sections of the limestone colossi from the upper porch, pieces of the sandstone sphinxes that had lined the avenue, and parts of kneeling statues of Hatshepsut in red and black granite. One seated red-granite statue, twice life-size, had been broken into many pieces but they were all in one place and could easily be assembled. The faces of some of the larger granite statues had been disfigured by chisels, fire, and hammers. As Winlock commented: "Thutmose III could have had no complaint to make on the execution of his orders, for every conceivable indignity had been

[1] H. E. Winlock: *op. cit.*, pp. 179, 180.

heaped on the likeness of the fallen Queen.'' One compensation was found in the fact that since these statues had been buried in the sand when they were smashed, the colours have been perfectly preserved.

The seated white marble statue of Hatshepsut in New York— the most beautiful sculpture of the queen—has an interesting history. Lepsius in 1843 had procured for the Berlin Museum the lower half of a white marble statue. In 1926, while clearing a section of the quarry, the Metropolitan Expedition unearthed the head of a similar statue and in the next season found other fragments. The description of the Berlin marble seemed to indicate that it was of the same material. Winlock wrote to Heinrich Schäfer, the director of the Berlin Museum, asking for a detailed description and sketches. The prompt reply confirmed Winlock's surmise that the material of the Berlin piece was identical with those parts in the possession of the Metropolitan Expedition. All the parts that were missing in Berlin—head, neck, arms, and the rear section of the throne—were just the parts which Winlock had. The sketches showed that the breaks fitted together perfectly and there were no pieces left over. Thus the possibility that there were two similar statues of the same material was ruled out.

Lepsius had also taken to Berlin the head of one of the granite sphinxes. It so happened that in this same season the Metropolitan Expedition had unearthed the body of a sphinx statue which, upon investigation, proved to be the one which belonged to the Lepsius head. The size, the breaks, the material and the texture all coincided perfectly. Mutually satisfactory arrangements were made with the result that the Berlin Museum shipped the marble body to New York and the Metropolitan Museum arranged for the granite sphinx body to be sent to Berlin. ''Thus,'' as Winlock concludes, ''Berlin got a most imposing granite sphinx, and the Metropolitan Museum acquired a complete, seated statue which will always be one of the prizes of its Egyptian Department.'' The seated cream-coloured marble statue of Hatshepsut is probably the most exquisitely carved sculpture to come out of Deir el Bahri and therefore must have occupied a prominent place in the temple. Usually the statues and reliefs of Hatshepsut show her with the beard of a king but here the sculptor, while retaining the head-dress and kilt of a man, has carved her face and body in a way that leaves no doubt as to her femininity.

This exchange was followed by others as the Deir el Bahri digging brought to light fragments of other statues. The end of the campaign found Winlock back in New York busy with marble jigsaw puzzles and his was the satisfaction of putting together several additional sculptures with pieces sent from Cairo and Berlin. The Metropolitan collection of Hatshepsut statues was completed by the addition of two fine granite sphinxes which originally lined the avenue to the temple.

Of the 35,000 objects in the Egyptian rooms of the Metropolitan Museum, the Hatshepsut collection is by far the most impressive and stands as eloquent witness to the painstaking work of the men who conducted the expedition and to those who were responsible for the installation and arrangement of the display.

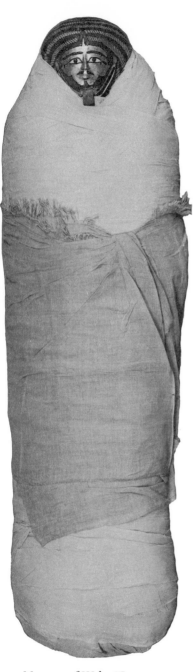

Mummy of Wah. (*Courtesy,
Metropolitan Museum of Art,
New York*)

Painted papyrus
cartonnage.
(*Courtesy, British Museum*)

Coffin of Meryet-Amun.
(*Courtesy, Metropolitan
Museum of Art, New York*)

Mummy of Meryet-Amun.
(*Courtesy, Metropolitan
Museum of Art, New York*)

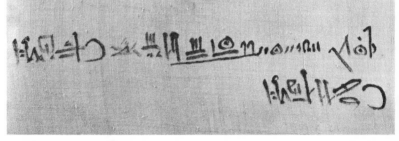

Inscription on the mummy of Meryet-Amun. (*Courtesy, Metropolitan
Museum of Art, New York*)

Chapter Ten

AMARNA

THE CITY OF THE HORIZON

The holy city of Akhetaton, better known as el-Amarna, arose magically out of the desert at the command of the heretic Pharaoh Ikhnaton.[1] It lasted for a quarter of a century and then vanished from the earth. But its ephemeral existence was great and glorious. Short-lived as it was, it left in the desert sands the indubitable evidence of a new and creative spirit in the world, a great revolution in art and religion. And that is where it stayed until its sudden death, for the reform of Ikhnaton never penetrated the national mind; it never touched the lives of the common people.

It requires a stretch of the imagination to stand today among the scanty ruins of Amarna—a desolate and unimposing place—and contemplate the romantic adventure of a young king, son of the most illustrious monarch of the Eighteenth Dynasty, transforming the desert into a dream city, a city of unsurpassed beauty with its temples, palaces, parks, public buildings, mansions, and spacious quays, pitting himself against the powerful Amon priests and all the vested interests and establishing a new religion and a new way of living, only to perish in the prime of life as the fulfilment of his dream collapsed about him.

In the sixth year of his reign, the battle with Amonism having been joined, Amenhotep IV changed his name to conform to his new cult of Aton and left Thebes never to return. The site chosen by the king for his new city was a stretch of barren land about 300 miles north of Thebes at a point where the eastern cliffs

[1] Or Akhenaton (Amenhotep IV).

retreat from the river in semicircular fashion for about six miles, leaving a plain some three miles wide between the river and the hills. This plain, protected on three sides by cliffs, was an ideal location. Previously, Ikhnaton and his engineers had spent several days on a demarcation expedition to set up boundary stelae. The stelae defined the larger domain of the Aton district, which also included the plain on the western bank of the Nile, all of which measured some 8 miles in length and from 12 to 18 miles east to west. The city proper occupied the bay in the hills on the east bank and was 6 miles long and 3 miles wide. Not all of this area, of course, was occupied. When completed, Akhetaton stretched along the river for 5 miles and backward towards the hills only for $\frac{1}{2}$-mile, utilizing the fertile strip bordering the river.

Several stelae indicate that the city was completed by the eighth year of the reign and that the court, with all official documents and personnel, had soon after been transferred from Thebes. The three main thoroughfares ran north and south and were intersected at right angles by several other streets. The main street, or King's Way, with the river on one side and the chief buildings on the other, started at Maru-Aton, the pleasure palace, and continued north past the Royal House, the Central Palace, the Great Temple, the North Palace and came to an end in the North City. Parallel to the King's Way ran High Priest Street, bordered by the mansions of the nobles, priests and government officials. Some of the estates in the North City had not yet been completed when the city was abandoned some eighteen years later.

The central section of Amarna was carefully planned. It consisted of the Great Temple, the Royal Magazines, the Hall of Foreign Tribute, houses of the priests, the royal estate, the foreign office, the "House of Life", where young scribes learned the art of writing and administration, houses of clerks, police barracks, armoury and parade grounds.

The Great Temple was planned by Ikhnaton to be the "mother church" for Atonism the world over. The enclosure measured $\frac{1}{2}$-mile in length and 350 yards in width, and was surrounded by a high wall. An avenue of sphinxes led to the House of Rejoicing, a smaller temple with two rows of columns flanking the centre aisle. At the end of each colonnade stood a carved limestone altar. Beyond this building, a ramp led to the Gem-Aton (The Finding of Aton). The inner court was open to the sky, permitting worship in the open air under the sun. The preliminary temples and the sanctuary itself were light, airy and cheerful in contrast to previous Egyptian temples, with their dark and mysterious chambers. Gem-Aton was composed of a great multitude of courts, passageways, ramps and altars. Mounting finally a long flight of stairs, the worshipper stood before the awesome high altar. Farther to the east lay the inner sanctuary, with an imposing façade and two tremendous pylons. Each pylon supported five masts from which fluttered brilliant pennants. Within the temple were offering tables and statues of Ikhnaton. Nearby stood the houses of the priests.

The temple contained no images, and Atonism depended upon no esoteric rites or elaborate secret ceremonies. However, the ritual did include offerings of food and wine. These offerings were consecrated by the king and queen after they had performed the rite of lustration and had burned the incense. The most prominent feature of the ceremony was music. A permanent choir and orchestra were attached to the temple and performed several hours each day. A special group of male chanters sang during the consecration of the offerings. Simultaneously, female musicians outside the temple played on tambourines and waved palm branches. Encircling the worship area were several small chapels, each leading to a series of gateways that opened on to six courts with temple buildings decorated in gay colours.

Worship was conducted at sunrise and sunset when the king and queen, or priests, officiated at the temple ceremony with the singing of the two hymns. "Thy rising is beautiful in the horizon of heaven, O living Aton, who givest life. Shining from the eastern horizon, Thou fillest Egypt with thy beauty. . . . Thy setting is beautiful, O living Aton, who guidest all countries that they make praise at thy dawning and at thy setting."

But the worship of Aton was not confined to the temple. It was in the gardens and groves of Amarna that the Pharaoh exclaimed: "O Lord, how manifold are thy works! The whole land is in joy because of thee. All that thou hast made leaps before thee. Eyes have life at the sight of thy beauty; hearts have health when the Aton shines. There is no poverty for him who hath set thee in his heart.''

Little occult mystery clung to the worship of Amarna. The priests were not ascetics, but lovers of truth and beauty. Ikhnaton discarded all magic—the tedious formulae for safe passage into the realm of Osiris, as well as the innumerable spirits, demigods, incantations and bogies. References in Atonism to death and the hereafter took on a spiritual meaning: the desire to be well remembered on earth and a prayer for the continuation of the light of Aton in the soul.

The royal estate occupied an area some 500 yards square. The palace itself, measuring 1,400 by 500 feet and having 500 pillars, lay on the west side of the King's Way. Fragmentary remains of the painted pavements of the palace are among the most striking examples of originality in the decorative art of antiquity. They give us just a hint of the magnificence of the original building and illustrate the naturalistic technique of Ikhnaton's artists, who were the first ever to depict rapid motion: bulls jumping through the air, calves galloping, fish swimming and ducks flying. They also painted everyday things: plants and flowers of many varieties and men at work in the fields.

From the palace, at the Window of the Appearances, the Pharaoh and his family presided over official and informal functions. The remains of brilliantly painted columns of the palm-frond style, inlaid with coloured glazes, were found in the queen's pavilion, and farther north, excavation unearthed many fragments of limestone relief as well as the death mask of Ikhnaton. Around the northern end of the royal estate ran a formal terraced garden, to the right of which stood the house of the king. The living-room of the house contained forty-two columns in six rows. Another hall of twenty columns led to private quarters of the king and queen. Back of the house were the royal magazines housing sealed wine jars, sacks of valuable objects, bales of cloth, grain, bread, spices, ancestral treasures and objects of foreign tribute. Connected to the king's house was a private temple called Hat-Aton, which was patterned throughout after the Great Temple. To the south stood the priests' quarters and the sacred lake.

At the extreme southern end of Amarna was Maru-Aton, a

royal park or grove dedicated to Aton and to the enjoyment of the outdoor life. Within this enclosure a temple had been built, thus combining the appreciation of the beauties of nature with the worship of their divine source. Maru-Aton consisted of two main areas, the smaller of which contained beautiful flower-beds, a lake and a reception hall. In the larger section another pleasure lake had been dug. 120 yards long and 60 yards wide, the lake was surrounded by ornate buildings and a plant aquarium. Near the shore was a rectangular island of flowers and shrubs. Crossing the bridge from the island, guests of the Pharaoh walked down a flowery path and through a colonnade to the temple. The pavements were decorated with frescoed panels showing marsh scenes of cattle jumping among papyrus brakes, and startled ducks taking flight. Still another royal residence, the North Palace, contained gardens, aviaries, enclosure for animals, a bird sanctuary and beautiful frescoes of bird life. One can picture Ikhnaton and Nefertiti entertaining their friends and visitors in this secluded and peaceful retreat.

In the first two years at Amarna, the land was allotted and the estates laid out along the main streets. A typical middle-class house occupied an area of 200 by 150 feet. The front entrance was flanked by two pylon towers. An avenue of trees led to the private open-air chapel. Behind the chapel ran a formal garden and an artificial lake or pool. The house itself consisted of a large living-room surrounded by guest rooms and store-rooms. The front door had a stone frame and the name of the owner was inscribed on the lintel. The roof of the house was supported by wooden columns set in stone. A corridor led from the central room to the sitting-rooms, bedrooms and bathrooms. The decoration of a private house generally consisted of a formal frieze of flowers and birds and hanging garlands. The servants' quarters, ovens and kitchen were separate and always on the east side of the house to avoid the prevailing west wind, and next to these were the stables. Unlike Egyptian temples and tombs, which were made of stone, the public buildings and houses of Amarna were made of mud-brick, but they lasted a long time in the extremely dry climate.

Just south of the royal estate stood the homes of the city officials, the most elaborate of which were those of Nakht, the new vizier who had replaced Ramose shortly after the occupation of Amarna; Paneshy, the Chief Servitor of the god; and Ranefer, Master of Horse. Here also lived Thutmose, sculptor of the famous head of Nefertiti. Still further to the south rose the faience and glass factories.

As the population increased, the city expanded towards the north. This section was called the North Suburb and was inhabited by minor officials and middle-class citizens. It also boasted the North Palace, with its exquisite wall-paintings of bird life and marsh scenes. Beyond the North Suburb was the North City, the seat of the queen's palace, to which Nefertiti may have retired after the death of her husband. The Customs House (used for the unloading and inspection of material entering from the north) was located at the extreme northern point of Amarna. A similar office was built at the southern end.

To the Egyptian his "House of Eternity" was even more important than his earthly home. Not the least significant feature of Amarna therefore was the necropolis. The rock tombs of the nobles were cut in the surrounding eastern cliffs. The importance of these tombs lies not in the recovery of mummies, for none has ever been found, but in the coloured wall-paintings and low reliefs. In some instances the bodies of the officials and priests were probably removed to Thebes when Amarna was deserted by the court. Like the Theban tombs, all have been defaced, some deliberately during the destruction of the city by the reactionary forces, others by later tomb robbers. It is through the tomb reliefs that we become intimately acquainted with the life and culture of Amarna—the public ceremonies, the private life of the royal family and the visits of foreign dignitaries. Even more important, however, are the hymns and texts relating to the new religion of Ikhnaton. From the tomb paintings we can reconstruct many events which took place during the reign: ceremonies for the receiving of tributes from foreign states, visits of the queen mother to Amarna, feasts and other royal functions.

The tomb of Mahu, chief of the Mazoi, the city police, is one of the best preserved in Amarna and contains a number of impressive reliefs: the vizier running along beside the royal chariot as it leaves the temple, the inspection of sentry posts by Mahu and the king, Mahu in the storehouse presenting a requisition from the vizier for supplies, the capture of foreign spies by Mahu and the appearance of the prisoners before the vizier. All of these are sculptured in exquisite detail. The wonder is that the quarriers, engineers, draftsmen, artists and sculptors were able to complete so many tombs in such a short time.

One of the most charming pieces of art to be recovered from the Amarna ruins is a coloured relief which pictures Ikhnaton and Nefertiti facing each other in an informal pose. Casually leaning on his staff, the king talks to his wife, who half teasingly holds a small bouquet of flowers to his nose for him to smell. In the other hand she holds a bouquet of lotus flowers. Her gown is ruffled by the breeze, as is the king's hair. The simplicity of this relief aptly illustrates the way in which the heresy of Ikhnaton expressed itself in the art and family life of the palace. The philosophy of naturalism so clearly seen in both the religion and art of Amarna is epitomized in the king's motto or guiding principle, "Living in Truth". The revolution in art was in fact an application of *maat*, "truthfulness". This naturalness had already appeared to a certain extent in the reign of Amenhotep III. Like the shift from the stylized art of the Middle Ages to the naturalism of the Renaissance, it was a change from the other-worldly to the secular.

One of the most unconventional scenes is found on a relief in the tomb of Huya. The royal family is celebrating the arrival in Amarna of the queen mother. Tuy, wearing the royal head-dress, sits facing the king and queen. Ikhnaton is eating what appears to be a skewer of charcoal-broiled *shish kebab*, while his lady, wearing only a simple skirt or apron, holds a whole roast duck in her hands. The queen mother is trying to decide whether to choose something from the heavily laden table of food before her or to take one of the cakes offered her by the young princess at her feet. Two large tables covered with plates of food stand before the king and queen. The other four children sit on the floor amusing themselves with games. Another relief from the same tomb shows the continuation of the celebration a few hours later when all are drinking wine. One princess stands on a footstool with a glass of wine in her hand while another, unnoticed by the rest, snatches some cakes. In these scenes the royal pair is often seen sitting together with their arms around each other and in one relief the queen is seated on the king's knee. These uninhibited scenes are typical of the Amarna reliefs, but it is a far cry from anything before or after in Egyptian art.

The close association of the king with his artists is plainly evident in a tablet which refers to the royal architect, Bek, as "the assistant whom his Majesty himself taught, chief of sculptors on the great and mighty monuments of the king". This inscription does not necessarily imply that Ikhnaton instructed his artists in the technical detail, but rather in the application of his principle "Living in Truth". The unprecedented realism of Amarna reliefs, some of which we have tried to describe, shows how thoroughly the artists were indoctrinated. Within the framework of that principle, they were undoubtedly free to portray things as they saw them, untrammelled by the dictates of hallowed tradition and court propriety. The revolution in art effected by the Amarna School influenced greatly the technique of human portraiture. Plant and animal life, marsh and river scenes had been portrayed in a fairly realistic manner in previous periods, so that the artists of Akhetaton were only continuing and accentuating that trend. The Amarna artists were unique, however, in their representations of the human figure. They depicted the daily events of life in a sincere and honest way. They pictured the king and his family unaffectedly enjoying the simple pleasures of domestic life. They modelled the human figure so realistically that one might think that some of their sculptures, such as the torso of one of the princesses, came from fifth-century Athens.

It would seem, in fact, that Ikhnaton's artists carried this realism almost to the point of caricature, particularly in picturing the king with a distinctly distended stomach. Some authorities feel that the king was afflicted with a disease which was characterized by the overdevelopment of the head, lips and lower part of the body. These peculiarities are shown in practically all of the Amarna reliefs and sculptures. If the king had such abnormalities, he may well have insisted on being depicted in this realistic manner. But his artists did not stop there. They began to exaggerate the abnormality and even pictured Nefertiti and the children in the same way. The habit seems to have become a fad, for later the priests and nobles were similarly drawn. Fragments of two colossal statues of Ikhnaton, which are now in Berlin, show a complete departure from the natural or realistic form. They are fantastic caricatures, with long and emaciated faces, high cheekbones, slit, almost closed eyes, large ears, long beard, thin arms and enlarged stomach. Such a grotesque style seems to represent an *art nouveau* or ancient school of impressionism. Some of the reliefs of the period pursue their baroque mannerisms still further. But this insistence ultimately caused the undoing of the Amarna School, for after Ikhnaton's death, artists completely rejected the exaggerative style and conscientiously returned to orthodoxy. Consequently, the normal continuity of artistic expression was lost, and the unique contribution of this period was not absorbed into the historic streams of Egyptian art except in the Nineteenth Dynasty, where certain traces of Amarna influence can be detected.

As we have already indicated, naturalism had not been entirely lacking in earlier Egyptian art, but before the Amarna period it played only a minor role. Traditional Egyptian painting or sculpture was primarily ideoplastic; that is, the form was used to symbolize an idea rather than a fact and was therefore conceptual in its aim rather than photographic. Thus, where the artistic expression was primarily ideological, realism could be only a subordinate factor and the work frequently lacked specific detail. The originality of the art of Amarna lay in its humanistic expression, in its aim to present an actual likeness rather than an ideological symbol.

This new philosophy of art produced a significant change. Now, instead of applying a conventional form to a particular subject and adding a minimum of new detail, the artist introduced a psychological element by portraying the subject in a unique or particular situation, with bodily posture and facial expression giving the sensation of an actual happening rather than producing a conventionalized pattern. In other words, the Amarna School depicted actual scenes from life and not abstract ideas. One tomb relief, for instance, pictures Mahu, chief of police at Amarna, receiving messengers. Nearby a brazier, with brightly burning coals, suggests that it is a chilly day. Such a touch of particularity shows the new realistic style.

Furthermore, the action of each picture is placed in its original setting—a palace, a field or a house—giving greater realism by providing the appropriate landscape or background. This does not imply perspective in the modern sense of the word, but it is an advance over all previous art.

Another "modern" characteristic of the work of Ikhnaton's artists is the unity of composition. The gestures or facial expressions of the various figures in a group combine to concentrate the viewer's attention on one central point. All the figures are related and are presented in a unified whole. Even in wall paintings, each section constitutes a unified scene with an important figure in the centre and subsidiary figures at the sides; formerly, such decorative murals were mechanically arranged in a series of disconnected scenes.

The murals of Amarna—found in the palaces, in the houses of the nobles and in the rock tombs—exist only in fragments, but enough remains to provide abundant evidence of the artists' complete absorption in the production of realistic representations rather than conceptual images.

The Green Room of the North Palace had large unbroken wall surfaces which were covered with one continuous picture, giving the appearance of wallpaper, except that there was no repetition of motif. The scene pictured is a marsh containing graceful papyrus plants. Lotus blossoms and green leaves float on the blue water. The bank is covered with grasses and weeds which bend under the weight of their buds. The thicket teems with life: rock pigeons and palm doves, small birds nesting with their young, the pied shrike and the black and white kingfisher. The diving kingfisher is just about to hit the water—an excellent example of Amarna realism. There is nothing original in marsh scenes with bird life and decorative borders, but the walls of the Green Room show a creativeness and freedom never before displayed in Egyptian art. Previously a papyrus thicket was shown only as a setting for a hunting expedition. Here is nature for nature's sake, a restful scene unmolested by the destructive activities of man.

Ikhnaton had hoped that Smenkhkara would succeed him but the latter mysteriously disappeared. At Ikhnaton's death the throne went to Tutankhamon who, in the second year of his reign, capitulated to the resurgent forces of Amonism, and returned the capital to Thebes where he occupied the throne for nine years.

He was succeeded by Ay, the nobleman and priest who had been close to Ikhnaton at Amarna, but who, like Horemheb, had found it not too difficult to change his religious loyalties as he changed residence from Amarna to Thebes. At any rate, Ay probably saw no reason for continuing to uphold a lost cause. It was in his tomb at Amarna that the great Aton-hymn was inscribed and there can be no doubt of his loyalty to Ikhnaton while at Amarna. After moving to Thebes, Ay built a new tomb for himself in the Valley of the Kings. His unimportant reign lasted for about three years, and, with his death, the Eighteenth Dynasty came to a close. A period of anarchy followed in which robbers plundered the tombs of Thutmose IV and other prominent kings.

The throne was seized in 1349 B.C. by Horemheb, who restored order and inaugurated a new era in the history of Egypt.[1]

FILES OF A FOREIGN OFFICE

Although Wilkinson and Lepsius had explored some of the rock tombs of Amarna in the middle of the nineteenth century, the City of the Horizon was really an unknown quantity until 1887. It was in that year that an Egyptian peasant woman, digging in a field on the outskirts of one of these little villages, stumbled upon some clay tablets in the sand dunes. They contained strange markings. She sensed that they might have some value and finally persuaded a fellow-villager to buy them for the equivalent of an American half-dollar. They were subsequently taken to numerous dealers who in turn sold them to archaeological authorities in Paris and Cairo, but these experts regarded them as worthless. Some were taken to Luxor and sold to dealers, and others were lost or ground to pieces. Finally a number of the tablets were bought by the Berlin Museum and the British Museum, where they were recognized as genuine documents of the fourteenth century B.C. written in the Babylonian cuneiform language.

The period immediately following the discovery was one of mystery and intrigue as Cairo authorities tried to secure the tablets from the natives by purchase or by force. Grébaut, the Director of the Service of Antiquities, ordered the police of Luxor to seize every house and shop containing antiquities and

[1] For discussion of the importance of Ikhnaton and his reform see my *The Heretic Pharaoh* (London, Robert Hale, 1962).

to arrest the owners. The order included the arrest of Wallis Budge who was known to be in on the hunt. Budge describes his experience as follows:

> I asked to see the warrants for the arrests, and he told me that M. Grébaut would produce them later on in the day. I asked him where M. Grébaut was, and he told me at Nakâdah a village about twelve miles to the north of Luxor, and went on to say that M. Grébaut had sent a runner from that place with instructions to the Chief of the Police at Luxor to do what they were then doing—that is, to take possession of the houses of all dealers and to arrest us. He then told Muhammad and myself that we were arrested.
>
> I told the police officer that I would not leave the town until the steamer arrived from Aswân, when I should embark in her and proceed to Cairo. When we had finished our meal the police officer took possession of the house, and posted watchmen on the roof and a sentry at each corner of the building. He then went to the houses of the other dealers, and sealed them, and set guards over them.
>
> In the course of the day a man arrived from Hajjî Kandîl, bringing with him some half-dozen of the clay tablets which had been found accidentally by a woman at Tell al-'Amârnah, and he asked me to look at them, and to tell him whether they were genuine or forgeries.
>
> When I examined the tablets I found that the matter was not as simple as it looked. In shape and form, and colour and material, the tablets were unlike any I had ever seen in London or Paris, and the writing on all of them was of a most unusual character and puzzled me for hours. By degrees I came to the conclusion that the tablets were certainly not forgeries, and that they were neither royal annals nor historical inscriptions in the ordinary sense of the word, nor business or commercial documents. The opening words of nearly all the tablets proved them to be letters or despatches, and I felt certain that the tablets were both genuine and of very great importance.
>
> I then tried to make arrangements with the men from Hajjî Kandîl to get the remainder of the tablets from Tell al-'Amârnah into my possession, but they told me that they belonged to dealers who were in treaty with an agent of the Berlin Museum in Cairo. Among the tablets was a very large one, about 20 inches long and broad in proportion. We now know that it contained a list of the dowry of a Mesopotamian princess who was going to marry a king of Egypt. The man who was taking this to Cairo hid it between his inner garments, and covered himself with his great cloak. As he stepped up into the railway coach this tablet slipped from his clothes

and fell on the bed of the railway, and broke in pieces. Many natives in the train and on the platform witnessed the accident and talked freely about it, and thus the news of the discovery of the tablets reached the ears of the Director of Antiquities. He at once telegraphed to the Mudîr of Asyût, and ordered him to arrest and put in prison everyone who was found to be in possession of tablets, and, as we have seen, he himself set out for Upper Egypt to seize all the tablets he could find.[1]

Altogether some 350 tablets were recovered and deciphered. The question immediately arose: "What were cuneiform inscriptions doing in Egypt and where did they come from?" The answer was not hard to find. Those tablets contained top secret correspondence from the files of the Egyptian Foreign Office. They were, in fact, letters written to the king of Egypt by his viceroys in all parts of the empire, pleading for help against invaders and warning of the impending loss of vassal states. Those letters provided the key to our understanding of one of the most critical periods of antiquity. They revealed for the first time valuable information about Babylonia, Canaan, Assyria, Mittani, the Hittites and the Amorites; and they recorded the first mention of the attempted invasion of Palestine by the Hebrews, two centuries or more before Joshua.

A governor in Syria wrote that his city was in danger of invasion and that he had not heard from the king of Egypt for many years. Ebed-Hepa, governor of Jerusalem, wrote frequently to Ikhnaton warning him that unless troops were dispatched soon Palestine would fall to the Habiri. It is not clear whether the name Habiri (Apiru) refers to a Hebrew tribe or not. If so, it would seem that some of the Hebrews were invading Canaan long before Joshua's conquest. Rib-Addi, governor of Byblos in Phoenicia, wrote some fifty letters warning the king of an impending attack upon his land by the Amurru (Amorites) under Aziru.

Along with the more recently discovered documents from Boghazköy, Ras Shamra, and Mari, the Amarna tablets have compelled a rewriting of the history of the ancient Near East. Their discovery drew the attention of the world to Amarna which immediately became one of the major sites for excavation in Egypt. Once again the pioneer was Flinders Petrie who went to

[1] *By Nile and Tigris* (London, John Murray, 1920).

Amarna in 1891. His investigations resulted in the discovery of Ikhnaton's palace and its painted pavements, wall-paintings, statues of Ikhnaton and Nefertiti, houses of the town, the site of the extensive faience and glass industry, and also some additional cuneiform tablets. The palm-leaf capitals of the palace were covered with coloured glazes. "They were," Petrie wrote, "a copy of the favourite cloison work of the Egyptian jewellers, in which minute segments of rich stones were set each in a fitting nest of gold so as to produce a brilliant device, in which every spark of colour was separated from the next by a line of gold. Here the jeweller's design was boldly carried into architecture on a large scale, and high capitals gleamed with gold and gem-like glazes."[1]

Petrie also made a preliminary survey of the entire site of Amarna in the course of which he came upon the boundary stelae. He was joined by Howard Carter who helped in the survey of the town. A search of the palace rubbish heaps revealed hundreds of pieces of imported Aegean pottery, indicating the coeval civilization of Crete and the Aegean islands. At the end of the season Petrie returned to Cairo with 132 cases of objects from the palace, many of which are now in the Ashmolean Museum at Oxford. He covered the pavements for protection and placed them under guard but they were destroyed by a disgruntled native helper. Fragments may now be seen in the Cairo Museum.

THE NEFERTITI BUST

The next important expedition to Amarna was that of the Deutsche-Orient Gesellschaft, a campaign that lasted from 1904 to 1914, and was under the direction of Ludwig Borchardt.[2] The work was concentrated on the excavation of the streets and houses at the eastern end of the city but the most striking find was the studio of the royal sculptor Thutmose, which contained

[1] For a complete report of the expedition with photographs in colour of the palace columns, the painted pavements and statuary, see W. M. Flinders Petrie: *Tell el-Amarna* (London, Methuen, 1894).

[2] See his *Ausgrabungen in Tell el-Amarna* (Berlin, Deutsche-Orient Gesellschaft Mitteilungen, 1911).

the painted limestone bust of Nefertiti.[1] It was on 6th December 1912 that Borchardt came upon the storeroom with its wonderful treasures.

In the magnificent head the sculptor has captured a poignancy and pensiveness of facial expression and an air of grace unexcelled in the history of art. Nefertiti impresses one as being completely modern. The details of this life-sized bust are so unbelievably real that it seems to come alive before one's eyes. It is carved from soft limestone and painted in blue, red, yellow, green, white, black and flesh colour.

It is nothing short of miraculous that this fragile statue should be found practically intact, after having been buried for nearly thirty-three hundred years. It is in perfect condition, except for some slight damage to the head-dress and ears and the absence of one eye. The right eye is made of rock crystal and the pupil of brownish wood. The absence of the left eye has provoked considerable discussion among archaeologists. Had Nefertiti suffered from an ophthalmic ailment, so common in Egypt at that time, and actually lost her left eye? A thorough search in the debris surrounding the bust failed to produce the missing eye, although pieces of the ear were found. The head appears to have been made without the left eye. On the other hand, other busts of the queen done by the same artist show no such defect. It is possible, therefore, that the present head was never completed. Borchardt suggested that since the head was meant to serve only as a studio model, it was thought necessary to insert only one eye.

Another question is posed by the fact that along with the almost perfectly preserved statue of the queen the archaeologists found a shattered statue of her husband. Why was the one destroyed and the other left untouched? After Ikhnaton's death and the removal of the court to Thebes, Nefertiti moved to the northern extremity of Akhetaton. The two busts were probably left by Thutmose on a shelf in his studio. The most logical explanation is that when the reactionaries from Thebes destroyed the city of Akhetaton they threw the king's statue to the floor and broke it into fragments, but had no particular reason for mutilating the

[1] For the history of the bust after its discovery see my *The Heretic Pharaoh* (London, Robert Hale, 1962), pp. 126–8.

statue of the queen. Perhaps it fell to the floor later, when the shelf deteriorated, injuring the ears and head slightly.

The queen wears a blue crown, level at the top, a type of head-dress peculiar to her. The artist has painted a band of gold and semi-precious stones around the crown and a headband of gold. The uraeus or royal serpent has been broken off. Two red ribbons hang from the nape of the neck. The collar of stone and gold is in the form of a double wreath of petals and matches the colour of the head-dress. Stucco and plaster were used to supplement the stone and as a foundation for the colouring.[1] Experts are usually of the opinion that painting a piece of sculpture is not only superfluous but inartistic. In this instance the sculptor may have regarded the colouring as purely secondary as the bust was intended as a studio model rather than a piece for exhibition. Be that as it may, the colouring succeeds in making the figure come alive, emphasizing, as it does, the crown, the collar, and the sensitive mouth and eyes. On the other hand, it is difficult to regard this masterpiece as merely a working model for use in the studio. The very fact that it is painted, along with its delicate modelling, may indicate that it was turned out as a finished piece of work for the queen herself. The sculptor worked directly on the stone with the help of preliminary lines drawn on the surface of the block, chiselling off one thin layer after another around the entire block until the head was completed to the satisfaction of the sculptor. This is known as freehand sculpture as contrasted to the later and modern method by which the portrait sculpture is formed in clay, a plaster cast of which is made and mechanically transferred to the stone or bronze. For the head of Nefertiti the artist undoubtedly had models, masks, and drawings before him. The contemplative observer sees the head not as a part of the whole but as a living and complete figure. It is a composition unlike anything in Egyptian history and that is the noteworthy thing about it. To call it un-Egyptian or decadent is a futile criticism in view of the universality of this figure.

Another peculiarity of the Nefertiti bust is the apparent im-balance between the ponderous head and the slender neck, a

[1] For Borchardt's chemical analysis of the colours and technical details of the sculpture by Richard Jenner see *The Head of Queen Nofrotete* (Ehemals Staatliche Museen, Berlin. Verlag G. Mann. Berlin, 1961).

Removing Naville's dump south of Neb-Hep-Re Temple at Deir el Bahri. (*Courtesy, Metropolitan Museum of Art, New York*)

James Henry Breasted, 1865-1935. (*Courtesy, Radio Times Hulton Picture Library*)

Giovanni Baptista Belzoni, 1778-1823. (*Courtesy, Robbins Portrait Collection*)

Statue of Queen Hatshepsut. (*Courtesy, Metropolitan Museum of Art, New York*)

contrast especially noticeable from the profile view. The massive top section with its forward pressure, starting at the bottom of the neck, would seem to be too heavy for the base. The artist's use of plaster has somewhat reduced the overweight but his experiment in equilibrium remains a startling success. The creator of this masterpiece had obviously passed through the first phase of the Amarna artistic revolution, which was one of exaggerated realism, and had arrived at a synthesis of traditional and "modern" forms.

There remains the final question: In the absence of any identification, can we be sure that this is the portrait of Nefertiti? In the first place, the head-dress indicates that it is a queen in which case there is the possibility that it might be the portrait of Meritaton, the wife of Smenkhkara, co-regent with Ikhnaton, or Ankhsenpaton, wife of Tutankhamon. These two were younger women whereas this is the portrait of an experienced and older person. The assumption that the head is that of Nefertiti is supported by comparison with other likenesses of hers. Family portraits in relief bearing the names of Ikhnaton and Nefertiti show the same prominent chin, long neck, brow, and nose. Such characteristics are in striking contrast also to the well-known features of Queen Tiy. It can be concluded with reasonable certainty therefore that the portrait is that of Nefertiti.

Along with the limestone bust, Borchardt found a brown sandstone head of Nefertiti which is in its own way just as beautiful. In addition to a damaged limestone bust of the king the studio contained about twenty heads and a number of models and masks. Whether these works of art were always kept in Thutmose's studio or had been gathered and stored there when the city was abandoned is not certain.

THE EGYPT EXPLORATION SOCIETY

After the First World War, the Egypt Exploration Society organized a protracted campaign, starting in 1921, under the direction of T. Eric Peet and Leonard Woolley, who devoted the first two years to the further clearing of the town, a project begun by Petrie and continued by the Germans. During this excavation the British discovered the village of the stone cutters and tomb makers. A later campaign, under the supervision of N. de Garis Davies, made a complete study of the paintings, sculptures, and inscriptions of the rock-tombs which line the eastern boundary of Amarna. The tombs unfortunately had been known, so that when it became evident that they contained valuable inscriptions, they were ransacked by natives of the nearby village of et-Till. Even some of the relief work was hacked out and sold. The Davies Expedition, however, succeeded in reproducing most of the wall-paintings and inscriptions before it was too late.[1] Participating in this expedition were F. L. Griffith, F. G. Newton, T. Whittemore, H. Frankfort and J. D. S. Pendlebury.

In 1923 the Society sent another team under the direction of Newton and Griffith. Associated with them were T. Whittemore, S. R. K. Glanville and W. B. Emery. They excavated the centre of the city, including some of the houses of the nobles as well as the North Palace.[2] One of the outstanding finds was the house of Paneshi, ''Chief Servant of the Aton in the Horizon of Aton'' in which was a limestone head of Ikhnaton.

The Society's excavations at Amarna were continued in 1926 by a team composed of Frankfort, Glanville, Davies and his wife.[3] They confined their activities to the northern city where they continued the work begun by Petrie and Carter on the Aton temple. Here they found several sacred bronze vessels and limestone reliefs. In the clearance of the official residence of Paneshy, they discovered two beautiful limestone blocks bearing reliefs of Ikhnaton, Nefertiti, and Meritaton, standing under the rays of the sun-disk, making offerings to Aton. The blocks were part of a sculptured altar in the form of a shrine. Also in the northern city they discovered and cleared the Hall of Foreign Tribute, which contained an elaborate relief of the king and queen receiv-

[1] See Henri Frankfort (ed.): *The Mural Paintings of Tell el-Amarna* (London, Egypt Exploration Society, 1929). This study has value not only as a record of Amarna art but for the light shed by the reliefs on the religious teachings of the king. The Davies publication of the Amarna tombs appeared 1903–08.

[2] See F. G. Newton and F. L. Griffith: *Excavations at el-Amarna: 1923–24;* two articles in the *Journal of Egyptian Archaeology*, Vol. X, Parts III, IV. October 1924.

[3] See H. Frankfort: *Preliminary Report on the Excavations at Tell-Amarna, 1926–27*, article in *Journal of Egyptian Archaeology*, Vol. XIII, Parts III, IV, October 1927.

ing imposts from foreign lands. Perhaps the most beautiful object found by the expedition was the red quartzite head of one of Ikhnaton's daughters. The wall-paintings found by Newton, in the North Palace, are fine examples of the purely secular art of Amarna. They are reproduced by N. de Garis Davies in the invaluable volume, *The Mural Paintings of Tell el-Amarna*. Further excavations of the Society resulted in the clearing of the mansions of the nobles, one of the finest of which was that of the vizier Nakht. These houses were spacious and contained large reception rooms, bedrooms, bathrooms and kitchens. The Amarna style of art is best illustrated in the rock-tombs of Huya, Merire I, Paneshi, and Penthu, which depict intimate scenes in the daily life of the royal household. Altogether twenty-five tombs were excavated at Amarna.[1]

REAPPRAISAL

In recent years there has been a tendency on the part of some Egyptologists to play down the originality and ultimate importance of the Amarna religious reform and Ikhnaton himself. This is, perhaps, a natural reaction to the enthusiastic accounts of earlier scholars and is not without some archaeological confirmation. The findings of such authorities as Pendlebury and Fairman, for instance, indicate that Ikhnaton at the time of his accession to the throne was ten or twelve years older than was formerly supposed; that the body found in the tomb of Queen Tiy was not that of Ikhnaton but Smenkhkara; that Nefertiti was estranged from Ikhnaton and lived with Tutankhamon in the North Palace while the king lived in the Central Palace with Meritaton and Smenkhkara; and that while Tutankhamon, under the influence of Nefertiti, remained faithful to Atonism until his removal to Thebes, Ikhnaton and Smenkhkara tried to effect a compromise with Amonism.[2]

---

[1] See H. Frankfort (ed.): *The Mural Paintings of Tell el-Amarna* (London, Egypt Exploration Society, 1929); James Baikie: *Egyptian Antiquities in the Nile Valley* (New York, Macmillan, 1932), pp. 245–63.

[2] See Leonard Cottrell: *The Lost Pharaohs* (New York, Holt, Rinehart, and Winston, 1961), pp. 231–5; also J. D. S. Pendlebury: *Tell el Amarna* (London, Lovat Dickson and Thompson Ltd., 1935).

Whatever truth may be embodied in this recei main features of the Amarna movement remain i movement we observe the power of an idea that he a brief but pregnant period in the face of priestly tr tary pressure, and popular desires. Ikhnaton himse spired prophet, teaching the doctrine of peace, p gospel of the simple life, and dedicating himself to ii. He anticipated the most advanced form of cosmic theism universal religion, later taught by Wordsworth, Spinoza, and Einstein, a naturalistic, yet spiritual world-view which is more in keeping with the space age than most of the parochial, sectarian systems of our day. His reform may have made little impression on the total civilization of Egypt; but if it was negligible in the history of Egypt, it looms large in the history of humanity.

Chapter Eleven

PAPYRI

Ancient scribes were ingenious in their utilization of natural resources for writing materials: the Chinese wrote on rice-paper and silk; the Burmese, on palm leaves; the Babylonians, on clay; and the Egyptians, on stone. But the Egyptians also wrote on papyrus. Some time before 3000 B.C. an unknown, unsung genius discovered a method by which the fibre of this plant could be converted into a highly serviceable form of paper.[1] Without that the literature of the Egyptians would be meagre indeed. The hieroglyphic inscriptions on stone, found on tomb and temple walls, columns, stelae, and sarcophagi, were for the most part royal annals, matters of state, and magical formula for the king's welfare in the hereafter. Papyrus, on the other hand, being better suited for longer documents and greater speed in writing, became the vehicle for literature as such: fiction, poetry, philosophy, wise sayings, medicine, astronomy, and religion. Inevitably it proved to be more practical than the slow and cumbersome method of chisel and stone. Fortunately, the dry climate and sand-mounds kept the papyri in a better state of preservation than many of the stone monuments, which were subject to the destructive forces both of nature and human nature. Egypt and papyrus are, in fact, synonymous terms for, while papyrus was used in Palestine, Greece, Rome, and Mesopotamia, none exists today which has not come from Egypt. Papyrus became universal and, having been used for almost 4,000 years, provides the clue

[1] παπύρος (Gr.), papyrus (Lat.), papier (Fr.), das Papier (Ger.), paper (Eng.).

to the history of language in the Near East and West, inasmuch as papyri records are found in hieroglyphic, hieratic, Demotic, Coptic, Aramaic, Hebrew, Arabic, Greek, and Latin. By the fourth or fifth century A.D. papyri gave way to parchment and a thousand years later parchment succumbed to paper.

The *Cyperus Papyrus* was a marsh reed that grew in all parts of Egypt, especially in the Delta, and usually attained a height of 8 or 10 feet. Its presence in the north caused it to be adopted as the symbol of Lower Egypt while the lotus became the symbol of Upper Egypt. Both were used in their open and bud form as the architectural motifs of the Egyptian temples. Papyrus sheets were made by cutting the pith or inner fibre into strips which were laid down vertically. Upon these, other strips were laid horizontally. The two layers were then glued together, pressed and rolled, and finally rubbed smooth with stone or bone. The sheet thus made varied in size; it was usually 6 inches in width by 9 inches in height, but at times was much higher. In long documents, sheet was glued to sheet as needed and rolled up in the form of a scroll. When completed, the roll was tied around the middle with a cord which in some cases was sealed with the owner's name. The papyrus book or codex came into use in the first three centuries of the Christian era. This resembled the parchment codex which was made by gluing the hairy sides of two sheep or antelope skins together, making a sheet that could be written upon on both sides. The sheets were then bound in book form—a more practical form than the scroll and which became the forerunner of the modern book.

The horizontal side of the papyrus was used for writing but the vertical side was also written upon when the material was expensive or scarce. The horizontal side is referred to as *recto* and the vertical as *verso*. The scribe used a reed pen, 8 or 10 inches long, made by bruising, and later cutting, the point like a quill pen. This was kept in a palette at one end of which were wells for the various coloured inks. When a scribe was engaged in elaborate work like the Book of the Dead with its polychrome vignettes, the palette had as many as twelve holes for the paints.[1]

---

[1] For complete treatment of papyrus, its manufacture and use, and also for editing and translation of the chief papyri see John A. Wilson's translations in *Ancient Near Eastern Texts Relating to the Old Testament*. Edited by James B.

The Greek papyri of the Ptolemaic and Roman periods are perhaps better known to the general public. These fragments from Oxyrhynchus and the Fayum, containing lost gospels, sayings of Jesus, private letters, copies of Greek and Roman classics, and family papers are most valuable, but it must be realized that they are from a period when dynastic Egypt was a thing of the past. Its dynastic history had long since ended and the country was governed by foreign rulers. The hieroglyphic and hieratic papyri of the Old, Middle, and New Kingdoms are longer, in many instances better preserved, and much more beautiful with their illuminated paintings and elaborate calligraphy. The earliest extant papyrus can be dated at about 3000 B.C. but there is evidence of the use of papyrus as early as 3500 B.C. By the New Empire (1580 B.C.) copies of the Book of the Dead were bought by all who could afford them with the result that today most of our papyri are funerary texts.

ANCIENT THIEVES AND MODERN HUNTERS

Ancient papyrus-hunting went hand in hand with tomb-robbery; in fact, one of the chief purposes of plundering a royal tomb was to recover the magic roll which had served to protect the king or nobleman in the Underworld. Some of the older papyri tell the story of adventurers who spent their lives in papyrus-hunting. This activity persisted from the First Dynasty to our own day.

As with other archaeological discoveries in Egypt, modern

Pritchard (Princeton, Princeton University Press, 1955); Adolf Deismann: *Licht vom Osten* (Tubingen, J. C. B. Mohr, 1923); Hans Lietzmann: *Griechische Papyri* (Bonn, 1910); George Milligan: *Selections from the Greek Papyri* (Cambridge, 1910); F. G. Kenyon: *The Paleography of Greek Papyri* (1899); William Schubart: *Das Alte Agypten und seine Papyrus* (1921); James Baikie: *Egyptian Papyri and Papyrus-Hunting* (London, Religious Tract Society, 1925); Camden M. Cobern: *The New Archaeological Discoveries* (New York, Funk and Wagnalls, 1917); Carl Wessely: *Aus der Welt der Papyri* (1914); E. J. Goodspeed and E. C. Colwell: *A Greek Papyrus Reader* (1935); Adolf Erman: *The Literature of the Ancient Egyptians*. Translated in English from *Die Literatur der Aegypten* by A. M. Blackman (London, Methuen, 1927); James H. Breasted: *Ancient Records of Egypt*, 4 vols. (Chicago, University of Chicago Press, 1906); A. S. Hunt: *Papyri and Papyrology*, Article in *Journal of Egyptian Archaeology*, Vol. I, Part II (April, 1914), pp. 81–92.

papyri-finds have been both accidental and deliberate. The first known papyri in modern times were some Greek and Latin fragments given by Johann Jakob Grynaeus to the Basel library towards the end of the sixteenth century. In the middle of the eighteenth century some charred rolls from a collection of Greek philosophical works were found at Herculaneum. In 1778 some Arabs found forty or fifty rolls in an earthen pot. Not knowing their value they burned practically all of them because they enjoyed the aromatic odour, but one of them was bought by a dealer and brought to Europe where it fell into the hands of Cardinal Stefano Borgia. It was the first papyrus edited and published in Europe and was called the Charta Borgiana Papyrus. The next modern reference to papyri was by Vivant Denon in his account of Napoleon's expedition to Egypt in which he writes of receiving a piece of papyrus that had been taken from a tomb and adds that he was conscience-stricken because of this violation of the sacred mummy. This did not stop him, however, from sharing the spoils of the tomb-robbers, as he confesses: "I was just going to scold those who, in spite of my urgent requests, had violated the integrity of this mummy, when I perceived in his right hand and under his left arm the manuscript of papyrus-roll, which perhaps I should never have seen without this violation: my voice failed me; I blessed the avarice of the Arabs, and above all the chance which had arranged this good luck for me; I did not know what to make of my treasure, so much was I frightened lest I should destroy it; I dared not touch this book, the most ancient book so far known; I neither dared to entrust it to anyone, nor to lay it down anywhere; all the cotton of my bed-quilt seemed to me insufficient to make a soft-enough wrapping for it."

During this period a Frenchman named Sallier had accumulated a number of papyri which when later translated by Champollion turned out to be the historical records of Ramses II and the Hyksos king Apepy.

After the *fellahin* learned of the value of papyri, they engaged in a wholesale ransacking of tombs for a century with untold damage to mummies. Equally unscrupulous was the frantic search of European travellers for *antika*, a fanatical hobby which made them accomplices in the "unbridled pillage of tombs", as Maspero described it.

Unlike the older papyri which were found along with mummies in tombs, their discovery being more or less incidental to other things, papyri from the Graeco-Roman period were found by themselves and only after prolonged search. Papyrus-hunting took on a scientific and specialized character at the end of the nineteenth and early part of the twentieth century. The hunting-grounds were the rubbish heaps of lost towns where practically nothing else of value could be expected. The hunters themselves were not interested in other quarry. Consequently, most of the well-known papyri found in the first half of the twentieth century are the result of deliberately planned work. The circumstances of their discovery are known, whereas the older documents showed up here and there in this or that collection with no known history other than the knowledge that some benefactor had purchased a papyrus from an Egyptian dealer or that a museum had acquired a document from the collection of a wealthy family. Little is known, therefore, of the exact date of writing, origin, and history of the famous Harris Papyri, the Tale of the Two Brothers, The Story of Setna and the Magic Rolls, and the Funerary Papyrus of Ani.[1]

THE GREAT HARRIS PAPYRUS

Papyrus Harris I was part of a group of five rolls found by some *fellahin* at Thebes in 1855. The rolls lay on the floor of a cliff tomb near Der el-Medinah, underneath a pile of mummies. They were sold to A. C. Harris of Alexandria. Papyrus Harris I was purchased from Mr. Harris's daughter by the British Museum.[2] This remarkable document, justifiably named the Great Harris Papyrus in view of its size (133 feet in length and 17 inches in height) as well as its contents, is in an excellent state of preserva-

---

[1] For discussion of the Teachings of Ptah Hotep and Amenemope, papyri not dealt with in this chapter, see my *The Heretic Pharaoh* (London, Robert Hale, 1962), pp. 64–6.

[2] The Harris Papyrus was first published by Birch: *Facsimile of an Egyptian Hieratic Papyrus of the reign of Ramses III, now in the British Museum* (London, 1896). For complete translation with commentary see James H. Breasted: *Ancient Records of Egypt*, Vol. 4, pp. 87–206. For a still more technical treatment see Adolf Erman: *Zur Erklärung des Papyrus Harris* (Sitzungberichte der Konigliche Preussischen Akademie der Wissenschaft, 1903), Vol. XXI, pp. 456–74.

tion. It contains 117 columns of twelve or thirteen lines each and is written in a beautiful hand. Coming from the reign of Ramses III and Ramses IV, it is a biographical account of the deeds and benefactions of the former monarch during his entire reign of thirty-one years. It was compiled at his death by his son probably as a funerary testimony to be used at the judgement seat of Osiris. These good works and gifts are listed in detail as constituting reasonable grounds for the god's favour and with them are prayers for the success of the son's reign. (In the mortuary inscriptions of Seti I similar prayers are found for the welfare of Ramses II.) According to Erman and Breasted, five scribes shared in the writing of the papyrus. The larger part of the document is given to the king's benefactions to the three temples of Karnak, Heliopolis, and Memphis. In addition to these, another section is devoted to other temples and the concluding chapter is a review of the king's military campaigns and domestic administration.

Ramses' gifts to the Karnak temple are an indication of the colossal wealth and strength of the Amon priesthood. It is recorded in this papyrus that Karnak possessed 5,164 divine images and 84,486 statues, statistics that were partially borne out by Legrain's phenomenal excavations.[1] The Amon priesthood possessed 433 temple groves in Egypt, eighty-three ships, forty-six temple workshops, 490,386 cattle, and 1,300 square miles of land—all given by Ramses and his immediate predecessors.

The concluding narrative of the Great Harris Papyrus describes the military events in the life of Ramses III, the last great campaigns in the dynastic history of Egypt, chief of which was the crushing of the attempted invasion of the Libyans from the west and the sea peoples from the north. The document also tells of Ramses' expedition to Punt, his exploration of the Sinai copper mines, and closes with a description of domestic peace and prosperity, an idyllic state of affairs which, needless to say, was greatly exaggerated. The fact is that the latter part of the reign was riddled with corruption and intrigue.

Another section of the Harris group (No. 500), a semi-fictional war-chronicle entitled "How Tahuti took the town of Joppa", dates from the Twentieth Dynasty, but the story relates

[1] See pp. 174–8.

to the period of Thutmose III. Tahuti, a veteran of the Syrian campaigns of Thutmose, here relates how by deception he was able to take his men into the town in large jars and how, when they were released, they overcame all opposition.

THE ADVENTURES OF WENAMON

The haphazard discovery of some of our best papyri is well illustrated in the "Report of Wenamon" which was accidentally found in 1891 by some *fellahin* in the village of El Hibeh in Upper Egypt. In the course of their search for wood to make a fire they unearthed this ancient roll of papyrus. Fortunately they realized that it had some value and sold it to a dealer in antiquities. Ultimately it came into the hands of M. W. Golenischeff who took it to St. Petersburg where he issued the first translation. Later it was translated successively by W. M. Müller, Erman, and Breasted.

Aside from the charm of this document as a literary master-piece, it has importance as a source of information on the relations between Egypt and Syria at the close of the Twentieth Dynasty. It comes from the time of Ramses XII when Hrihor, the High Priest of Amon, was the actual ruler of Thebes while Nesubenebded governed Tanis in the Delta. Hrihor dispatched an official by the name of Wenamon to buy cedar from Lebanon for the construction of a new sacred barge for Amon. The messenger took with him an image of the god as a gift to the prince of Byblos. Upon his return to Thebes, Wenamon made out a full report of his adventurous journey.[1]

Wenamon left Thebes on the sixteenth day of the eleventh month of year twenty-three of Ramses XI. At Tanis he boarded a merchant ship plying the Mediterranean. Arriving at Dor, a petty kingdom of the Thekel and first port of call, he was robbed of the gold and silver he had brought with him to buy the timber. On the voyage from Tyre to Byblos he ran across some of the Thekel from Dor who had his money, as he supposed, and he seized it from them. Upon his arrival at Byblos, Zakar-baal, the prince, refused to see him, since he did not carry the proper credentials as an envoy of the king. Some twenty days later, as

[1] Erman and Breasted are convinced of the authenticity of this report.

he was about to leave, a young nobleman persuaded the prince to receive Wenamon. He had left his credentials with Nesubenebded at Tanis and carried only his image of Amon, which was not calculated to impress the prince very much. At first Wenamon was refused the timber; so he sent to the ruler of Tanis for more money upon receipt of which the prince had the required lumber cut and shipped.

> He said to me: "Behold, if thou art true, where is the writing of Amon, which is in thy hand? Where is the letter of the High Priest of Amon, which is in thy hand?" I said to him: "I gave them to Nesubenebded and Tentamon." Then he was very wroth, and he said to me: "Now, behold, the writing and the letter are not in thy hand! Where is the ship of cedar, which Nesubenebded gave to thee? Where is its Syrian crew? He would not deliver thy business to this ship-captain [——] to have thee killed, that they might cast thee into the sea. From whom would they have sought the god then? And thee, from whom would they have sought thee then?"
>
> Then I was silent in this great hour. He answered and said to me: "On what business hast thou come hither?" I said to him: "I have come after the timber for the great and august barge of Amon-Re, king of gods. Thy father did it, thy grandfather did it, and thou wilt also do it." So spake I to him.
>
> He said to me: "If the ruler of Egypt were the owner of my property, and I were also his servant, he would not send silver and gold, saying: 'Do the command of Amon.' It was not the payment of [tribute] which they exacted of my father. As for me, I am myself neither thy servant nor am I the servant of him that sent thee. If I cry out to the Lebanon, the heavens open, and the hogs lie here on the shore of the sea."

As Wenamon prepared to sail for Egypt the men from whom he had taken the money appeared, intent upon his arrest. Through the prince's good offices, however, he managed to evade the Thekel thieves and set sail. His ship was driven off course by gales and ran aground at Cyprus. The inhospitable Cypriotes were on the point of putting him to death when a native who spoke Egyptian interceded with the queen of Cyprus and Wenamon was saved.

How Wenamon fared in Cyprus and how he returned to Egypt we are not told, for the rest of the report is lost. It is evident from this document that during the Twentieth Dynasty Lebanon and other former provinces were no longer dominated by Egypt and had become independent.

THE STORY OF SINUHE

The tale of Sinuhe is in poetic form and breathes such an air of reality, as Breasted observes, that "it is not to be disregarded as a historical source". This hieratic papyrus from the Middle Kingdom and now in the Berlin Museum, was first published by Lepsius.

The occurrence of the story of Sinuhe in several versions during the Middle and New Kingdoms can only mean that this tale had become a classic, famous not only for its content but perhaps even for its literary form. Sinuhe lived during the reigns of Amenemhet I and his son and co-regent Sesostris I in the Twelfth Dynasty. The author of this biographical sketch does not provide us with a continuous narrative but selects certain episodes which are arbitrarily pieced together.

Sinuhe introduces himself as a "henchman who followed his lord and a servant of the king's harem, waiting on the princess, the greatly praised, the Royal Consort of Sesostris, the Royal Daughter of Amenemhet". The story opens with the announcement of the king's death: "In the year thirty on the ninth day of the third month of Inundation, the god entered his horizon. King Amenemhet flew away to heaven and was united with the sun, and was united with his creator. The two great portals were shut; the courtiers sat with their heads on their knees and the people grieved." At the time of the king's death Prince Sesostris was in the Delta campaigning against the Libyans. Upon receipt of the news, he returned at once to Memphis. Sinuhe, who was with the prince, presumably for political reasons, fled into Syria.

I stole away — — —,
To seek for myself a place of concealment.
I placed myself between two bushes,
To [avoid] the way which they went.
I proceeded up-stream,
Not intending (however) to reach the court;
I thought there was fighting (there).

I arrived at Kedem (*Kdm*);
I spent a year and a half there.
Emuienshi, that sheik of Upper Tenu, brought me forth
Saying to me: "Happy art thou with me,
(For) thou hearest the speech of Egypt."
He said this, (for) he knew my character,
He had heard of my wisdom;
The Egyptians who were there with him, bare witness of me.

"Behold, thou shalt now abide with me;
Good is that which I shall do for thee."
He put me at the head of his children,
He married me to his eldest daughter,
He made me select for myself of his land,
Of the choicest of that which he had,
On his boundary with another land.

After many years, Sesostris, learning of Sinuhe's whereabouts, requested that he return to Egypt:

Horus, Life-of-Births, Two Crown-Goddesses, Life-of-Births, King of Upper and Lower Egypt, Khperkeré, Son of Ré, Sesōstris, that liveth for ever and ever.

A royal decree unto the henchman. Behold, this decree of the King is brought to thee to instruct thee as here followeth: Thou hast traversed the foreign lands and art come forth from Kedemi to Retenu, and land gave thee to land, by the counsel of thine own heart. What hast thou done that aught should be done against thee? Thou didst not curse, that thy speech should be reproved, and thou didst not so speak in the council of the magistrates, that thine utterances should be thwarted. (Only) this thought, it carried away thine heart - - - -. *But* this thine heaven, that is in the palace, yet abideth and prospereth to-day; *she hath her part* in the kingdom of the land, and her children are in the council-chamber. Thou wilt long subsist on the good things which they give thee, thou wilt live on their bounty. Come back to Egypt, that thou mayest see the Residence wherein thou didst grow up, that thou mayest kiss the earth at the Two Great Portals, and mingle with the Chamberlains.

Sinuhe was touched by this decree and made plans to return. He was well received, especially by the queen who "uttered an exceeding loud cry".

I was placed in the house of the king's son, and a bath was therein.

Years were made to pass away from my body, I was shaved, and my hair was combed. A load of dirt was given over to the desert, and the filthy clothes to the Sand-farers. I was clothed in finest linen and anointed with the best oil. I slept on a bed, and gave up the sand to them that be in it. Meals were brought me from the palace, three times and four times a day, over and above that which the royal children gave, without cessation. And so live I, rewarded by the king, until the day of my death cometh.[1]

THE TALE OF THE TWO BROTHERS

The Tale of the Two Brothers is part of the Papyrus d'Orbiney in the British Museum. It was written by a scribe named Enana who lived during the reigns of Merneptah and Seti I. Based on an earlier myth about Anubis (Anpa) and another divinity, Bata, it became in time a popular fairy-tale throughout Egypt.

The opening lines describe the simple peasant life of the two brothers. Bata, the younger, lives with Anpa and his wife and "serves them as a son". He "tended the cattle in the field, ploughed and reaped for him, and did for him all the tasks that are in the field".

The younger brother was a good worker with no equal in the whole land and the strength of a god was in him."

One day when Bata had come back to the house for some seed-corn, Anpa's wife tried to seduce him. Bata refused her attentions. Fearful of what might result, the wife told her husband that Bata had made advances to her. Anpa prepared to kill his younger brother but Bata saw him coming and fled to the other side of a canal. He called to Anpa and explained the true situation. Anpa was chagrined because of the injustice wrought upon his brother but Bata was determined to leave the country and go to the Valley of the Acacia. Anpa returned to the house and "slew his wife, cast her body to the dogs and remained in mourning for his younger brother".

The second part of the story describes the strange adventures of Bata in the Land of the Acacia and is just as allegorical and fantastic as the first part is simple and realistic. When Bata left home he spoke to his brother as follows:

[1] Based on translations of Erman and Breasted.

I shall draw out my heart by art magic (said he), and shall place it on the top of the Acacia; and when my foe shall cut down the Acacia, and my heart falls to the ground, thou shalt come to seek it. Though the search cost thee seven years, do not be discouraged; but when once thou hast found my heart place it in a jug of fresh water; then I shall live again, and shall repay the evil which my foe has done me. Now thou shalt know when aught happens to me, by these signs. The jug of beer which is brought to thee shall foam over, and when thou callest for a cup of wine, it shall be muddy. Verily thou shalt not delay, once these things have happened.

What follows in the Valley of the Acacia is a strange and incomprehensible series of miraculous events which come to a close with Bata turning into a bull and returning to Egypt with his elder brother on his back, after which he becomes king of Egypt. Undoubtedly the allegorical details of the Acacia story were more intelligible to the ancient Egyptians than to us and they resemble elements in the folk-lore of other old cultures.[1]

THE STORY OF THE DOOMED PRINCE

The fictional literature of ancient Egypt more than any other type reveals the unconventional, characteristic ideals of the ordinary man without priestly interpretation, theological interpolation, or official formulae. The Story of the Doomed Prince is one of the world's great fairy-tales. It forms a section of Papyrus Harris 500 and was first brought to light by Georg Ebers. The date of this papyrus is not definitely known but it seems to reflect the spirit of the Eighteenth Dynasty. Many important lines are missing but the lacunae can be supplied by the reader's imagination.

A certain king, who had had no son, rejoices in the birth of an heir. He is told, however, that the boy will die by a crocodile, a serpent, or a dog. The son goes out to seek his fortune and marries the daughter of a Naharin prince. He tells her of the three-fold threat against his life and she suggests that he first kill

[1] For translation of *The Tale of the Two Brothers* see W. M. Flinders Petrie: *Egyptian Tales* (London, Methuen, 1895), Second Series, pp. 36–86; Adolf Erman: *The Literature of the Ancient Egyptians*. Translated into English by A. M. Blackman (London, Methuen, 1927), pp. 150–61.

Model of the estate of a Tell el-Amarna noble.

Dr. A. H. Gardiner shakes hands with the guardian of the tomb of Tutankhamon. (*Courtesy*, *Radio Times Hulton Picture Library*)

Unfinished head of Nefertiti in bronze quartzite.
(Courtesy, Hirmer Verlag, Munich)

the dog who "runs always before you". The prince refuses to kill his faithful companion. They return to Egypt to live in a city where a great crocodile was kept near their house. One day, while the prince is asleep, a serpent approaches him. His wife gives the serpent milk to drink until it is too full to move and then kills it. Later the prince goes hunting with his dog. The dog pursues the quarry to a river bank where the crocodile grabbed the youth and said, "I am thy fate who has been pursuing thee, and . . ."

At this point the papyrus breaks off, leaving the modern reader with the task of finishing in his own mind this fateful tale. If the story does have an ulterior meaning, it would seem to be that the aspect of fate or destiny was by the Eighteenth Dynasty becoming a part of the Egyptian consciousness, whereas formerly life was usually taken in stride with no hint of mystery or foreordination.

FUNERARY PAPYRUS

Nine-tenths of the extant Egyptian literature is religious in character and nine-tenths of this religious literature is devoted to the funerary aspects of religion. The ancient Egyptian was not indifferent to his earthly life by any means but he was deeply concerned for his well-being in the next life. The result of this preoccupation in the hereafter was the Book of the Dead with its various recensions such as the Book of Knowing What is in the Underworld, the Book of the Gates, and the Book of Breathings. The funerary literature is therefore enormous but much of it is repetitious. In view of its paramount importance, one would expect some standardization of the material or some canonized form, but all copies of the Book of the Dead vary in length and, to some extent, content. No two rolls, in fact, have been found with the same selection of texts. The Book of the Dead is really a misnomer, since no such entity ever existed. The length and quality of the ritual text buried with an individual depended on what the family could afford as well as on the conscientiousness of the scribe who did the work, for he knew that once the document was written and put in the coffin, no one else would ever see it. For this reason some copies of the Book of the Dead are less accurate than others. In later times—from the Twenty-first

16

Dynasty onward—the texts were very carelessly written with long omissions.

The oldest form of the Book of the Dead is found in the Pyramid Texts of the first five or six dynasties. These were made only for kings and were inscribed on pyramid walls. The popularization of the cult of Osiris occurred in the Middle Kingdom as seen in the Coffin Texts which were made for all who could afford them. Here there is a greater emphasis on the moral qualifications of the individual as he is judged in the Hall of Osiris. But writing on coffins was an expensive process. Consequently, with the further democratization of the cult of immortality, the Book of the Dead in the New Empire came to be written on papyrus. This meant that all classes could share in the blessings of the hereafter, the quantity and quality of the ritual papyrus depending on the means of the purchaser.

The most famous funerary papyrus is that of Ani. It was purchased for the British Museum by E. A. W. Budge in 1888. Its history is unknown. It is 78 feet in length, 15 inches in height, and contains sixty-six chapters. It is known for its accuracy of writing and for its beautiful vignettes.[1] The judgement scene from the Ani Papyrus is the best known and most frequently reproduced of these illuminations. Ani stands before the judgement seat with his wife behind him. Before them stands the balancing scales, one containing Ani's heart and the other the feather of Truth. Anubis, the Guide of the Underworld, tests the balance. The gods of Destiny, Good Fortune, and Birth stand nearby, while the god Thoth, the scribe, records the result of the weighing. Behind him Ammit, a composite monster, stands ready to devour Ani's heart if it does not balance the feather. Above is the jury of twelve gods who hear the confession of the deceased.

The text of the papyrus contains an invocation, a shorter repudiation of sins, and a longer one, the so-called Negative Confession. Rather than a negative confession this really is a positive testimony on the part of the deceased that he had done no wrongs. Forty-two such assertions were made:

I have not done iniquity. I have not committed robbery with

[1] Another beautiful funerary papyrus is the Hunefer which is also in the British Museum.

violence. I have done violence to no man. I have not committed theft. I have not slain man or woman. I have not made light the bushel. I have not acted deceitfully. I have not purloined the things which belong to God. I have not uttered falsehood. I have not carried away food. I have not uttered evil words. I have attacked no man. I have not killed the beasts which are the property of God. I have not acted deceitfully. I have not laid waste ploughed land. I have never pried into matters. I have not set my mouth in motion against any man. I have not given way to anger concerning myself without a cause. I have not defiled the wife of a man. I have not committed any sin against purity. I have not struck fear into any man. I have not violated sacred times and seasons. I have not been a man of anger. I have not made myself deaf to words of right and truth. I have not stirred up strife. I have made no man to weep. I have not committed acts of impurity or sodomy. I have not eaten my heart. I have abused no man. I have not acted with violence. I have not judged hastily. I have not taken vengeance upon the god. I have not multiplied my speech overmuch. I have not acted with deceit or worked wickedness. I have not cursed the king. I have not fouled water. I have not made haughty my voice. I have not cursed the god. I have not behaved with insolence. I have not sought for distinctions. I have not increased my wealth, except with such things as are my own possessions. I have not thought scorn of the god who is in my city.

It is clear from this recital that the Egyptian wished to be free, or at least claim that he was free, of such social sins as adultery, violence, cruelty, unkindness, and misrepresentation, and to have practised such individual virtues as self-restraint, dignity, integrity, open mind, and good will. Just how sincere this confession was in the mind of the average Egyptian is an open question. It may represent Shakespeare's character who protests too much, a sop to one's conscience, or a mere device to gain entrance to the Elysian fields, used by men who were all too conscious of having committed the very sins which they repudiate! It is thus conceivable that with most people the judgement-seat confession was nothing more than a magic formula, purchased by the individual and placed beside him in the coffin. Just how much moral sensitivity *per se* the Egyptians had is a moot question but the requirements for entrance into the realm of Osiris did produce some ethical standards. However, as in later cultures, ethical ideas tended to turn into commercial transactions and the individual who had the price bought his ticket to heaven regardless of his character.[1]

MEDICAL AND SURGICAL PAPYRI

The medical and surgical papyri go back almost as far as the funerary papyri—and for a good reason. Although the custom of embalming the dead belonged to the realm of religion, it must have had an immediate and direct influence upon medical knowledge. The practice of mummification, in which the viscera were removed and the nature and relative position of the internal organs were observed, gave to the Egyptians a knowledge of anatomy and physiology that no other ancient people had, a knowledge, for that matter, denied to later peoples who either cremated their dead or, for religious reasons, prohibited vivisection and anatomical study.

In spite of their scientific knowledge, however, the Egyptians relied upon magic which permeated every aspect of daily life. In all prescriptions for sickness and injury we find incantations and magic spells along with scientific medical procedures. One could hardly expect such an old civilization to be free from the ideas of demon possession, fetishism, and superstition—phenomena which have persisted down into our own times. The purpose of the magical spells, manual or oral, was to reinforce the actual remedy. Sometimes the two are indistinguishable just as today the mental and spiritual element is always present in the physician-patient relationship. There is, on the other hand, a logical explanation for the mixture of magic and science. In the case of a headache or a wound, for instance, caused by an enemy's sword, cause and effect were obvious and the treatment was a scientific one; but in the case of internal disorders, diagnosis being impossible, the sickness was assigned to demon possession. That was the difference between a headache and a stomach ache.

The reputation of Egyptians for their knowledge of medicine and surgery is not only attested by the reports of Homer, Herodotus, Cyrus, Darius and other ancient writers, but is substantiated by original documents—the medical papyri, which

[1] For moral aspects of the "Confession" see my *The Heretic Pharaoh* (London, Robert Hale, 1962), pp. 62, 63.

constitute the oldest *materia medica* in the world. As was the case with the funerary literature, the medical papyri are recensions of an older book of medicine. The longest and best preserved of these is the Ebers Papyrus. It was found in 1862 and in 1873 was acquired by Georg M. Ebers. It is now in the University of Leipzig. This papyrus dates from the Eighteenth Dynasty but, as previously noted, was a copy of a much earlier general treatise. The roll contains 110 columns which have been broken down into 877 sections. The material consists of recipes and household remedies. Many ailments are merely cited but for others specific drugs are prescribed including instructions for dosage and method of administering the remedy. Two of the remedies from Ebers Papyrus are as follows:

Memorandum on the Use of the Castor Oil Tree
As Found in the Ancient Writings of the Wise Men

When a person rubs its stalk in water and applies it to a head which is diseased, he will immediately become as if he had never been ill.

When a person who suffers from constipation chews a little of its berry along with beer, then the disease will be driven out of the sick one's body.

Also, a woman's hair will increase in growth by using the berries. She crushes them, makes them into one, puts them in oil, and anoints her head therewith.

Furthermore, the oil from its berries is pressed out as an ointment for the use of any person who has the *uba*-abscess-with-stinking-matter. Lo, the evil will fly as though he had suffered nothing! For ten days he anoints himself afresh daily in the morning in order to drive the abscess away.

Remedy to Drive Away Indigestion

Take a casserole, half-filled with water, half with onions. Let it stand for four days. See that it does not become dry. After it has stood moist, beat to a froth one-fourth of the third part of the contents of this vessel, and let him who suffers from the vomiting drink it for four days so that he may become well immediately.[1]

[1] From C. P. Bryan (editor and translator): *Papyrus Ebers* (London, Geoffrey Bles, 1930).

The Edwin Smith Papyrus or Book of Surgery was found with the Ebers Papyrus and is now in the possession of the New York Academy of Medicine. It was first edited and translated by James H. Breasted in an outstanding volume.[1] This papyrus comes from the hand of a seventeenth-century B.C. scribe who copied the general treatise which to him was an archaic document. It is 15 feet in length and its seventeen columns contain forty-eight cases dealing with ailments of all kinds, some of them being remarkably modern in diagnosis and treatment. It displays an anatomical knowledge far in advance of the Middle Ages and mentions over a hundred anatomical terms. It is doubtful if the author understood the nervous system since he used the same term to describe nerves, muscles, arteries, and veins. Just how much was known about blood vessels is unclear. In one passage it would seem that there is a hint of the circulation of the blood but it probably indicates only a knowledge of the connection of the pulse and the beating of the heart: "The beginning of the science of the physician; to know the movement of the heart and to know the heart; there are vessels attached to it for every member of the body." A statement follows that by placing the finger on the body in the region of the heart or on the head or arms the action of the heart will be noticed.

The Edwin Smith Papyrus also exhibits a considerable knowledge of the brain. It speaks of the convolutions of the brain as being like "corrugations which form on molten copper", a rather realistic description. The author explains that "when opening, in a compound fracture of the skull, the membrane or skin enveloping the brain which is rent, breaks open the fluid in the interior of the head"—the earliest known reference in medical history, according to Breasted, to the meningeal membrane. Here also is the first reference in history to the brain as "the centre of nervous control", the surgeon having noticed that injury to the brain disturbed the normal control of the other parts of the body. In this connection the author observes that in the case of a compound comminuted fracture of the skull which displays no visible external contusion, "his eye askew because of

---

[1] *The Edwin Smith Surgical Papyrus* (Chicago, University of Chicago Press, 1930).

it on the side of him having that injury which is in his skull; he walks with a shuffle on that side."

The Smith Papyrus differs from the Ebers and other medical works in that it is not a recipe book but a manual of surgical cases. It is true, however, that where the author prescribes therapeutic treatment following the surgery, the element of magic appears, showing that in ancient Egypt surgery was far ahead of medicine. The cases prescribed for are chiefly contusions, fractures, cuts, and bruises—injuries probably received in the construction of great monuments and temples. The surgeon was dealing with the result of visible causes and his work was therefore outside the realm of magic. The author divides the cases into three groups, distinguishing cases that can be treated from those which are difficult or impossible.

Here also is the first mention of mechanical appliances and aids. These include a lint, made from a vegetable tissue and used for absorption or stoppage of blood, linen swabs, bandages of linen, adhesive tape ("to be applied to the two lips of the gaping wound"), stitching, cauterizing material, and splints of various kinds. A typical example of the procedure of the Edwin Smith manuscript is as follows:

[Case 10] A Gaping Wound at the Top of the Eyebrow.

Examination
If thou examinest a man having a wound in the top of his eyebrow, penetrating to the bone, thou shouldst palpate the wound, and draw together for him his gash with stitching.
Diagnosis
Thou shouldst say concerning him: "One having a wound in his eyebrow. An ailment which I will treat."
Treatment
Now after thou hast stitched it, thou shouldst bind fresh meat upon it the first day. If thou findest that the stitching of his wound is loose, thou shouldst draw it together for him with two strips of plaster, and thou shouldst treat it with grease and honey every day until he recovers.[1]

In addition to the Ebers and Smith Papyri, several other documents are worthy of mention. The *Hearst Papyrus* from the

[1] From J. H. Breasted: *Edwin Smith Surgical Papyrus*, Vol. I, pp. 225–33.

Eighteenth Dynasty was discovered at Deir el-Ballas in Upper Egypt in 1899 and is now at the University of California. It consists of fifteen columns and contains some 250 prescriptions. The material resembles the Ebers Papyrus, both probably having come from a common source. The sixth section of the *Chester Beatty* group (British Museum) contains prescriptions and remedies chiefly for rectal ailments. The *Berlin* and *London* Medical Papyri complete the list of earlier medico-magical treatises. There are also fragments from the Ptolemaic period.

The heritage of the modern world from Egypt in the field of medicine is indeed impressive: the use of drugs and herbs, knowledge of human and comparative anatomy, detection of various diseases, and vivisection.[1]

PETRIE AT GUROB

As we have explained earlier, the great papyri of the Old, Middle, and New Kingdoms were not *discovered* but mysteriously appeared here and there and ultimately found their way to the various museums of the world. The papyri of the Ptolemaic and Roman eras, on the other hand, were found by deliberate search in the rubbish mounds of lost towns. The town dumps of the Fayum and Oxyrhynchus have yielded tens of thousands of papyri thrown there by the inhabitants century after century. This accumulation of waste material has provided for the modern scholar a complete and revealing commentary on the daily life and thought of the common people of that age. The inscriptions of the earlier periods were formal or literary; the papyrus material of Graeco-Roman times was, as a rule, personal and domestic, relating not to public and historical matters but to the intimate details of family life. True, this period also gave up copies of Greek and Roman classics and important theological documents but the chief value of its papyri is the revelation of the life of the average man in Egypt from the fourth century B.C. to the fourth century A.D.

Scientific papyrus-hunting started in 1889 with the excavations

[1] For a summary of the contribution of Egypt to this field see Warren R. Dawson: *Medicine*. Article in *The Legacy of Egypt*; edited by S. R. K. Glanville (Oxford, Clarendon Press, 1942), pp. 179–97.

of Flinders Petrie at Gurob in the Fayum, a town built by Thutmose III and destroyed five hundred years later. The coffins found in the Ptolemaic period were extremely crude but within them Petrie found a most unusual form of mummy-case called "cartonnage", which consisted of layers of damp linen stuck together with paste and covered with stucco. The linen and stucco were pressed while wet into the shape of the body in much the same way that soft clay would be sculptured on a model. The stucco was skilfully moulded and painted with the result that the finished mummy-case had the appearance of a life-like statue from head to feet. In later Ptolemaic times, papyrus was substituted for linen, either glued with the stucco or merely soaked and placed one sheet on top of the other and covered with plaster. The contents of the waste-paper baskets of the neighbourhood were gathered by the embalmer and made into a *papier-maché* covering for the mummy he was preparing for burial. Thus it happened that the cartonnage of a mummy-case would contain the private letters or business papers of one person. In some cases the papyri turned out to be valuable copies of Greek poetry. Naturally, having been glued or soaked together, they were hard to extricate from the mummy and harder still to decipher. Larger pieces of papyri, which had merely been soaked in water and placed on top of each other, were in a much better state of preservation.

Petrie's finds in the cartonnage-coffins at Gurob included copies of Plato's *Phaedo* and Euripides' *Antiope* from the third century B.C. or earlier, antedating all previously known Greek manuscripts by many years. At Hawara in 1889 Petrie found in a lady's coffin a large roll containing most of the second book of the Iliad. The Homer Papyrus, as it was called, was rolled up and served as a head-rest for its owner, "a young and beautiful woman with little ivory teeth and long black silky hair", as Amelia Edwards wrote at the time. The dead woman must have been a Greek person with such scholarly interests that she had her Homer buried with her.[1] Still older was the Greek manuscript of the *Persae* of Timotheus, found in the coffin of a Greek soldier and dating from the fourth century B.C.

At the present time Professor André Bataille, director of the Institute de Papyrologie of the Sorbonne, is engaged in retrieving

[1] The manuscript is in the Bodleian Library at Oxford.

sheets of papyrus from third-century B.C. mummies by spraying
them with hot diluted hydrochloric acid which dissolves the
plaster. The wad of papyrus is then laid on a wire tray over a
tank of steaming water and the sheets are separated by tweezers.
Recently among the receipted bills, accounts, inventories, and
contracts from a town in the Fayum, he came upon a dozen fine
pieces of papyri which, when fitted together, turned out to be
a hitherto unknown play of Menander from the third century B.C.
The play is entitled *The Sicyonian* and consists of 400 clearly
written lines in Greek.

GRENFELL AND HUNT

The richest source for Graeco-Roman papyri, surpassing all
others, was Oxyrhynchus, a town that flourished from the third
century B.C. to the fifth century A.D. and then was unheard of
until the remarkable expeditions of B. P. Grenfell and A. S. Hunt
brought it to the attention of the modern world.[1] Oxyrhynchus,
the modern Behneseh, a few miles south of the Fayum, was the
chief city of the nineteenth nome of Egypt and was named after
the fish which was worshipped in that region. It was also an
important centre of the early Christian monastic movement and
contained a number of strong churches. Grenfell and Hunt,
assisted by D. G. Hogarth, were sent to Egypt by the Egypt
Exploration Society in 1895 with the specific purpose of finding
papyri. Their successful operations at Arsinoe, Tebtunis, and
Oxyrhynchus continued until 1907.[2]

The most spectacular, and from a biblical standpoint, the most
significant find at Oxyrhynchus was the papyrus known as the
Logia or Sayings of Jesus. In January 1897, Grenfell and Hunt
tackled one of the rubbish heaps of the town and on the second
day of their search they picked up a scrap of papyrus, written in
uncial Greek characters, containing the word ΚΑΡΦΟΣ, meaning
"mote". The word had a familiar ring and upon examination the

[1] For history of the Graeco-Roman Branch of the Egypt Exploration Society
see A. S. Hunt: *Twenty-five Years of Papyrology*. Article in *Journal of Egyptian
Archaeology*, Vol. VIII, Parts II, IV. October, 1922, pp. 121–2.
[2] See Bernard P. Grenfell, Arthur S. Hunt and David G. Hogarth: *Fayum
Towns and their Papyri* (London, Egypt Exploration Fund, 1900).

fragment proved to be part of a collection of sayings of Jesus from the early part of the third century. The page measured roughly 6 by 4 inches and contained eight Logia, four of which are new, not being found in the New Testament. The text is as follows:

. . . and then shalt thou see clearly to cast out the mote that is in thy brother's eye.

Jesus saith, Except ye fast to the world, ye shall in no wise find the kingdom of God; and except ye keep the sabbath, ye shall not see the Father.

Jesus saith, I stood in the midst of the world, and in the flesh was I seen of them, and I found all men drunken, and none found I athirst among them, and my soul grieveth over the sons of men, because they are blind in their heart . . .

Jesus saith, Wherever there is one . . . alone, I am with him. Raise the stone and there thou shalt find me, cleave the wood and there I am.

Jesus saith, A prophet is not acceptable in his own country, neither doth a physician work cures upon them that know him.

Jesus saith, A city built upon the top of a high hill, and stablished, can neither fall nor be hid.[1]

Although these sayings resemble in the main the canonical gospels, there is present a certain apocryphal or esoteric element, noticeable especially in Logion III, which is not typical of Jesus' attitude towards Sabbath-day rules. The importance of the fragment lies in the fact that it was the forerunner of many such lost documents which show how widespread and voluminous were the early Christian writings, both canonical and uncanonical.

In 1903 Grenfell and Hunt returned to Oxyrhynchus to find a second and larger sheet containing five additional Logia of Jesus most of which are incomplete. They were written on the *verso* side of a real estate document, indicating that papyrus must have been rather valuable at the time. These sayings have to do mainly with the theme of the Kingdom of Heaven and resemble some of the canonical teachings but on the whole have even a less authentic ring than the first group, if one can speak of authenticity at all in such matters. The strangeness of the thought may indicate

[1] From B. P. Grenfell and A. S. Hunt: ΛΟΓΙΑ ΙΗΣΟΥ; *Sayings of our Lord* (New York, Henry Froude, 1897), pp. 10–15.

a later date—probably towards the end of the third century. Even in the first century the Christian message was being influenced by Gnostic, Docetic, and other thought-forms so that by the third century Christianity had become a thoroughly syncretistic religion containing many foreign elements. Grenfell and Hunt found several other gospel-fragments belonging to the second and third centuries and which resemble the Gospel of the Egyptians, the Gospel of Thomas, and other non-canonical literature.

The rubbish heaps of Oxyrhynchus also yielded many classical texts among which were six speeches of Hyperides, Aristotle's treatise on the Constitution of Athens, the *Hellenica*, a lengthy history of Greece during the years 396 and 395 B.C., Plato's *Symposium*, the *Paeans* of Pindar, fragments of Sappho, the story of Acontius and Cydippe by Callimachus, the Appeal of Appianus before Marcus Aurelius, and a list of Olympic victors for the years 480 to 468 B.C. and 456 to 448 B.C. Such discoveries give us a hint of the high cultural standing of this Hellenized Egyptian city of 2,200 years ago.

From Oxyrhynchus also came a pell-mell of non-literary papyri which provide a vignette of ancient domestic life that no classic or formal documents could possibly contain. How the papyri came to be found in such quantities is explained by Grenfell:

> It was not infrequent to find large quantities of papyri together, especially in three mounds, where the mass was so great that these finds most probably represent part of the local archives thrown away at different periods. It was the custom in Egypt to store up carefully in the government record offices at each town official documents of every kind dealing with the administration and taxation of the country; and to these archives even private individuals used to send letters, contracts, etc., which they wished to keep. After a time, when the records were no longer wanted, a clearance became necessary, and many of the old papyrus rolls were put in baskets or on wicker trays and thrown away as rubbish. In the first of these "archive" mounds, of which the papyri belong to the end of the first and beginning of the second century, we sometimes found not only the contents of a basket all together, but baskets themselves full of papyri. Unfortunately, it was the practice to tear most of the rolls to pieces first, and of the rest many had naturally been broken or crushed in being thrown away, or had been subsequently spoiled by

damp, so that the amount discovered which is likely to be of use, though large in itself, bears but a small proportion to what the whole amount might have been.[1]

The gigantic waste-paper basket that was Oxyrhynchus contained a rich store of raw materials from which we can reconstruct the social history of a provincial town. These casual documents lay bare the intimate life of ordinary people: their business dealings, their family life, their complaints, their private worries, their problems, and attitudes. What makes these glimpses of personal life important is that they were *unimportant*. They are fresh and unstudied utterances never meant for the public eye or posterity. It is this absence of pose, official air, and artificiality that lends authenticity to these fragments and makes them invaluable to the social historian. They enable us, as C. H. Roberts says, "to catch the inhabitants of this ancient world off their guard in their ordinary business and in their private correspondence, to look at government from the point of view of the governed."[2]

In this kaleidoscopic picture of daily life presented by the thousands of documents recovered by Grenfell and Hunt, nothing is more revealing than the private letters, a few of which may be cited. Here is a parent who is withdrawing his son from a school (or apprenticeship) because of his unsatisfactory work:

> You have written to me about little Anastasius, and as I am in your debt, be sure you will be paid in full. Nothing of what has been told you is true except that he is stupid and a child and foolish. He wrote me a letter himself quite in keeping with his looks and empty wits. And since he is a child and stupid, I will fetch him home. I am keeping his letter to show you when I come. Chastise him; for ever since he left his father, he has had no other beatings and he likes getting a few—his back has got accustomed to them and needs its daily dose.

Here is a man preparing for a gay party at his home:

> Demophon to Ptolemaeus, greeting. Make every effort to send me the flute-player Petous with both the Phrygian flutes and the rest; and if any expense is necessary, pay it, and you shall recover it from me. Send me also Zenobius the dancer, with a drum and the

[1] From *Oxyrhynchus and its Papyri*, Egyptian Exploration Fund Report 1896–97.
[2] *The Legacy of Egypt*. Edited by S. R. K. Glanville (Oxford, Clarendon Press, 1942), p. 254.

sacrifice; and let him wear as fine clothes as possible. Get the kid also from Aristion and send it to me; and if you have arrested the slave, deliver him to Semptheus to bring to me. Send me as many cheeses as you can, a new jar, vegetables of all kinds, and some delicacies, if you have any. Good-bye. Put them on board with the guards who will assist in bringing the boat.

A high official at Alexandria writes to Asclepiades, Director of Revenue in the Fayum, giving directions for the entertainment of a Roman senator who is about to visit the district. The letter was carried by another official named Hermias and presented to Horus the scribe of Asclepiades:

Hermias to Horus, greeting. Appended is a copy of the letter to Asclepiades. Take care that action is taken in accordance with it. Good-bye. The 5th year, Xandicus 17, Mecheir 17.

To Asclepiades, Lucius Memmius, a Roman Senator, who occupies a position of great dignity and honour, is making the voyage from Alexandria to the Arsinoite nome to see the sights. Let him be received with the utmost magnificence, and take care that at the proper spots the guest-chambers be prepared, and the landing-stages to them be completed, and that the appointed gifts of hospitality be brought to him at the landing-place, and that the things for the furnishing of the guest-chamber, and customary tid-bits for Petesuchus and the crocodiles, and the necessaries for the view of the Labyrinth, and the offerings and sacrifices, be provided. In short, take the greatest pains in everything, that the visitor may thereby be well satisfied, and display the utmost zeal. . . .

A wife writes of her concern for her husband:

I am constantly sleepless (she writes), filled night and day with the one anxiety for your safety. Only my father's attentions kept my spirit up, and on New Year's Day I assure you that I should have gone to bed fasting but that my father came in and compelled me to eat. I implore you therefore to take care of yourself and not to face the danger without a guard; but just as the strategos here leaves the bulk of the work to the magistrates, you do the same.

Theon, a spoiled boy, writes to his father:

Theon to Theon his father, greeting. You did a fine thing! You have not taken me away along with you to the city! If you refuse to take me along with you to Alexandria, I won't write you a letter, or speak to you, or wish you health. And if you do go to Alexandria, I won't take your hand, or greet you again henceforth. If you refuse to take me, that's what's up! And my mother said to Archelaus, "He upsets me: off with him!" But you did a fine thing! You sent me gifts, great ones, husks!! They deceived us there, on the 12th, when you sailed. Send for me then, I beseech you. If you do not send, I won't eat, I won't drink. There now! I pray for your health. Tubi 18. Deliver to Theon from Theonas his son.

Such is the unconscious revelation of human nature in Graeco-Roman Egypt provided by these and countless other letters.[1]

The other sites of the Grenfell and Hunt excavations were the Fayum towns of Arsinoë, Kom Ushim, Umm et Atl, Kasi el Barnat, Wadfa, Prolemais, and Tebtunis.[2] At the last-mentioned site they found many valuable papyri inside mummified crocodiles. While digging in a crocodile cemetery, a workman, disgusted with finding nothing but crocodiles, smashed one to pieces and found that the creature had been wrapped in a papyri-cartonnage. Many others were stuffed with papyri in the process of mummification. Some of the materials thus found were official documents of the Ptolemaic government!

Before leaving the subject of papyri, mention should be made of a recent find which rivals in importance the Dead Sea Scrolls. This was the discovery in 1945 of some forty-eight hitherto unknown Gnostic documents from the third and fourth centuries of our era near Nag Hammadi in Upper Egypt, an event which has stimulated a new world-wide interest in Gnosticism and, although only a fraction of the thousand pages of papyri have been edited and published to date, it has provoked a considerable discussion on the part of experts.[3] *The Gospel of Truth*, one of the

[1] For a more exhaustive study of letters and other documents from the Ptolemaic period see James Baikie: *Egyptian Papyri and Papyrus Hunting* (London, Religious Tract Society, 1925); Camden M. Cobern: *The New Archaeological Discoveries* (New York, Funk and Wagnalls, 1917).

[2] For official report see their *Fayum Towns and their Papyri* (London, Egypt Exploration Fund, 1900).

[3] For an authoritative treatment of the Nag Hammadi Library see F. L. Cross (ed.): *The Jung Codex* (London, 1955) and H. C. Puech: *Coptic Studies in Honor of W. E. Crum* (Boston, 1950). The first volume of the Coptic Gnostic texts was published by P. Labib (*Coptic Gnostic Papyri in the Coptic Museum at Old Cairo.*

Nag Hammadi texts already edited and translated, has added greatly to our knowledge of Valentinian Gnosticism. This codex was first acquired by a Belgian antiquarian and was purchased by Guilles Quispel for the Jung Institute in Zurich in 1952. It was named the Jung Codex in honour of the famous founder of the Institute.[1]

It will be perceived by this time that our debt to Egypt arises no less from its papyri than from its temples, tombs, and pyramids, as the grandfather of Charles Darwin poetically pointed out as early as 1789, one year after the first papyrus-discovery of modern times was made:

The Greek Papyri

PAPYRA, throned upon the banks of Nile,
Spread her smooth leaf, and waved her silver style.
—The storied pyramid, the laurel'd bust,
The trophied arch had crumbled into dust;
The sacred symbol, and the epic song,
(Unknown the character, forgot the tongue),
With each unconquer'd chief or sainted maid,
Sunk undistinguished in oblivion's shade.
And o'er the scatter'd ruins Genius sigh'd,
And infant Arts but learned to lisp and died.
Till to astonish'd realms PAPYRA taught
To paint in mystic colours Sound and Thought,
With Wisdom's voice to print the page sublime,
And mark in adamant the steps of Time.

Cairo, 1956), one of which is the *Gospel of Thomas* which incidentally contains the sayings of Oxyrhynchus Papyri. Another text included in Labib's edition is *The Gospel According to Thomas* translated into English by A. Guillaumont, H. Ch. Puech, G. Quispel, W. Till, and Yassah Abd al Masih (New York, 1959). In 1930 seven Manichaean documents from the Fayum were recovered. These were written in Coptic.

[1] See Phalor Labib: *Coptic Gnostic Papyri in the Coptic Museum at Old Cairo* (Cairo, 1956); F. L. Cross (ed.): *The Jung Codex* (London, 1955) (containing monographs by W. C. van Umnik, Henri-Charles Puech, and Gilles Quispel) Jean Doresse: *Nouveaux textes gnostiques coptes découvertes en Haute-Égypte*, in *Vigilia Christianae* (Amsterdam, 1949); Michael Malinine, Henri-Charles Puech, and Gilles Quispel: *Evangelium Veritatis* (Zurich, 1956); Hendrik Grobel: *The Gospel of Truth* (New York, 1960).

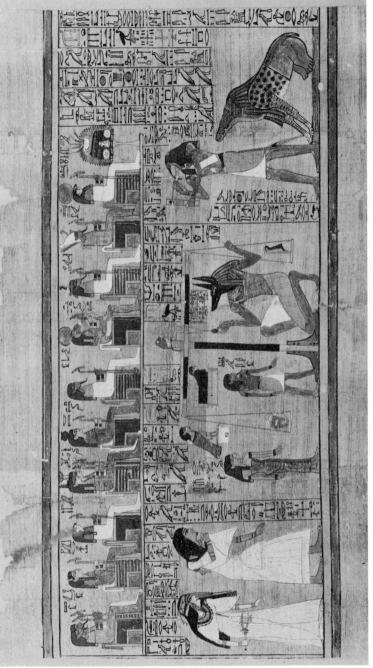

Judgement scene from the Ani Papyrus. (*Courtesy, British Museum*)

Philae: capitals of the West Colonnade submerged. (*Courtesy, Museum of Fine Arts, Boston*)

Chapter Twelve

NUBIA AND THE NEW HIGH DAM

A CULTURAL VICTORY

In the salvage of the priceless monuments and archaeological wealth of Nubia, the cause of international co-operation won a victory unprecedented in the cultural history of man. Ineffective thus far in the prevention of war, the organization of nations at least triumphed in the cause of peace and human values. Confronted with the fact that the erection of the New High Dam meant the disappearance of all the magnificent temples lining the banks of the Nile for three hundred miles and realizing that they could not accomplish the rescue alone, the governments of Egypt and the Sudan in 1959 appealed to UNESCO. Only by mobilizing international support could a project of this magnitude succeed. It became clear to all thinking people that these artistic, religious, and historical treasures, reflecting the ideas and high aspirations of the greatest civilization of antiquity, belong not just to the two countries where the monuments happen to be located but to the world, are a part of the common heritage, and that their disappearance would be a terrible loss to all mankind.

It goes without saying that archaeologists and historians had originally regarded with dismay the proposal to erect the High Dam. As over against the antiquarian there was the humanitarian consideration. The problem of survival for the twenty-seven million people inhabiting the Nile Valley had to be solved either by birth control or water control. The first being an unlikely method as far as the *fellahin* were concerned, the second was, at least in the mind of the government, an absolute necessity. It was a case of drowning the past to save the future, a choice between

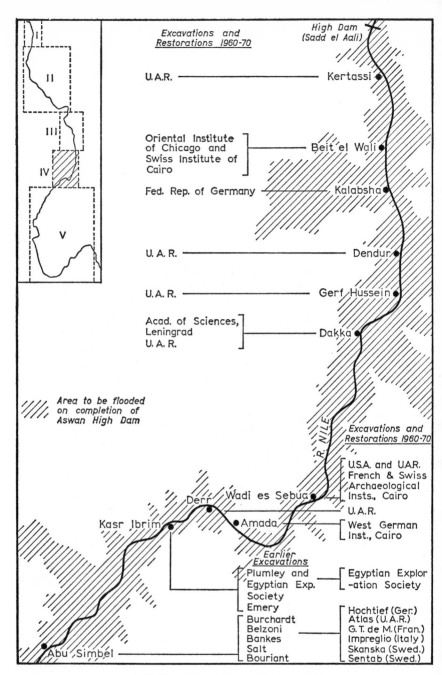

EGYPTIAN EXCAVATIONS Part IV

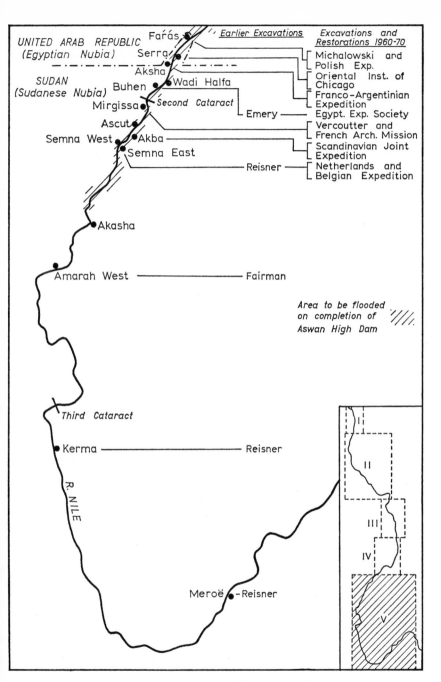

EGYPTIAN EXCAVATIONS Part V

culture and agriculture, between providing for the welfare of modern man or preserving the cultural deposit of ancient man. The New High Dam would be a wall against hunger in a land where ninety-nine per cent of the people live on four per cent of the land, "living like ants on a long stick of candy", the long thin stripe called the Nile. The advisability of birth control remains imperative, however, for with an annual population growth of over three per cent, the New High Dam might hold back the great flood of water but cannot hold back the tide of human beings.

The old dam at Aswan, begun in 1898, was completed in 1902. It was raised successively in 1907–12 and in 1929–34. Sadd el Aali, the New High Dam, will correct all fluctuations in the annual inundation of the river. No longer will the Egyptian fear the twin disasters of too much or not enough water. The reservoir will increase the food production of the country by one-half, some 2,500,000 acres of desert will be brought under cultivation; and Egypt's hydro-electric output will be increased tenfold.

The challenge was accepted when Vittorino Veronese, Director-General of UNESCO, in 1960 invited the member states of the United Nations, as well as public and private institutions, to participate on a new and unparalleled scale in the task of salvaging the monuments of Nubia. Shortly thereafter all archaeological expeditions were assigned and the race against the rising waters was on. Five years later, with the exception of Philae and Abu Simbel, the task had been accomplished by the combined effort of fifty-five nations and the battle of Nubia was won. The barrier across the Nile below Aswan was closed in May 1964 and the waters began to transform the ancient land of Cush into a tremendous lake. Some twenty temples were relocated on higher ground and many untouched areas of Upper Nubia were explored and excavated, revealing hitherto unknown temples, tombs and early Christian churches.

NUBIA: TERRA INCOGNITA

Nubia is the name given to the territory between Aswan and Kerma, or, roughly, between the First and Third Cataracts. Egyptian Nubia is the portion lying north of Wadi Halfa and

Sudanese Nubia is the section to the south. This land, at least the Sudanese part, has never been thoroughly surveyed or explored. Archaeologically speaking it was really an unknown land. Previous excavations supplied invaluable information regarding early man in the upper Nile Valley. In the period just after the Second World War, the two men who were chiefly responsible for Sudanese excavation were the British archaeologists A. J. Arkell and P. L. Shinnie, who built what later became the Sudanese Department of Antiquities. Arkell's work was confined to the Paleolithic Era as a result of which our knowledge of the Stone Age people has increased tremendously. Shinnie's research laid the foundation for the current reconstruction of the history of the three Christian kingdoms which arose from the mission sent from Constantinople in the sixth century.

Aswan, at the First Cataract and head of navigation, was the natural frontier of Egypt, but the desire for gold, ebony, ivory and slaves from the Sudan drove the ancient Egyptians farther and farther up the Nile in spite of transportation difficulties. This operation necessitated forts and trading-posts along the hazardous route. Early in their history the Egyptians came to regard both Lower and Upper Nubia as an integral part of Egypt proper. Theban power and administration were extended to Wadi Halfa at the Second Cataract and beyond. Fortified trading posts were established as far as Kerma, gateway to the land of Cush. These fortifications, strategically located through Nubia, were manned by garrisons of Egyptian and African troops. Somers Clarke, Alan H. Gardiner, and Flinders Petrie made studies of the region and listed fourteen of these fortresses. Buhen, at the Second Cataract and one of the principal military posts, was recently excavated by W. B. Emery for the Egypt Exploration Society.[1] His expedition uncovered the remains of a Middle Kingdom town with brick walls, moats, ramparts, look-out towers and apertures in the walls of the town for bowmen. The centre of the town was a citadel called "The Walls of Amenemhet". A colony of Egyptian officials lived here and administered the lucrative trade with Thebes.

Before the Second World War an expedition of the Egyptian Exploration Society, directed by H. W. Fairman, excavated at

[1] See *Illustrated London News*, September 12, 1959, pp. 249–51.

Amarah West, about 100 miles south of Wadi Halfa. This town, founded during the reign of Seti I, was originally an island in the Nile but sandstorms from the north had filled in the north channel and also covered up its ruins. Fairman found a temple of Ramses II and the governor's palace.

Earlier excavations at Kerma (1913) by G. A. Reisner, head of the Harvard-Boston Museum of Fine Arts expedition, shed much light on the daily life of the Egyptians in this colony as well as the manner of their burials. The tumuli tombs of the Egyptian administrators showed extensive evidence of human sacrifice.[1] The presence of hundreds of bodies indicated that the members of the household were buried along with the governor to accompany him on his homeward journey.

Egyptian control of Nubia and Cush was strong during the Twelfth Dynasty under the Amenemhets and the Senusrets. In addition to the Nubian trade, expeditions were sent to Punt by way of the Red Sea, an enterprise later revived by Queen Hatshepsut. Under Thutmose I sporadic revolts sprang up in Cush and during the reign of Thutmose III Nubia and Cush were subdued and trade flowed freely to Thebes. Egyptian influence was felt as far south as Napata at the Fourth Cataract.

By the Ramesside period the commercial impact of Egypt on Nubia was supplemented by the religious, as excavated temples throughout this region bear witness. The six principal sanctuaries in Nubia were at Beit el Wali, Gerf Hussein, Wadi el-Sebua, Derr, Abu Simbel, and Akasha. These temples, which clung to the west bank of the Nile, facing the rising sun, were further proof of the sustained Egyptianization of Nubia. Each had its hierarchy of priests and representatives at Thebes and each was the nucleus of an Egyptian-African community.

Following the reign of Ramses III, Egypt proper was beset with corruption at home and revolt abroad with the result that Herihor, the viceroy of Nubia, seizing the military and ecclesiastical power, became the first Pharaoh of the Twenty-first Dynasty.[2] Native Egyptian rule, already weakened, collapsed

---

[1] See John A. Wilson: *The Culture of Ancient Egypt* (Chicago: University of Chicago Press, Phoenix Books, 1959), p. 139.

[2] In the opinion of some scholars Herihor was chief priest of Amon at Thebes and did not become Pharaoh of the Twenty-first Dynasty.

under Libyan domination and the seat of power shifted to Upper Nubia and Cush. Napata and Meroë emerged as capitals of the new Kingdom of Cush. The Cushite king Piankhy invaded Egypt as far as the Delta, overcame the Libyans, and returned to Napata as virtual ruler of all Egypt, Nubia and Cush. His conquest of Egypt is recorded on a stele from 731 B.C. in the Amon temple at Jebel Barkal in the Napata region. His successors moved the capital to Thebes and Tanis and repelled the Syrians who were in the ascendancy at the time. Later, however, the Cushite kings lost all of Egypt which was ruled by the Saite princes. Assyrian, Persian, and Greek conquests followed and the weakened domination of Egypt by Cush came to an end. The Cushite kingdom continued with its capital at Napata and Meroë. For a thousand years the kings of Cush were buried in pyramid tombs in the Napata district. By reason of his excavations of the pyramids at Nuri, Reisner was able to determine an approximate chronology of these Pharaohs from the sixth to the fourth century B.C. In a similar expedition at Meroë he established the dates of the reigns from 308 B.C. to A.D. 355.

Ptolemaic Egypt gave way to Roman conquest which crushed Nubia and Cush. In the fourth century Christianity infiltrated Egypt and Ethiopia but it was not until the sixth century that Nubia became Christian. The territory was divided into three Christian kingdoms: Nobatia in Nubia and Kauria and Alwah in Cush. King Silko, presumably ruling over these three kingdoms, was the first Christian monarch. Many churches were built in the 500 years that followed. Most of them were converted temples in which much of the former Egyptian decoration was left alongside of the Christian symbolism. The Ramses temple at Wadi el-Subua was among the first to be re-dedicated as a church in the middle of the sixth century. Later, new churches were built at Faras, capital of Nobatia and Kasr Ibrim, both of which became influential Christian centres. Those that were newly built, being of mud-brick and plaster, were not durable. The administration of the Christian churches was organized along Byzantine lines. Recent excavations have produced evidence that Christian Nubia from the sixth to the twelfth century was a thriving and prosperous country in spite of the Moslem conquest. Architecture and painting also bore a distinct Byzantine character.

Many wall-paintings have been uncovered in these whitewashed Nubian churches. Naturally the change from the Egyptian religion to Christianity was a syncretistic one. The resurrected Osiris now became the resurrected Christ; Isis, suckling the child Horus, was now Mary holding the infant Jesus; the Book of the Dead joined the Gospels; the *ankh*, symbol of life, became the cross; and the Egyptian Therapeutae were reincarnated in the Christian anchorites. In time, however, the Nubian church threw off Egyptian influence and became typically Coptic in worship and doctrine as refugees from Lower Egypt infiltrated the region.

Spectacular finds that have been made at Faras, Meinarti, Serra, Debeira, and Mirgissa and other sites in early Christian Nubia will be described later in this chapter.

THE SACRED ISLE

Philae, "Pearl of Egypt", as Herodotus called it, emerged late in Egyptian history. It was sacred to the worship of Osiris and Isis. Here were the Sacred College and Osiris Sanctuary in which the death and resurrection of the saviour-god was re-enacted. On one of the portals the following words are inscribed:

> The Holy Mound is the sacred golden domain of Osiris and his sister Isis. It was predestined therefore from the beginning (of the world) . . . Let there every day be divine service by the appointed high priest; let there be a libation to Isis, Lady of Philae, when the libation of each day is poured. Let there be no beating of drums or playing of harps or flutes. No man shall ever enter here; no one, great or small, shall tread upon this spot. No one here shall raise his voice during the sacred time of the days when Isis, Lady of Philae, who is enthroned, shall be here to pour the libation each tenth day. Isis, Lady of Philae, will embark for the Sacred Mound on the holy days, in the sacred bark of which the name is . . . (effaced).

Before the first Aswan Dam was built Philae was an island of enchantment, a group of five temples nested in a grove of palm trees and mimosas. To come upon this "vision of Paradise", after crossing the grim desert must have been an unforgettable experience for any traveller. It is still a thing of beauty to one who, in the summer months when the water of the reservoir is low, threads his way in a boat around the giant pylon of the Isis temple or through the graceful papyrus columns of the portico, stopping to admire the wall-reliefs which show the Pharaoh making offerings to the gods. Even in the winter months, when only the flat top of the pylon protrudes above the waters of the lake, there is the mysterious charm of the submerged isle.

Philae is one of three islands belonging to the granite shelf of the First Cataract. The other two, farther to the west, are el-Heseh and Bigeh, the latter also having been connected with the worship of Isis. It was from Philae that the Isiac cult spread throughout the Graeco-Roman world to become fused with the theology and ritual of early Christianity especially in the concept of the death and resurrection of the god.

Philae itself is now about to be resurrected. Of the various proposals for salvaging the island, two were suggested during the construction of the first dam in 1902: raising the temples on the same site or dismantling and rebuilding elsewhere. At that time it was decided to leave the island as it was. The foundations of the buildings were reinforced and the inscriptions systematically recorded. In spite of the successive raisings of the dam in 1907–12 and 1929–34, the temples have put up a brave fight against the erosive effects of the water. The fact of being submerged for nine months each year has proved to be more beneficial than a partial immersion because the stone was thereby cleansed from the damaging effects of salt. It therefore appears that the previous situation would be preferable to a fluctuation of the water level in which case the water would cut into the buildings causing them to crumble and disintegrate. One might say that the monuments of Philae have thus been preserved for the present rescue operation.

The plan submitted by the Netherlands government and approved by the United Arab Republic would isolate the island from the rest of the lake by surrounding it with a series of small dams, thus preserving the temples in their original setting. Three dikes would link the islands together and connect each one to the river bank to form a semicircular protection. The level of the reservoir within this continuous dike would not be affected by the fluctuation of the water between the Aswan Dam and the

New High Dam and the island would be entirely above the water.[1]

By this plan the island will be protected by an artificial lake within a larger artificial lake, a "double-boiler" effect, as it has been described. In 1960 a Dutch team carried out preliminary surveys and made soundings, gathering accurate data on water levels, geology, alignment of the dams, water evaporation, wind velocity, effect of waves and water seepage. The plan calls for a depth in the new Philae lake of 328 feet with a pumping system to keep the level constant in the face of evaporation and seepage. Operations on the Philae project are not scheduled to begin before 1968. This delay is caused by the fact that only when the new dam is completed can the water be contained so as to permit work on dry land. Once more—after 2,000 years—Philae will appear in its original form. The Kiosk of Trajan and the Temple of Isis will again be mirrored in the waters and visitors will stroll through the colonnades and under the palm trees as a famous Egyptian queen once did.

THE FATE OF ABU SIMBEL

The modern traveller upon seeing the façade of Abu Simbel for the first time and vainly searching for a phrase adequate for the occasion might well look to the colourful utterances of previous visitors: John L. Borckhardt in 1813, the first explorer in modern times to explore Abu Simbel; Belzoni in 1817, who cleared the sand from the façade; William Bankes and Henry Salt who in 1819 continued Belzoni's work; Champollion in 1829; and W. H. Yates in 1841; and finally James H. Breasted who in 1906 wrote:

> Not only is it one of the most remarkable buildings in the world, but also a storehouse of numerous historical records. . . . None of our party will ever lose the impressions gained during the weeks spent under the shadow of the marvelous sun-temple. In storm and sunshine, by moonlight and in golden dawn, in twilight and in midnight darkness, the vast colossi of Ramses had looked out across the river with the same impassive gaze and the same inscrutable smile.

[1] For further technical considerations see *The UNESCO Courier*, October 1961, pp. 16–20.

I have turned in my couch in the small hours and discovered the gigantic forms in the starlight, and been filled with gladness to have had the opportunity of doing anything to preserve the surviving records of the age that produced them . . . such matchless works.

Engineers who have been probing the rock walls for internal stresses, boring holes with diamond-tipped drills and surveying the mountain of rock preparatory to the actual salvage operation, ignore the awe-inspiring sight of the temple silhouetted against the moon or pierced by the rising sun; but they do marvel at the genius of their ancient predecessors who performed this marriage of the colossal with the beautiful, and joined science to nature to produce an architectural masterpiece. The engineers of Ramses must have had a profound knowledge of geology, for they knew that the rock was of such a consistency that it could house the interior of the temple and would lend itself to the carving of the façade and friezes. They knew how to use the hard sandstone banks which alternated with the soft layers, using the more compact strata for the temple ceilings and interior halls. They must have known about the porosity of the rock and the solvent powers of the water-table below the escarpment and the possible dissolution of the rock itself. They must have known about weathering and the durability of the stone. Their lives depended on such knowledge for theirs was the task of building a lasting structure which would embody the immortality of the gods and the Pharaoh himself. In doing so, they contrived to fit the designs of the two temples into the natural landscape, thus creating one of the wonders of the ancient world. They knew enough about astronomy so to build that on two days each year one long beam of the rising sun would penetrate the darkness of the long pillared nave to the innermost sanctuary 200 feet within the mountain and rest upon the silent figure of the sun-god Ra-Horakhti.

This mysterious rendezvous with the sun with its interplay of rock and sunlight and the climactic illumination of the gods of the inner sanctuary can hardly have been the result of chance. Such a spectacle, demonstrating the relationship between the construction of the temple and the rising sun with its accompanying ritual, is an intriguing sequence. The temple is not oriented precisely on an east-west axis but faces slightly to the north-east.

As the sun rises above the hills on the east bank of the river, it lights up the frieze of dancing baboons on the top of the temple façade. In Egyptian mythology baboons assisted in the daily birth of the sun-god Ra as he rose from the nocturnal darkness of the underworld. The baboons danced with delight in celebration of this daily victory over darkness and death and saluted Ra as he started his journey over the blue sky. The solar drama continues as moments later the sun strikes the figure of Ra-Horakhti, standing in a niche under the baboon frieze and directly over the entrance to the underground temple. The god's falcon head supports the sun-disk and cobra. On either side of the statue are reliefs showing the Pharaoh offering the supreme gift to the god: the image of *Maat*, the goddess of universal harmony, justice, and truth. Ramses identified himself with this god, the representation of which is indicated in the sceptre (*user*) at the right side of the statue and the figure of *Maat*, thus combining to give the name Usermaat-Ra, the king's second title.

As the sun rises still higher, it bathes the four colossi of Ramses, and finally, as we have observed, twice in the year illuminates the first court, and then follows the corridor, which becomes narrower and narrower, until it shines on the three enthroned deities, Amon, Ramses, and Ra-Horakhti. Ptah, the fourth god, remains in darkness.[1]

The four sitting statues on the temple façade, 67 feet in height, are taller than the Colossi of Memnon at Thebes. Clinging to the legs of the statues are members of the royal family. In the First Court or Hypostyle Hall are eight quadrangular pillars from each of which is carved an Osiride statue of Ramses. Bas-reliefs covering the walls tell the story of Ramses' foreign conquests chief of which was the controversial battle of Kadesh. This historical relief, 58 feet long and 26 feet high, from a military point of view is probably the most detailed and informative in all Egypt. It shows the strategy of the opposing armies who were hidden behind hills and walls, the interrogation of spies, peasants retreating with their cattle to safety, army life in the camp with horses being fed, doctors treating the wounded and soldiers eating. The

[1] For detailed discussion of the astronomical aspects of this curious phenomenon see *Ramses' Mysterious Encounter at Dawn*, Article by Jan K. van der Haagen in *The UNESCO Courier*, October 1962.

inscription is considered outstanding as an example of poetic narrative; and the accompanying illustrations equal the text in beauty and detail. One of the figurative representations shows Ramses in a chariot pursuing the enemy. The reins are tied around his waist in order to leave his hands free to shoot with his bow. Flanking the central corridor are eight rock-hewn chambers used for the storage of treasures. Proceeding through the main hall to the inner sanctuary, we see the figures of the three gods to whom the temple is dedicated and Ramses himself.

Cut into the sandstone rock on the terrace of the temple is the "Marriage Stele", one of the most precious records of the past. It tells of the marriage of Ramses II to the daughter of the king of the Hittites. Copies of this inscription were sent by Ramses to be immortalized on the walls of other Egyptian temples. Although damaged to some extent by erosion, the Abu Simbel inscription is by far the most complete and best preserved. It was first studied by Lepsius in 1843 and again at the end of the nineteenth century by the French Egyptologist, E. Bouriant. In connection with the present operation at Abu Simbel, UNESCO scholars have spent many months copying the stele by night with the aid of electric reflectors. The background for the text of the inscription was Ramses' war with the Hittites, which was probably not so overwhelmingly successful as some of his records claim. A peace treaty was drawn up in 1269 B.C. between Ramses and Muwattali, the Hittite king. Later, in order to cement better relations between the two countries the diplomatic marriage was arranged.[1]

Not far from the temple of Ramses and separated by a sandy gully is the temple of Queen Nefertari. Its façade, 88 feet wide and 39 feet high, is ornamented by six colossal statues, each 33 feet in height. They are in two groups, one on each side of the portal, and in each group the queen stands between figures of the Pharaoh. At their feet are their children. The inner court contains painted reliefs of the king and queen. From this hall a corridor leads to the sanctuary. On one of the buttresses of the

[1] For the latest translation of the text see Jaroslav Cerny: *The Sun was a Witness at Pharaoh's Marriage*, an article in *The UNESCO Courier*, February 1960, p. 33. The marriage, it seems, took place on a cloudy day but on the appearance of the Pharaoh the sun came through the clouds to be a witness to the union.

façade is the beautifully carved hieroglyph: "Ramses, strong in Truth, beloved of Amon, made this divine abode for his royal wife, Nefertari, whom he loves."

Now, with the spotlight of fate focused on Abu Simbel, twentieth-century engineers face the task of matching the stupendous technical achievement of their ancient forebears in this most challenging salvage project of modern times. Several plans were suggested for rescuing the temples from the rising waters. One plan, submitted by a French firm, called for a rock-filled dam which would enclose the two temples. This would provide a space in front of the temples from which to view them, but the dam, being higher than the façade, would destroy the original design of the structure in relation to the rising sun as well as preventing a view from the Nile. Other objections were the prohibitive cost and the problem of seepage.

The Italian plan, which was favoured for some time by UNESCO and the government of the United Arab Republic, proposed to lift the temples bodily 206 feet by means of hydraulic jacks. This meant cutting the temples away from the mountain and encasing them in concrete boxes. They would then be raised so that they would bear the same relation to the river but on an elevation just above the level of the new reservoir. The two temples would be lifted separately and would be raised one-sixth of an inch at a time by 300 jacks, each one with a thousand-ton lift. With each foot, concrete blocks would be inserted to bear the weight evenly. The technical complications connected with such a plan became obvious and it was abandoned.

The government of the United Arab Republic finally accepted the Swedish plan according to which the temples were cut into blocks of no more than thirty tons each in weight and then raised to the top of the cliff where they were reassembled. The re-erected temples, elevated 64 metres and placed 180 metres farther inland, now have the same orientation and the surrounding area has been landscaped so as to present the same appearance which the whole site originally had. The operation called the International Joint Venture, was entrusted to the German firm of Hochtief A.G. in association with Atlas (UAR), Grands Travaux de Marseille (France), Impreglio (Italy), Skanska (Sweden) and Sentab (Sweden). The contract was signed on 16th November

1963 and the work began immediately. The cost of the project was estimated at approximately $37 million.

First of all the temples had to be protected from the rising waters of the Nile by a cofferdam surrounding the whole site. The most delicate operation of all was the cutting of the blocks and their transportation to a safe place for temporary storage. Because the sandstone of Abu Simbel is brittle and lacks the cohesiveness the stone blocks as they were cut were strengthened by the injection of chemical agents. The façades of the temples were protected by sloping sand-fills which provided access to the portrait statues and protected the façades as the cuttings were made. The next step was the excavation of the rock above and behind the temples, thus freeing the buildings and making it possible to dismantle the roofs and walls of the temple rooms. The excavation was carried out by means of compressed-air drills, pneumatic hammers and rock chisels. Meanwhile a scaffolding was erected in all the temple-rooms to support the ceilings and walls.

The Abu Simbel project, expected to be finished by 1970, was not without its hindrances. Aside from the hazardous task of removing the bas-relief and statues without injury, there was the difficulty of transporting construction material from Europe to such a remote spot. Climatic conditions were particularly unfavourable to foreign personnel. The staff numbered fifty foreign and forty Egyptian technicians and some 800 labourers. While most of the workers knew little about the history and cultural value of the temples before arriving at Abu Simbel, now that they were involved in the salvage of these monuments of art they were keenly interested in its successful accomplishment. Early in the morning of 18th October 1966, the blazing Egyptian sun rose over the desert; its first rays penetrated deep into the inner sanctuary of the temple and came to rest on the figure of the god just as Ramses' engineers had planned it 3200 years ago. The race against the rising waters had been won and the four colossal figures sat together in their new home.

EGYPTIAN NUBIA

Perhaps the building of the New High Dam was an archaeological blessing in disguise, for it has turned the attention of the world to this almost forgotten land and the secrets it holds. The searchers discovered not only treasures of art but new light on the buried pages of history and have unearthed new traces of pre-historic man in the Sudan. As an added incentive to the partici-pating institutions the governments of the United Arab Republic and the Sudan arranged to give all expeditions fifty per cent of the excavation finds in Nubia. In addition, the strict laws govern-ing foreign concessions enacted by the Egyptian government after the First World War were generously modified. The government also agreed to offer as grants-in-return to contributing countries five Pharaonic temples and many ancient treasures. Among the latter are the famous head of Ikhnaton from the Karnak temple, a well-known Osiriac statue of Thutmose III, a sandstone statue of an Egyptian scribe from Karnak, and other monuments of the Eighteenth Dynasty and earlier.

The UAR government designated four sites as the new homes for the dismantled temples of Egyptian Nubia. The temples of Kalabsha, Kertassi and Beit-el-Wali were taken to a site near Aswan; those from Sebua and Dakka to Wadi es Sebua; the Amada temple and the tomb of Pennut to a higher level near Amada; and the chapel of Jebel Shams and the rock temple of Abu Oda will join the temples of Ramses II and Nefertari on the hill above Abu Simbel. In Sudanese Nubia a park was created near the Khartoum Museum to accommodate the temples of Aksha, Semna-West and Semna-East.

The first important excavation site, as we survey the area from north to south, was Beit-el-Wali, the joint concession of the Oriental Institute of Chicago and the Swiss Institute of Cairo with Dr. Keith C. Seele and Dr. Herbert Ricke as co-directors and Labib Habachi, formerly of the Egyptian Antiquities Service, as chief archaeological consultant. Beit-el-Wali was the site of a small Ramesside rock-hewn temple, one of twenty-three in Nubia marked for dismantling. It was cut out of the face of the cliff on the west bank of the river. The task of the expedition was to cut the temple away from the rocky cliff and place it on a higher elevation near Aswan. The Beit-el-Wali temple is noted for its reliefs which describe Ramses' Asian and Nubian campaigns. Part of the value of these polychrome reliefs lies in their portrayal in great detail of ancient life in Nubia.

North Cemetery at Meroë, capital of the Cushite kingdom. (*Courtesy, Museum of Fine Arts, Boston*)

Uncovering the top of a coloured fresco in the Christian church discovered at Faras. Polish expedition. (*Courtesy, Unesco, Paris*)

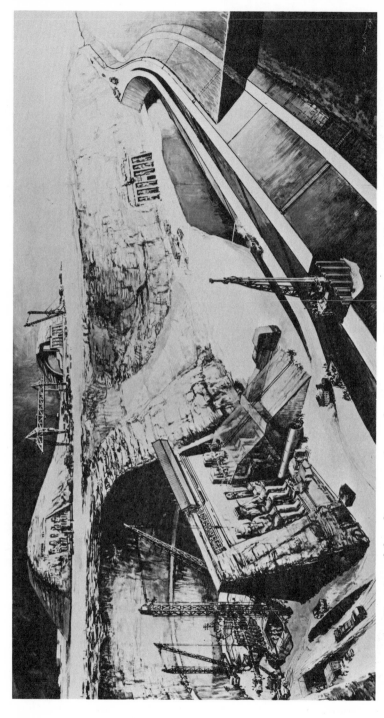

Drawing of the salvage operation under way at Abu Simbel in 1964. (*Courtesy, Unesco, Paris*)

A few miles south of Beit-el-Wali is Kalabsha, known as the "Luxor of Nubia" and seat of the largest and best-preserved, free-standing temple in Nubia. This temple, a fine example of Graeco-Roman architecture, was erected in the Ptolemaic period (332–30 B.C.) and was dedicated to Mandulis, the Nubian sun-god, and is almost as large as the Notre Dame of Paris. The reliefs, which have to do with the worship of Mandulis, were never finished. One inscription, added in A.D. 249 and written in Greek, orders all swineherds to keep their pigs out of the sanctuary! Paintings of biblical scenes show that the building was taken over by the Christians and used as a church. The temple consists of a massive pylon, an open peristyle court, a hall of pillars, and an inner sanctuary. An outer wall encloses the entire sacred area. The temple was dismantled in 1962 and in the following three years was rebuilt on the west bank of the Nile thirty kilometres to the north. The project was conducted by the Federal Republic of West Germany. The task of dismantling, transporting, and reconstructing the temple became a giant jigsaw puzzle. Some 1,600 blocks of sandstone, some of which weigh 20 tons, had to be lifted and placed on boats to be carried to the new site near Aswan where they were marked and stored. Twelve thousand cubic metres of rock were removed by dynamite to prepare the new building site. This was the first time in history that a building of such size has been taken apart stone by stone and put together again on another site. The operation revealed to the engineers the technical problems faced by the ancient Egyptian architects and builders. Ceilings and pillars had collapsed and required careful restoration and reliefs were protected from further damage. Today the temple stands on its new site ready for visitors who will see it almost as it was 2,000 years ago.

The temple of Dakka, like Philae and Kalabsha, was submerged for eight months of the year with only the tops of the pylons visible. It is a Graeco-Roman sanctuary, built in the third century B.C. and dedicated to Thoth, god of wisdom and writing. The low reliefs are in a perfect state of preservation. The Academy of Sciences of Leningrad is responsible for the transfer of the temple to a spot near Wadi es Sebua, a little farther to the south. Archaeologists had for many years believed that a temple of Horus from the fifteenth century B.C. existed in the same region but no part of it had ever been seen. In 1963 when the partially submerged Dakka avenue of sphinxes was being dismantled, to the amazement of the excavators the missing temple appeared beneath the avenue itself. As the workers eagerly dug into the sand there came into view a temple that had been buried for 3,500 years. It had been built by Thutmose III to the god Horus. The temple of Sebua, like that of Dakka, was approached by an avenue of sphinxes which for nine months each year were covered up to their crowns by the Nile water. When Ramses II built el Sebua, he listed the names of his children, numbering more than one hundred, on the walls. The inner court contains a wealth of low and incised reliefs. Christian frescoes painted over old reliefs indicate the conversion of the temple into a Christian church. In one instance the peeling plaster produces a palimpsest which shows Ramses offering flowers to Saint Peter! Contributions from the United States and the United Arab Republic made possible the dismantling and removal of the Sebua temple in 1964. In the previous year another new temple emerged from the sand just south of Wadi es Sebua. It turned out to be one of the larger temples of ancient Egypt. Built during the reign of Amenhotep III (1411–1375 B.C.) it had an architectural style that anticipated the Abu Simbel temples. Under the altar the archaeologists found an object which served as a theological symbol of ancient Egyptian cosmology. It was a representation of the egg of fertility which, according to the sacred texts, was placed on the primeval hill of creation. Another important discovery at Wadi es Sebua was that of a Coptic vase which apparently was used in connection with the conversion of the temple of Sebua into a Christian church.

Thirty-five miles north of Abu Simbel the Nile traveller suddenly comes upon a gigantic promontory 200 feet high jutting out into the river. This massive cliff, towering over its surroundings like the Rock of Gibraltar, is called Kasr Ibrim and was an ancient fortress. The Egypt Exploration Society of Great Britain sent an expedition to this citadel in 1961 and in the ensuing five years found it to be an archaeological gold mine with a continuous history from 1570 B.C. to A.D. 1812 when it was abandoned. The 1963–64 expedition under the direction of

J. M. Plumley discovered the remains of a magnificent church which contained the untouched tomb of a fourteenth-century Christian bishop. Wrapped in his clothes were two scrolls each 16 feet long. One of the scrolls, in Coptic, was the official pronouncement of the bishop's consecration and appointment to the See of Faras and Kasr Ibrim. The other was a translation of the same document in Arabic. Professor Plumley dated the scrolls at A.D. 1372. Their importance is that they show that Christianity, rather than being wiped out by Islam in the twelfth century, as it had formerly been thought, existed in the fourteenth and probably early fifteenth century. The 1964–65 season resulted in equally important finds. Underneath a Christian house the excavators found an earthenware pot containing nine leather scrolls written in Old Nubian as well as manuscript fragments in Greek, Coptic, Old Nubian, and Arabic.

The Kasr Ibrim excavations by the Egypt Exploration Society are also important because of the light they have shed upon the pre-Christian peoples of Nubia: the ancient Egyptians, and the Meroites. The work of Professor Walter B. Emery in the cemeteries of this site has greatly increased our knowledge of the X-group people who lived at Kasr Ibrim until the sixth century of the Christian era.

One of the most spectacular finds in the Nubian campaign was a Christian church of the seventh century, discovered at Faras in the Sudan by the Polish expedition under Professor C. Michalowski. This is the largest church ever found in Nubia. On the interior walls were found 169 brilliantly coloured frescoes along with inscriptions in Greek, Coptic, and old Nubian. The paintings are as fresh and vivid as the day they were executed. One of them shows the archangel Michael protecting Shadrach, Meshach, and Abednego from the fiery furnace. Another, measuring 7 by 4 metres, pictured the Nativity. Others include scenes from both the Old and New Testament, paintings of the Virgin and apostles, and a series of twenty-seven portraits of bishops who were installed at Faras. At the end of this enormous cathedral Michalowski found the tomb of Bishop Johannes, the probable founder who died in 606. Beneath the church were the remains of a temple built by Thutmose III. The basilica was abandoned in the twelfth century when Nubia became Moslem. It was built of stone and fired brick, the stones having been taken from the temples of Thutmose III and Ramses II.

Perhaps the greatest thrill of the Polish expedition was the discovery that the removal of the frescoes revealed others underneath and in some cases a third layer of paintings. To free the frescoes from the sand, remove from the wall, separate one layer of paintings from another and prepare for transportation required extreme patience and skill. First the fresco was cleaned and sprayed with a protective coating; next, tissue paper impregnated with beeswax was applied to the surface; then, a veil of muslin was spread over the tissue and hot beeswax was ironed on to it. When the fresco was dry and stiff it was pried loose from the wall with delicate instruments. After it was detached from the wall, it was attached to a wooden frame and pulled on to a thicker packing frame for transporting. Of the 169 frescoes fifty-two were given to Poland by the government of the Sudan and the rest were sent to Khartoum. Polish specialists at Warsaw and Khartoum examined the paintings to discover, if possible, the secret of the seventh-century artists who did such brilliant work. It was clear at the outset that the Nubian painters were influenced by Byzantine art but had an unmistakable style of their own.

A few miles south of Faras the Oriental Institute of Chicago expedition of 1962 at Serra cleared another fort and found inside the fortifications the remains of early Christian buildings. At Debeira the Scandinavian Joint Expedition found the tomb of Prince Amenemhet of the sixteenth century B.C. A vertical shaft 22 feet deep led to a 40-foot horizontal passage which in turn ended at the burial chamber. This was empty, but vases, canopic jars and other objects indicated that it had once been a rich tomb. In the tomb-chapel Professor Save-Söderbergh, the director of the expedition, found a magnificent grey granite stele containing names and titles of Prince Amenemhet. The titles bear witness to the complete Egyptianization of Nubia by 1500 B.C.

SUDANESE NUBIA

The first important site in Sudanese Nubia is Buhen, the seat of a temple built by Queen Hatshepsut and later enlarged by Thutmose III. The unusual feature of this temple is the colonnade which has alternating square pillars and round columns. The inner courts are decorated with polychrome reliefs and many of the paintings have retained their original colours. Buhen was also a Middle Kingdom fortress and commercial centre. The fortress was discovered in 1958 by Walter B. Emery who has conducted two expeditions for the Egypt Exploration Society at this site. His excavations threw much light on the nature of the pharaonic military installations of the Middle Kingdom. Buhen was one of a series of strongholds erected to defend the strategic area of the Second Cataract which divided Upper and Lower Nubia. Partially destroyed in the seventeenth century B.C., it was rebuilt and strengthened in 1570 B.C. An interesting feature of Emery's excavation was the discovery of the skeleton of a horse of the Middle Kingdom, indicating that the horse was used in Nubia earlier than previously thought. It is possible that the Nubians had acquired horses from Arabia and used them before the Egyptians. The remains of the fortress at Buhen having been made of mud-brick, could not be saved, but the temple, one of the finest in Sudanese Nubia, was dismantled and reconstructed at Khartoum in 1963. Buhen was also an industrial town containing blast furnaces for the melting of copper. In 1962 Emery found mortars, stone hammers, and crucibles with pieces of copper that had dropped to the ground. Not the least of his finds at Buhen were pieces of inscribed pottery and clay sealings which bore the names of Fourth- and Fifth-dynasty kings. A trench cut across the whole town site contained mud-bricks which may date from the First Dynasty. An expedition at a cemetery twenty miles from Buhen also uncovered sealings of the First Dynasty. It would seem from these finds that Egypt had dealings with Nubia several centuries earlier than is usually believed.

One of the most noteworthy expeditions in Sudanese Nubia was that of Mirgissa where the French Archaeological Mission under Professor Jean J. Vercoutter has excavated the Middle Kingdom fortress (*c.* 2000 B.C.), situated on a hill overlooking the Second Cataract. In front of the fortress on the plain, the French found the ruins of a town of the same period with walls 30 feet high and intact houses with stairs and roofs. Nearby was a slipway used by Nile boatmen in the low-water season when the rapids were impossible to cross. The boats were dragged over wooden poles superimposed upon the mud path. These have disintegrated but their indentations and the marks made by the boats remain, as does a footprint in the dried mud made nearly four thousand years ago by one of the last sailors to pull a boat along the roadway.[1] The desert-highway for ships was made by laying down a layer of Nile silt on the sands, after which wooden poles were placed across the road in the manner of railroad ties. Middle Kingdom Egyptians also transported huge granite statues over such roads but without using the poles. Colossi were hauled on sledges, a task made comparatively easy by pouring water on the silt ahead of the sledge, thus providing a slippery surface.[2] The discovery of the slipway at Mirgissa in 1964 confirms the conjecture that the ancient Egyptians travelled up and down the Nile throughout the year.

Other finds made by the French expedition at Mirgissa included over 3,000 execration texts (names of enemy tribes), an unplundered cemetery containing many pieces of pottery and funerary objects and a royal cemetery with untouched tombs.

The Scandinavian Joint Expedition and the expeditions of the Museum of New Mexico and the University of Colorado have extended our knowledge of Nubian prehistory and paleology. At Akba the Scandinavian Expedition found some 3,000 groups of pictographs which had been carved on the huge granite boulders of the desolate valley around 8000 B.C. Pictured on the rocks were giraffes, elephants, hippopotami, and several extinct African animals. Evidence was produced by the Museum of New Mexico excavators that the Nile is less than 50,000 years old and that before it had carved out its present course, a number of large rivers had flowed through the same region. Along the banks of these streams, extending twenty miles into the desert, prehistoric men lived and made tools. It was found that the annual flood of the Nile 10,000 years ago was probably three times the width of

[1] Centuries later the Greeks employed the same idea in dragging ships across the Isthmus of Corinth.

[2] The blocks of limestone used for the construction of the pyramids of Lahun and Giza were rolled over such a mud track reinforced by wooden rollers.

the present-day overflow. By 3500 B.C. the decreased rainfall in Africa had resulted in the present narrow Nile Valley.

EXODUS

In our preoccupation with the archaeological campaign in this vast open-air museum of Nubia, we are apt to overlook the fact that before and during the history-making excavations, a mass exodus of people was being made and the villages that formerly dotted the banks of the Nile had turned back into the desert. The Nubian mud-brick houses, already disintegrating, would soon be part of the Nile silt. Mosques, cemeteries, and fruit groves would soon be lost to view.

The exodus for 100,000 Nubians in Egypt began in 1963. For the northern Nubians, at least the men, the crisis was not a new one, for they had to re-settle in 1912 and 1933 when the Aswan Dam was heightened. Many of the men in Egyptian Nubia had migrated to Cairo and other northern cities to find jobs as cooks, waiters, servants, drivers, mechanics, and guides. Those remaining simply escaped the rising waters of the Nile by moving their huts farther up the cliffs. But now the women and children and the older folk had to leave their homeland and put down their roots elsewhere. The government established a community for the displaced at Kom Ombo forty miles north of Aswan where 25,000 houses, 138 stores, thirty-three mosques, and thirty-six schools were erected. There the Nubians began their new life. For the women the change, physically speaking, was a welcome one. Stone houses and concrete floors are better than adobe and mud. And there are schools, clinics, playgrounds, and movies. The adjustment was not easy but there were reminders of their former life. New villages were given the names of some forty old towns of Nubia. The new homes, although more modern, are more crowded since the resettlement area is only one-tenth the size of their former land. Their economic condition improved as they engaged in sugar-cane farming. Some of these people may one day return to Nubia, for the desert on both sides of the new reservoir will soon be made arable by the overflowing water, thus permitting new settlements to arise.

The Sudanese Nubians were removed to the Atbara River

beyond the Fourth Cataract and to Khashm Girba near the Ethiopian frontier. By the summer of 1965 the resettlement was completed. Life for the Nubians became much more prosperous with better houses, more land, and opportunity for work in the cotton and wheat fields.

So Nubia, like some lost continent in the Atlantic Ocean, is lost to view. One of the cradles of civilization, Stone Age gateway to the interior of Africa, land of the cataracts, early source of gold, ivory, and ebony, seat of the ancient kingdoms of Nabata and Meroë, scene of early Christian churches and later Moslem mosques, battleground of Kitchener and Gordon—Nubia has vanished from the earth. But not from the memory of man, for the records of its culture will remain, thanks to the archaeologist, and its influence on civilization will live as long as man survives.

GLOSSARY

ANKH: the sign for life, worn by the living to prolong life and by the dead to renew life, is one of the most common hieroglyphic symbols.

BA: The immaterial element or soul of the deceased represented by a human-headed bird which returns to the body in the hereafter.

CANOPIC JARS: Vessels, usually of alabaster, in which the Egyptians preserved the viscera of the deceased in the tomb with the mummy.

CARBON-14 DATING: A method of age-determination by examining the amount of carbon-14 left in organic matter. The disintegration of this unstable element proceeds at a known definite rate; thus the approximate date of any sample of organic matter can be ascertained.

CARTONNAGE: A form of mummy-case, consisting of layers of damp linen stuck together with paste and covered with stucco and then painted. Usually found in the Fayum. In later Ptolemaic times, papyrus was substituted for linen.

CARTOUCHE: The use of this symbol which encircled a royal name was aimed at the preservation of the deceased in perpetuity or as long as the solar disk continued to revolve in the sky. The cartouche was an adaptation of the emblem of the sun on the horizon.

CENOTAPH: An empty tomb of a king who is buried elsewhere.

CLERESTORY: The part of a temple or church which rises above the outer walls and contains windows or openings which light the interior.

COLOPHON: An inscription placed at the end of a manuscript or codex, indicating the scribe's identity.

COLOSSI: Statues of heroic size carved out of sandstone, limestone or granite. The largest and best known were sculptured for Amenhotep III and Ramses II.

COLUMNS: Round, faceted or fluted pillars used as supports for ceilings in temples and made from stone. The capital and shaft took their form from a plant. The varieties of columns were as follows: the palmiform (circular shaft, capital of palm-leaf shape); lotiform (ribbed shaft, capital in the form of a closed or open lotus-bud); papyriform (ribbed shaft and capital closed or open in form of papyrus plant); also composite forms such as papyrus-lotus columns at Karnak. There were twenty-seven kinds of composite columns.

CROOK: From predynastic days the crook was used as a royal sceptre and symbol of authority.

DJED-PILLAR: Hieroglyphic symbol or amulet signifying "stability", "durability", a talisman for the living and protective amulet for the dead. Probably derived from an early agricultural fetish.

EPIGRAPHY: The recording and decipherment of ancient inscriptions for the sake of their preservation.

FELLAH (Pl.: Fellahin): An Egyptian peasant.

FLAIL: Emblem of royal authority, consisting of three long streamers suspended from a handle. Kings were usually portrayed holding the crook and the flail crossed on the breast.

GRAFFITI: Crudely scratched inscriptions found on ancient Egyptian monuments.

HEB-SED: A royal ceremony in which the coronation was re-enacted. It was performed in an inner court of the temple.

HYPOSTYLE: The hall of a temple the roof of which rests on rows of columns.

ILLUMINATION: Adornment of a manuscript with brilliant colours and miniature designs.

KA: The double or guardian spirit of the deceased associated with him in the next life.

KIOSK: A pavilion or portico with open sides, the roof being supported by columns.

MAAT: Symbol of truth, justice, cosmic order, personal integrity, action according to that which is "right". Represented by the crouching figure of a goddess, the daughter of Ra; used as the weight of truth placed on the scale opposite the heart of the deceased person in the Judgement Hall of Osiris. The Vizier as Priest of Maat spoke in accordance with *Maat* (in truth).

MASTABA: The first form of tomb in the development of the pyramid. It was a rectangular structure made of brick and had a flat roof and slanting sides.

NECROPOLIS: A cemetery.

PAPYRUS: A tall sedge or marsh plant the pith of which was made by the ancient Egyptians into a writing material. Now found chiefly in the Upper Nile Valley.

PECTORAL: A symbolic ornament in the form of a wide necklace made of gold and precious stones worn on the breast of a king or member of the royal family.

PERISTYLE: A system of roof-supporting columns on four sides of a building.

PHOENIX: Sacred bird of Egypt; symbol of the sun and the rejuvenation of the soil; connected with the theme of creation.

POTSHERD: A fragment of pottery.

PYLON: A portal or gateway of a temple having a truncated pyramidal form.

SCARAB: Sacred emblem of creation made in the form of a dung-feeding beetle and representing resurrection and renewal of life. It was placed in the tomb as a guarantee of eternal life.

SCEPTRE: A symbol for well-being or health, a modification of the crook. Usually associated with the *ankh* and the *tet*.

SERDAB: A chamber built inside a pyramid or mastaba tomb and containing a statue of the king. The only opening was a narrow slit in one wall on a level with the head of the statue.

SHADOOF: A counterpoised sweep, consisting of a long pole pivoted at the top of a post, used to raise water in Egypt.

STELE: A slab of stone bearing an inscription celebrating an important event, marking a boundary, serving as a gravestone or announcing a royal edict.

TEMENOS: The stone enclosure wall of a pyramid.

TET: Djed-Pillar. Osirian symbol for stability or prosperity usually found in association with the *ankh* and the sceptre of health.

TUMULUS: An artificial mound made over a grave, usually found in Nubia.

UNCIAL: A manuscript done in large square capital letters.

URAEUS: The hooded head of the coiled cobra was an emblem of the sun-god Ra. It was worn on the forehead of the king or queen as part of the royal head-dress.

USHABTI: A small mummiform model of a servant or member of the royal household, placed in the tomb of a king or noble for the purpose of performing menial tasks for the deceased in the next world.

UTCHAT: The symbolic eye, originally representing the right eye of Horus, came to signify health and happiness. From this sign came the modern pharmaceutical symbol for drug prescriptions.

WADI: A dry river-bed or channel in the desert.

CHRONOLOGY

There are as many dating systems for Egyptian history as there are Egyptologists. Any one of them is at best approximate, especially concerning the dynasties preceding 1200 B.C. The following dates therefore are not to be regarded as precise. The dating of some reigns (Hatshepsut, Ikhnaton) depends upon whether or not the co-regency is included in the reign. The dynastic dates of the Old Kingdom are given, but the reigns of the individual kings are uncertain and are therefore omitted.

The arrangement of Egyptian history by dynasties derives from the lists of the priest Manetho who served under Ptolemy Philadelphus (285–247 B.C.). These lists have been preserved by Josephus (first century A.D.) and some early Christian historians. Some of the chronological lists used by Manetho are extant, one of which is the Turin Papyrus, written during the reign of Ramses II. Other lists appear on monuments at Sakkarah and Karnak. The Palermo Stone from the Fifth Dynasty contains valuable information about the early dynasties. In addition to the above records, chronological data have been ascertained from various monuments, tombs, royal annals and letters (such as the Amarna tablets). The following list of dates is an eclectic one, based partly on Kurt Lange, John A. Wilson, William S. Smith, and James H. Breasted.

Archaic Period

Accession of Menes	3400 (3500) B.C.
First and Second Dynasties (Thinite)	3400–2980

Old Kingdom

(THIRD DYNASTY–SIXTH DYNASTY)

Third Dynasty (Memphite)	2980–2900
Zoser	
Snefru	

Fourth Dynasty (Memphite)	2900–2750
Khufu or Cheops	
Khafre	
Menkure	
Fifth Dynasty (Memphite)	2750–2625
Sixth Dynasty (Memphite)	2625–2475
Pepi I	
Pepi II (reign of 90 years)	
Seventh and Eighth Dynasties (Memphite)	2475–2445

Middle Kingdom

(NINTH DYNASTY–SEVENTEENTH DYNASTY)

Ninth and Tenth Dynasties	
(Heracleopolitan)	2445–2160
Eleventh Dynasty (Theban)	2160–2000
Nibheptre Mentuhotep IV	2160–2000
Twelfth Dynasty (Theban)	2000–1788
Amenemhet I	2000–1970
Sesostris I (or Senusert or Usertesen)	1980–1935
Amenemhet II	1938–1903
Sesostris II	1906–1887
Sesostris III	1887–1849
Amenemhet III	1849–1801
Thirteenth Dynasty (Theban)	1788
Fourteenth Dynasty (Xoite)	
Fifteenth and Sixteenth Dynasties	to
(Hyksos or "Shepherd Kings")	
Seventeenth Dynasty (Theban)	1580

New Kingdom or New Empire

(EIGHTEENTH DYNASTY–TWENTIETH DYNASTY)

Eighteenth Dynasty (Diospolite)	1580–1305
Ahmose I (or Ahmes)	1580–1557
Amenhotep I (or Amenophis)	1557
Thutmose I (or Thothmes)	to
Thutmose II	1501
Thutmose III and	1501
Queen Hatshepsut (or Hatasu)	to 1447

Amenhotep II	1447–1420
Thutmose IV	1420–1411
Amenhotep III	1411–1375
Ikhnaton (or Amenhotep IV)	1375–1358
Smenkhkara	1358
Tutankhamon	
Ay	to
Horemheb	1303
Nineteenth Dynasty	1305–1200
Ramses I	1303–1302
Seti I	1302–1290
Ramses II	1290–1224
Mer-ne-Ptah	1224–1214
Syrian interregnum	1202–1197
Twentieth Dynasty	1200–1090
Set-nakht	1197–1195
Ramses III	1195–1164
Ramses IV	1164–1157
Ramses V	1157–1153
Ramses VI	1153–1149
Ramses VII	1149–1152
Ramses VIII	1142–1138
Ramses IX	1138–1119
Ramses X	1119–1116
Ramses XI	1116–1085
Twenty-first Dynasty	
(Tanite Dynasty; priest kings in Thebes)	1085– 950
Smendes	1085
Herihor (Thebes)	to 1054
Psusennes I (Pasebkhanu)	1054
Paynozem (Thebes)	to 1009
Amen-em-ipet	1009–1000
Sa-amen	1000–984
Psusennes II (Pasebkhanu)	984–950
Twenty-second Dynasty	
(Bubasite) Libyan kings	950–730
Sheshonq I	950–929
Osorkon I	929–893
Takelot I	893–870
Osorkon II	870–847

Sheshonq II	847
Takelot II	847–823
Sheshonq III	823–772
Pami	772–767
Sheshonq IV	767–730

Partly contemporaneous with Twenty-second Dynasty:

Twenty-third Dynasty	817 (?)–730 B.C.
Pedibast	817–763
Sheshonq V	763–757
Osorkon III	757–748
Takelot III	748
Rud-amen	to
Osorkon IV	730
Twenty-fourth Dynasty	730–715
Tef-nekht	730–720
Bocchoris (Bakenrenef)	720–715

Partly contemporaneous with Twenty-third and Twenty-fourth Dynasties:

Twenty-fifth Dynasty (Kushite: Ethiopian)	751–656
Kashta	
Piankhy	751–716; Conquest
	of Egypt: *circa* 730
Shabako	716–701 (?)
Shebitku	701–690
Taharqa	690–664
Tanwetamani	664–653

Saite Period: 663 to 525 B.C.

Twenty-sixth Dynasty	663–525
Psamtik I (Wah-ib-ra)	663–609
Necho (Nekau, Wehem-ib-ra)	609–594
Psamtik II (Nefer-ib-ra)	594–588
Apries (Haa-ib-ra)	588–568
Amasis (Ahmes-sa-neith, Khnum-ib-ra)	568–525
Psamtik III (Ankh-ka-en-ra)	525

Foreign Domination

Persian Period: 525 to 332 B.C.

Twenty-seventh Dynasty (First Persian Domination)	
	525–404
Cambyses	525–522

Darius I	522–485
Xerxes	485–464
Artaxerxes I	464–424
Darius II	424–404
Twenty-eighth Dynasty	404–398
Amyrtaios	404–398
Twenty-ninth Dynasty	398–378
Nepheritis I (Naifaaurud)	398–392
Akhoris (Haker)	392–380
Psammouthis (Psamut)	380–379
Nepheritis II (Naifaaurud)	379–378
Thirtieth Dynasty	378–341
Nectanebo I (Nekht-nebef)	378–360
Teos	360–359
Nectanebo II (Nekht-hor-heb)	359–341
Thirty-first Dynasty (Second Persian Domination)	
	341–332
Artaxerxes III (Ochos)	341–338
Arses	338–335
Darius III (Codoman)	335–330
Ptolemaic Period	332– 30
Alexander the Great	332–323
Ptolemy I (Soter)	323–283
Ptolemy II (Philadelphus)	285–247
Ptolemy III (Euergetes I)	247–221
Ptolemy IV	221–203
Ptolemy V (Epiphanes)	203–181
Ptolemy VI (Philometor)	181–145
Ptolemy VII (Euergetes II)	170–163, 145–116
Ptolemy VIII (Soter II)	116–108, 88– 80
Ptolemy IX (Alexander)	108– 88
Ptolemy X	80
Ptolemy XI (Auletes)	80– 51
Ptolemy XII	51– 48
Cleopatra VII	
Ptolemy XIII	47– 44
Cleopatra VII	
Cleopatra VII	44 (?)–30
Ptolemy XIV (Caesarian)	

BIBLIOGRAPHY

Prologue: INDESTRUCTIBLE EGYPT

Aldred, Cyril. *The Development of Egyptian Art.* London: Tiranti, 1952

Baikie, James. *A Century of Excavation in the Land of the Pharaohs.* London: Religious Tract Society, 1924

Baikie, James. *Egyptian Antiquities in the Nile Valley.* London: Methuen, 1932

Borchardt, Ludwig. *Aegypten; Landschaft, Volksleben, Baukunst.* Berlin: Wasmuth, 1929

Breasted, James H. *A History of Egypt.* London: Hodder and Stoughton, 1906

Breasted, James H. *Ancient Records of Egypt* (5 vols.). Chicago: University of Chicago Press, 1906–7

Breasted, James H. *Development of Religion and Thought in Ancient Egypt* (Introduction by John A. Wilson). London: Hodder and Stoughton, 1912

Breasted, James H. *The Dawn of Conscience.* London: Scribner's Sons, 1935

Bruce, James. *Travels to Discover the Source of the Nile* (Ed. C. F. Beckingham). Edinburgh: Edinburgh University Press, 1964.

Brunton, W. M. *Kings and Queens of Ancient Egypt.* London: Hodder and Stoughton, 1926

Budge, E. A. Wallis. *The Gods of the Egyptians.* London: Methuen, 1904

Budge, E. A. Wallis. *The Literature of the Ancient Egyptians.* London: Dent, 1914

Budge, E. A. Wallis. *The Mummy.* Cambridge: Cambridge University Press, 1894

Capart, J. *Primitive Art in Egypt.* London: Grevel and Co., 1905

Ceram, C. W. *Gods, Graves, and Scholars* (Translated by E. B. Garside). London: Gollancz; Sidgwick and Jackson, 1952

Bibliography 291

Ceram, C. W. *The March of Archaeology* (Translated by R. and C. Wilson). New York: Knopf, 1958

Cottrell, Leonard. *The Lost Pharaohs*. London: Evans, 1962

Davidson, Marshall B. (ed.) *The Horizon Book of Lost Worlds* (Narrative by Leonard Cottrell). New York: American Heritage Publishing Company, 1962

Davies, Nina M. and Gardiner, A. H. *Ancient Egyptian Paintings* (3 vols.). Cambridge: Cambridge University Press, 1936

Dawson, Warren R. *Who Was Who in Egyptology*. London: Egypt Exploration Society, 1951

Edwards, Amelia B. *Pharaohs, Fellahs and Explorers*. London: Osgood and McIlvaine, 1891

Edwards, Amelia B. *A Thousand Miles Up the Nile*. London: Routledge, 1889

Elisofon, Eliot. *The Nile* (Foreword). London: Thames, 1964

Emery, Walter Bryan. *Archaic Egypt*. Harmondsworth, Middlesex: Penguin Books, 1961

Engelbach, Reginald (ed.). *Introduction to Egyptian Archaeology with special reference to the Egyptian Museum, Cairo*. Cairo: Department of Egyptian Antiquities of the Egyptian Museum, 1946

Engelbach, Reginald. *The Problem of the Obelisks*. London: Unwin, 1923

Erman, Adolf and Ranke, H. *Aegypten und Aegyptischen Leben im Altertum*. Tübingen: Mohr, 1923

Erman, Adolf. *Die Religion des Aegypter*. Berlin: W. de Gruyter and Co., 1934

Erman, Adolf. *The Literature of the Ancient Egyptians* (Translated by A. M. Blackman). London: Methuen, 1927

Frankfort, Henri. *Ancient Egyptian Religion. An Interpretation*. Oxford: Oxford University Press, 1948

Frankfort, Henri. *Kingship and the Gods*. Cambridge: Cambridge University Press, 1948

Frankford, H., Frankfort, H. A., Wilson, J. A. and Jacobsen, T. *The Intellectual Adventure of Ancient Man*. Cambridge: Cambridge University Press, 1947

Gardiner, Alan. *Egypt of the Pharaohs*. Oxford: Oxford University Press, 1961

Giedion, S. *The Eternal Present*, vol. 11: *The Beginnings of Architecture*. London: Oxford University Press, 1963

Glanville, S. R. K. (ed.). *The Legacy of Egypt*. London: Oxford University Press, 1942

Glanville, S. R. K. *The Growth and Nature of Egyptology*. Cambridge: Cambridge University Press, 1947

Hayes, W. C. *The Scepter of Egypt:* part 1. New York: Harper, 1953

Hoyningen-Huene and Steindorf, G. *Egypt* (Second revised edition). New York: Augustin, 1945

Lange, Kurt and Hirmer, Max. *Aegypten: Architektur, Plastik, Malerei in Drei Jahrtausenden*. Munich: Hirmer, 1955

Maspero, Gaston. *Manual of Egyptian Archaeology*. London, 1895

Maspero, Gaston. *Egypt: Ancient Sites and Modern Scenes* (Translated by Elizabeth Lee). London: Unwin, 1910

Maspero, Gaston. *The Dawn of Civilization*. London: Christian Knowledge Society, 1910

Mertz, Barbara. *Temples, Tombs and Hieroglyphs*. London: Gollancz, 1964

Montet, Pierre. *Eternal Egypt* (Translated by Doreen Weitman). New York: New American Library of World Literature, 1964

Murray, Margaret A. *The Splendour that was Egypt*. London: Sidgwick and Jackson, 1949

Petrie, W. M. Flinders. *A History of Egypt*. London: Methuen, 1924

Petrie, W. M. Flinders. *A History of Egypt from the Earliest Kings to the Sixteenth Dynasty*. London: Methuen, 1923

Piggott, Stuart (ed.). *The Dawn of Civilization*. London: Thames and Hudson, 1962

Posener, Georges. *Dictionary of Egyptian Civilization*. New York: Tudor Publishing Company, 1959

Pritchard, James B. (ed.). *Ancient Near Eastern Texts Relating to the Old Testament*. London: Oxford University Press, 1955

Pritchard, James B. *The Ancient East in Pictures Relating to the Old Testament*. London: Oxford University Press, 1955

Säve-Söderbergh, Torgny. *Pharaohs and Mortals*, London: Hale, 1963

Singleton, Esther. *Egypt as Described by Great Writers*. New York: Dodd, Mead, 1911

Smith, W. Stevenson. *A History of Egyptian Sculpture and Painting in the Old Kingdom* (Second edition). London: Oxford University Press, 1950

Smith, W. Stevenson. *Ancient Egypt: As represented in the Museum of Fine Arts, Boston*. Boston: Museum of Fine Arts, 1960; Boston: Beacon Press, 1961

Smith, W. Stevenson. *The Art and Architecture of Ancient Egypt*. Baltimore: Penguin, 1958

Steindorff, George and Seele, Keith C. *When Egypt Ruled the East*. Cambridge: Cambridge University Press, 1942

Weigall, Arthur E. P. *The Treasury of Ancient Egypt*. London: Blackwood, 1911

Wilkinson, Gardner. *The Manners and Customs of the Ancient Egyptians* (5 vols., third edition). London: Murray, 1847

Wilson, John A. *Signs and Wonders Upon Pharaoh*. Chicago: University of Chicago Press, 1964

Wilson, John A. *The Culture of Ancient Egypt*. Cambridge: Cambridge University Press, 1956

Wilson, John A. and others. *The Intellectual Adventure of Ancient Man*. Cambridge: Cambridge University Press, 1947

Wood, Roger and Drower, Margaret S. *Egypt in Colour*. London: Thames and Hudson, 1964

Chapter One

THE LOST LANGUAGE

Budge, E. A. Wallis. *An Egyptian Hieroglyphic Dictionary* (2 vols.). London: Murray, 1920

Budge, E. A. Wallis. *Egyptian Language*. London: Routledge and Kegan Paul, 1951

Budge, E. A. Wallis. *The Decrees of Memphis and Canopus* (3 vols.). London: Trench Trübner and Co., 1904

Budge, E. A. Wallis. *The Rosetta Stone*. London: Religious Tract Society, 1929

Budge, E. A. Wallis. *The Mummy; Chapters on Egyptian Funeral Archaeology*. Cambridge: Cambridge University Press, 1925

Ceram, C. W. *Gods, Graves, and Scholars* (Translated by E. B. Garside). London: Gollancz, 1952

Cleator, P. E. *Lost Languages*. London: Hale, 1959

Deuel, Leo. *Testaments of Time: The Search for Lost Manuscripts and Records*. New York: Knopf, 1965

Elgood, P. G. *The Ptolemies of Egypt*. Bristol: Arrowsmith, 1938

Erman, Adolf. *Die Hieroglyphen*. Berlin: Göschen, 1912

Erman, Adolf. *Neuaegyptische Grammatik* (Second edition). Leipzig: Engelmann, 1933

Gardiner, Alan H. *Egyptian Grammar* (Third edition). London: Oxford University Press, 1957

Gardiner, Alan. *My Working Years*. London: Coronet Press, 1964

Hartleben, Hermine. *Champollion, sein Leben und sein Werk* (2 vols). Berlin, 1906

Oldham, Frank. *Thomas Young, FRS, Philosopher and Physician*. London: Arnold, 1933

Wood, A. *Thomas Young*. Cambridge: Cambridge University Press, 1954

Chapter Two

EARLY EXPLORATION

Bankes, William John. *Geometrical Elevation of an Obelisk from the Island of Philae*. London: Murray, 1821

Belzoni, Giovanni Battista. *Narrative of the Operations and Recent Discoveries in Egypt and Nubia*. London: Murray, 1820

Browne, William George. *Travels in Africa, Egypt and Syria: 1792–98*, London: T. Cadell Jr., 1799

Borckhardt, John Lewis. *Travels of Mr. Borckhardt in Egypt and Nubia*. London: Phillips, 1819

Carter, Harry (translator). *The Histories of Herodotus*. New York: Heritage, 1958

Clair, Colin. *Strong Man Egyptologist*. London: Oldbourne, 1957

Dawson, Warren R. *Charles Wycliffe Goodwin, 1817–1878: A Pioneer in Egyptology*. London: Oxford University Press, 1934

Denon, Dominique Vivant. *Travels in Upper and Lower Egypt* (Translated by A. Aikin). London: Phillips, 1803

Disher, M. Wilson. *Pharaoh's Fool*. London: Heinemann, 1957

Edwards, Bela Bates. *Biography of a Self-Taught Man*. London, 1869

Halls, J. J. *Life of Henry Salt* (2 vols.). London, 1834

Hamilton, H. C. and Falconer, W. *The Geography of Strabo*. London: Bohn, 1857

Henniker, Frederick. *Notes During a Visit to Egypt, Nubia, the Oasis, Mt. Sinai, and Jerusalem.* London, 1823

Herold, J. Christopher. *Bonaparte in Egypt.* New York: Harper and Row, 1962

Lane, Edward William. *Account of the Manners and Customs of the Modern Egyptians* (2 vols.). London, 1836

Legh, Thomas. *Narrative of a Journey in Egypt and the Country beyond the Cataracts* (Second edition). London: Murray, 1817

Mayes, Stanley. *The Great Belzoni.* London: Putnam, 1959

Norden, Friderik Ludwig. *Drawings of Some Ruins and Colossal Statues at Thebes in Egypt.* New Haven: Sydney's Press, 1814

Norden, Friderik Ludwig. *Travels in Egypt and Nubia* (Translated by Peter Templeton). London: Davis and Reymers, 1757

Pococke, Richard. *Travels in Egypt.* London, 1755

Sandys, George. *A Relation of a Journey begun Anno Domini 1610.* London: Cotes-Allot, 1627

Vyse, Richard William Howard. *Operations Carried on at the Pyramids of Gizeh in 1837.* Appendix by J. S. Perring. (3 vols.) London: Fraser, 1840–42

Wilkinson, John Gardiner. *The Manners and Customs of the Ancient Egyptians* (3 vols.; revised edition). London: Murray, 1879

Chapter Three

ORDER OUT OF CHAOS

Deuel, Leo. *The Treasures of Time.* London: Souvenir, 1962

Ebers, George. *Richard Lepsius. A Biography* (Translated by Z. D. Underhill). New York: Gottsberger, 1887

Lepsius, Karl Richard. *Denkmaeler aus Aegypten und Aethiopien.* Leipzig: Heinrichs, 1897–1913

Lepsius, Karl Richard. *Discoveries in Egypt and Ethiopia* (Ed. K. R. H. Mackenzie). London, 1852

Mariette, Auguste. *Outlines of Ancient Egyptian History* (Translated by M. Brodrick). London: Murray, 1892

Mariette, Auguste. *The Monuments of Upper Egypt* (Tarnslated by Alphonse Mariette). London, Alexandria and Cairo, 1877

Murray, Margaret A. *The Splendour that was Egypt*. New York: Philosophical Library, 1949

Petrie, W. M. Flinders. *A History of Egypt*. London: Methuen, 1924

Petrie, W. M. Flinders. *Arts and Crafts of Ancient Egypt* (Second Edition). London: Foulis, 1910

Petrie, W. M. Flinders. *Inductive Metrology*. London: Saunders, 1877

Petrie, W. M. Flinders. *Kahun, Gurop, and Hawara*. London: Paul, Trench, Trübner and Co., 1890

Petrie, W. M. Flinders. *Methods and Aims in Archaeology*. London: Macmillan, 1904

Petrie, W. M. Flinders. *Seventy Years in Archaeology*. London: Sampson, Low and Co. (1931)

Petrie, W. M. Flinders. *Ten Years' Digging in Egypt*. London: Religious Tract Society (1923)

Petrie, W. M. Flinders. *The Funeral Furniture of Egypt*. London: British School of Archaeology

Chapter Four

PYRAMIDS

Baikie, James. *Egyptian Antiquities in the Nile Valley*. London: Methuen, 1932

Borchardt, Ludwig. *Das Grabdenkmal des Königs Nefer-ir-ke-re*. Leipzig: Heinrichs, 1909

Borchardt, Ludwig. *Das Grabdenkmal des Königs Chephren*. Leipzig: Heinrichs, 1912

Borchardt, Ludwig. *Das Grabdenkmal des Königs Sahure* (vols. 1 and 2). Leipzig: Heinrichs, 1910–13

Borchardt, Ludwig. *Die Enstehung der Pyramide und Baugeschichte der Pyramide bei Medum nachgewiesen*. Berlin: Springer, 1928

Borchardt, Ludwig. *Die Pyramiden, ihre Enstehung und Entwicklung*. Berlin: Curtis, 1911

Borchardt, Ludwig. *Längen und Richtungen der vier Grundkanten der grossen Pyramide bei Gise*. Berlin: Springer, 1926

Brown, R. H. *The Fayum and Lake Moeris*. London, 1892

Brunton, Guy. *Lahunl: The Treasure*. London: British School of Archaeology in Egypt, 1920

Clarke, S. and Engelbach, R. *Ancient Egyptian Masonry.* Oxford: Clarendon Press, 1930

Cottrell, Leonard. *The Mountains of Pharaoh.* London: Hale, 1956

De Camp, L. Sprague. *The Ancient Engineers.* London: Souvenir, 1963

Drioton, E. and Lauer, J. P. *Sakkara, the Monuments of Zoser.* Cairo: French Institute of Oriental Archaeology, 1939

Dunham, Dows. *El Kurru.* Cambridge: Harvard University Press, 1950

Edwards, I. E. S. *The Pyramids of Egypt.* Baltimore: Penguin, 1947

Emery, W. B. *Excavations at Sakkara: Great Tombs of the First Dynasty.* Cairo: Government Press, 1954–58

Emery, W. B. *Excavations at Sakkara: The Tomb of Hemaka.* Cairo: Government Press, 1938

Engelbach, Reginald and Clarke, Somers. *Ancient Egyptian Masonry.* London: Oxford University Press, 1930

Fakhry, Ahmed. *The Bent Pyramid of Dashur.* Cairo, 1954

Fakhry, Ahmed. *The Monuments of Sneferu at Dashur.* Cairo, 1954

Fakhry, Ahmed. *The Pyramids.* Chicago: University of Chicago Press, 1961

Firth, C. M., Quibell, J. E., Lauer, J. P. *The Step Pyramid.* Cairo: French Institute of Oriental Archaeology, 1935

Goneim, M. Zakariah. *Excavations at Sakkara: Horus Sekhem-khet.* Cairo: French Institute of Oriental Archaeology, 1957

Goneim, M. Zakariah. *The Buried Pyramid.* London: Longmans, 1956

Hassan, Selim. *Excavations at Giza* (8 vols.). London: Oxford University Press, 1932–53

Hayes, W. C. *The Entrance Chapel of the Pyramid of Sen Wosret I.* Bulletin of the Metropolitan Museum of Art, No. 29, November 1934

Hölscher, U. *Das Grabdenkmal des Königs Chephren.* Leipzig, 1912

Junker, H. *Grabungen auf dem Friedhof des Alten Reiches bei dem Pyramiden von Giza* (4 vols.). Vienna, 1929–41

Lange, Kurt and Hirmer, Max. *Aegypten.* Munich: Hirmer Verlag, 1955

Lansing, Ambrose. *The Museum's Excavation at Lisht.* Bulletin of the Metropolitan Museum of Art, No. 28, April, 1933

Lauer, Jean-Philippe. *Le Problème des Pyramides d'Egypte.* Paris: Payot, 1948

Lythgoe, A. M. *The Treasure of Lahun.* Bulletin of the Metropolitan Museum of Art, December 1919. Part 2

Mace, A. C. *The Egyptian Expedition: Excavations at Lisht.* Bulletin of the

Metropolitan Museum of Art, No. 3, 1908; No. 9, 1914; No. 16, 1922; No. 17, 1922

Petrie, W. M. Flinders. *Medum*. London: Nutt, 1892

Petrie, W. M. Flinders. *The Pyramids and Temples of Giza*. London: Field and Tuer, 1883

Petrie, W. M. Flinders. *Ten Years Digging in Egypt*. New York: Revell, no date

Reisner, George A. *A History of the Giza Necropolis*, vol. 1. Cambridge: Harvard University Press, 1942

Reisner, George A. *A History of the Gaza Necropolis*, vol. 2. (Completed and revised by W. Stevenson Smith). Cambridge: Harvard University Press, 1955

Reisner, George A. *Excavations at Napata*. Bulletin of the Museum of Fine Arts, Boston. 1917: vol. 15, no. 89

Reisner, George A. *Hetepheres, Mother of Cheops*. Bulletin of the Museum of Fine Arts, Boston. Special supplement to vol. 25. May 1927

Reisner, George A. *Known and Unknown Kings of Ethiopia*. Bulletin of the Museum of Fine Arts, Boston. 1918: vol. 16, no. 97

Reisner, George A. *Mycerinus: The Temples of the Third Pyramid at Giza*. Cambridge: Harvard University Press, 1931

Reisner, George A. *The Development of the Egyptian Tomb down to the Accession of Cheops*. Cambridge: Harvard University Press, 1936

Reisner, George A. *The Empty Sarcophagus of the Mother of Cheops*. Bulletin of the Museum of Fine Arts, Boston. 1928: vol. 26, no. 157

Smith, W. Stevenson. *The Art and Architecture of Ancient Egypt*. Baltimore: Penguin, 1958

Smith, W. Stevenson. *The Tomb of Hetepheres I*. Bulletin of the Museum of Fine Arts, Boston. 1953: vol. 51, no. 284

Smyth, Piazzi. *Our Inheritance in the Great Pyramid*. London: Daldy, Isbister, 1877

Hamilton, H. C. and Falconer, W. (Translators). *The Geography of Strabo* (3 vols.). London: Bohn, 1857

Vyse, Colonel Richard W. H. *Operations Carried on at the Pyramids of Gizeh in 1837* (3 vols.). London: Fraser, 1840–42

Winlock, Herbert E. and Mace, Arthur C. *The Tomb of Senebtisi at Lisht*. New York: Gilliss Press, 1916

Winlock, H. E. *The Treasure of El Lahun*. New York: Metropolitan Museum of Art, 1934

Chapter Five

FROM PETRIE TO GONEIM

Borchardt, Ludwig. *Das Grabdenkmal des Königs Nefer-ir-ke-re.* Leipzig: Heinrichs, 1909

Borchardt, Ludwig. *Das Grabdenkmal des Königs Chephren.* Leipzig: Heinrichs, 1912

Borchardt, Ludwig. *Das Grabdenkmal des Königs Sahure* (vols. 1 and 2). Leipzig: Heinrichs, 1910–13

Borchardt, Ludwig. *Die Enstehung der Pyramide und Baugeschichte der Pyramide bei Medum nachgewiesen.* Berlin: Springer, 1928

Borchardt, Ludwig. *Die Pyramiden, ihre Enstehung und Entwicklung.* Berlin: Curtis, 1911

Borchardt, Ludwig. *Längen und Richtungen der vier Grundkanten der grossen Pyramide bei Gise.*

Goneim, M. Zakariah. *Excavations at Sakkara: Horus Sekhem-khet.* Cairo: French Institute of Oriental Archaeology, 1959

Goneim, M. Zakariah. *The Buried Pyramid.* London: Longmans, 1956

Petrie, W. M. Flinders. *Medum.* London: Nutt, 1892

Petrie, W. M. Flinders. *Ten Years' Digging in Egypt.* London: Religious Tract Society (1923)

Petrie, W. M. Flinders. *The Pyramids and Temples of Giza.* London, 1883

Reisner, George A. *A History of the Giza Necropolis,* vol. 1. Cambridge: Harvard University Press, 1942

Reisner, George A. *A History of the Giza Necropolis,* vol. 2 (Completed and revised by W. Stevenson Smith). Cambridge: Harvard University Press, 1955

Reisner, George A. *Excavations at Napata.* Bulletin of the Museum of Fine Arts, Boston. 1917: vol. 15, no. 89

Reisner, George A. *Hetepheres, Mother of Cheops.* Bulletin of the Museum of Fine Arts, Boston. Special supplement to vol. 25. May 1927

Reisner, George A. *Known and Unknown Kings of Ethiopia.* Bulletin of the Museum of Fine Arts, Boston. 1918: vol. 16, no. 97

Reisner, George A. *Mycerinus: The Temples of the Third Pyramid at Giza.* Cambridge: Harvard University Press, 1931

Reisner, George A. *The Development of the Egyptian Tomb down to the Accession of Cheops.* Cambridge: Harvard University Press, 1936

Reisner, George A. *The Empty Sarcophagus of the Mother of Cheops.* Bulletin of the Museum of Fine Arts, Boston. 1928: vol. 26, no. 157

Chapter Six

TOMBS

Bacon, Edward. *Digging for History.* New York: Day, 1960

Baikie, James. *A Century of Excavation in the Land of the Pharaohs.* London: Religious Tract Society, 1924

Baikie, James. *Egyptian Antiquities in the Nile Valley.* London: Methuen, 1932

Breasted, James Henry. *Ancient Records of Egypt* (5 vols.). Chicago: University of Chicago Press, 1906–7

Brunton, W. M. *Kings and Queens of Ancient Egypt.* London: Hodder, 1925

Budge, E. A. W. *The Book of the Dead: the Chapters of Coming Forth by Day* (3 vols). London, 1898

Capart, Jean. *Lectures on Egyptian Art.* London: Oxford University Press, 1928

Capart, Jean. *Thebes: the Glory of a Great Past* (In collaboration with Marcelle Wernrouck). London: Allen and Unwin, 1926

Carter, Howard and the Earl of Carnarvon. *Five Years Exploration at Thebes.* London, 1912

Davies, Nina M. and Gardiner, Alan H. *Ancient Egyptian Paintings* (3 vols.). Cambridge: Cambridge University Press, 1936

Davies, Norman de Garis. *Five Theban Tombs.* London: Egypt Exploration Fund, 1915

Davies, Norman de Garis. *The Tomb of Nakht at Thebes.* New York: Metropolitan Museum of Art, 1917

Davies, Norman de Garis. *The Tomb of Rekhmire at Thebes.* New York: Metropolitan Museum of Art, 1943

Davies, Norman de Garis and Gardiner, Alan H. *The Tomb of Amenemhet.* London: Egypt Exploration Society, 1915

Davis, Theodore M. *Tomb of Ouiya and Touiyou.* London: Constable, 1907

Davis, Theodore M. *The Tomb of Thutmosis IV*. London: Constable, 1904

Davis, Theodore M. *Tomb of Queen Tiyi*. London: Constable, 1910

Dawson, Warren R. *Egyptian Mummies*. London, 1924

Dunham, Dows. *The Royal Cemeteries of Kush I, El Kurru*. London: Oxford University Press, 1951

Dunham, Dows. *The Royal Cemeteries of Kush II, Nuri*

Emery, Walter B. *Excavations at Sakkara: Great Tombs of the First Dynasty*. Oxford: Egypt Exploration Society, 1954

Emery, Walter B. *Excavations at Sakkara: Great Tombs of the First Dynasty* (2 vols.). Cairo: Government Press, 1949–58

Emery, Walter B. *Excavations at Sakkara: 1937–1938, Hor Aha*. Cairo: Government Press, 1939

Emery, Walter B. *The Royal Tombs of Ballana and Qustul*. Cairo: Government Press, 1938

Emery, Walter B. *Excavations at Sakkara: the Tomb of Hemaka*. Cairo: Government Press, 1938

Mace, A. C., Winlock, Herbert E. *The Tomb of Senebtisi at Lisht*. New York: Gilliss Press, 1916

Nelson, Harold H. and Hölscher, Uno. *Work in Western Thebes: 1931–33*. Chicago: University of Chicago Press, 1934

Peet, T. Eric. *The Great Tomb Robberies of the Twentieth Egyptian Dynasty*. Oxford: Clarendon Press, 1943

Pettigrew, Thomas J. *A History of Egyptian Mummies*. London: Longman, 1834

Quibell, J. E. *Archaic Mastabas: Excavations at Sakkara: 1912–1914*. Cairo: Service des Antiquités, 1923

Quibell, J. E. *Excavations at Sakkara: 1906–1907*. Cairo: Service des Antiquités, 1907–8

Quibell, J. E. and others. *Excavations at Sakkara: 1907–1938*. Cairo: Service des Antiquités, 1927

Reisner, George A. *The Tomb of Hetep-heres, the Mother of Cheops* (Revised by W. Stevenson Smith). *A History of the Giza Necropolis*, vol. 2. Cambridge: Harvard University Press, 1955

Reisner, George A. *A History of the Giza Necropolis*, vol. 2 (Completed and revised by W. Stevenson Smith). Cambridge: Harvard University Press, 1955

Reisner, George A. *The Development of the Egyptian Tomb down to the Accession of Cheops*. London: Oxford University Press, 1936

Smith, Joseph Lindon. *Tombs, Temples and Ancient Art.* Norman: University of Oklahoma Press, 1956

Vandier, Jacques (ed.). *Paintings from Tombs and Temples.* New York: New York Graphic Society, 1954

Winlock, H. E. *Excavations at Deir el Bahri: 1911–31.* London: Macmillan, 1943

Winlock, H. E. *Models of Daily Life in Ancient Egypt from the Tomb of Meket-re at Thebes.* London: Oxford University Press, 1955

Chapter Seven

TUTANKHAMON

Budge, E. A. Wallis. *Tutankhamen, Amenism, Atenism, and Egyptian Monotheism.* London: Hopkinson and Co., 1923

Carnarvon, the Earl of, and Carter, Howard. *Five Years Exploration at Thebes: 1907–1911.* London and New York: Frowde, 1912

Carter, Howard and Mace, A. C. *The Tomb of Tutankhamen* (3 vols.). London: Cassell, 1923–33

Desroches-Noblecourt, Christiane. *Tutankhamen: Life and Death of a Pharaoh.* Greenwich: New York Graphic Society, 1963

Fox, Penelope. *Tutankhamon's Treasure.* London: Oxford University Press, 1951

Piankoff, Alexandre. *The Shrines of Tutankhamon.* New York: Harper and Row, 1962

Weigall, Arthur. *Tutankhamen and Other Essays.* London: Butterworth, 1923

Chapter Eight

TEMPLES

Aldred, Cyril. *The Development of Ancient Egyptian Art.* London: Tiranti, 1952

Baikie, James. *Egyptian Antiquities in the Nile Valley.* London: Methuen, 1932

Borchardt, Ludwig. *Aegyptische Tempel mit Umgang.* Cairo: Selbstverlag des Herausgebers, 1938

Breasted, James H. *The Temples of Lower Nubia*. Article in American Journal of Semitic Languages and Literatures XXIII (1906–7), pp. 1–64.

Breasted, James H. *The Monuments of Sudanese Nubia*. Article in American Journal of Semitic Languages and Literatures XXV (1908–9), pp. 1–110

Capart, Jean. *Thebes*. London: Allen and Unwin, 1926

Frankfort, H. *The Cenotaph of Seti I at Abydos* (2 vols.). London: Egypt Exploration Society, 1933

Frankfort, H., De Buck, A., Gunn, B. *The Cenotaph of Seti I* (2 vols.). London: Egypt Exploration Society, 1933

Gardiner, Alan H. (ed.). *The Temple of King Sethos I at Abydos* (3 vols.). Chicago: University of Chicago Press, 1933–5

Lange, Kurt and Hirmer, Max. *Aegypten: Architektur, Plastik, Malerei in Drei Jahrtausenden*. Munich: Verlag, 1955

Murray, Margaret A. *Egyptian Temples*. London: Sampson Low, Marston and Co., 1931

Naville, Edouard. *Excavations at Abydos*. Article in *Journal of Egyptian Archaeology*, vol. 1, part III. July 1914

Nelson, Harold H. *Series of Medinet Habu V* (5 vols.). Chicago: University of Chicago Press, 1930–56

Nelson, Harold H. *The Excavations of Medinet Habu* (4 vols.). Chicago: University of Chicago Press, 1934–51

Quibell, J. E. *The Ramesseum*. London: Quaritch, 1898

Riefstahl, Elizabeth. *Thebes in the Time of Amenhotep III*. Norman: University of Oklahoma Press, 1964

Smith, Earl Baldwin. *Egyptian Architecture as Cultural Expression*. New York: Appleton-Century, 1938

Smith, Joseph Lindon. *Tombs, Temples and Ancient Art* (Ed. Corinna L. Smith). Norman: University of Oklahoma Press, 1956

Smith, W. Stevenson. *The Art and Architecture of Ancient Egypt*. Baltimore: Penguin, 1958

Whittemore, Thomas. "The Ibis Cemetery at Abydos: 1914". Article in *Journal of Egyptian Archaeology*, vol. 1, part IV. October, 1914

Wilson, John A. *Signs and Wonders Upon Pharaoh*. Chicago: University of Chicago Press, 1964

Chapter Nine

DEIR EL BAHRI

Baikie, James. *Egyptian Antiquities in the Nile Valley*. London: Methuen, 1932

Capart, Jean. *Thebes*. London: Allen and Unwin, 1926

Lange, Kurt and Hirmer, Max. *Aegypten: Architektur, Plastik, Malerei in Drei Jahrtausenden*. Munich: Verlag, 1955

Naville, Edouard. *The Temple of Deir el-Bahri* (4 vols.). London: Egypt Exploration Fund, *no date*

Smith, W. Stevenson. *The Art and Architecture of Ancient Egypt*. Baltimore: Penguin, 1958

Winlock, Herbert E. *Excavations at Deir el-Bahri: 1911–31*. London: Macmillan, 1943

Winlock, Herbert E. *The Tomb of Queen Meryet-Amun at Thebes*. New York: Metropolitan Museum of Art, 1932

Chapter Ten

AMARNA

Anthes, Rudolf. *An Essay on Contemplation of the Nofretete Head*. Berlin: Ehemals Staatliche Museen, 1961

Baikie, James. *The Amarna Age*. London: Black, 1926

Borchardt, Ludwig. *Ausgrabungen in Tell el-Amarna*. Berlin: Deutsche Orient-Gesellschaft Mitteilungen: no. 46, 1911

Borchardt, Ludwig. *Portraets der Königen Nofretete*. Leipzig: Heinrichs, 1923

Bratton, F. Gladstone. *The Heretic Pharaoh*. London: Hale, 1962

Brunton, W. M. *Great Ones of Ancient Egypt*. London: Hodder, 1929

Budge, E. A. Wallis. *By Nile and Tigris*. London: Murray, 1920

Campbell, Edward Fay. *The Chronology of the Amarna Letters*. London: Oxford University Press, 1964

Cottrell, Leonard. *The Lost Pharaohs*. London: Evans, 1962

Davies, Norman de Garis. *The Rock Tombs of el-Amarna*. London: Egypt Exploration Society, 1903–1908

Frankfort, Henri. "Preliminary Report on the Excavations at Tell el-Amarna, 1926–27". Article in *Journal of Egyptian Archaeology*, vol. 8, parts 3 and 4. October 1927

Frankfort, Henri (ed.). *The Mural Paintings of el-Amarna*. (Contributors: N. de Garis Davies, Nina de Garis Davies, H. Frankfort, F. G. Newton, T. Whittemore, S. R. K. Glanville.) London: Egypt Exploration Society, 1929

Frankfort, Henri (ed.). *The Rock Tombs of Tell el-Amarna*. London: Egypt Exploration Society, 1929

Griffith, F. L. "Excavations at Tell el-Amarna, 1923–24". Article in *Journal of Egyptian Archaeology*, vol. 10, parts 3 and 4. October 1924

Lange, Kurt. *König Echnaton und die Amarna Zeit*. Munich: Verlag, 1951

Mercer, S. A. B. and Hallock, F. H. (ed,.). *The Tell el-Amarna Tablets*. London: Macmillan, 1939

Newton, F. G. "Excavations at el-Amarna, 1923–24". Article in *Journal of Egyptian Archaeology*, vol. 10, parts 3 and 4. October 1924

Pendlebury, J. D. S. *Tell el-Amarna*. London: Lovat, Dickson and Thompson, 1935

Pendlebury, J. D. S. *Tell el-Amarna: the City of Akhenaten*. Part I by T. Eric Peet and C. Leonard Woolley; part II by H. Frankfort and J. D. S. Pendlebury. London: Egypt Exploration Society, 1923–51

Petrie, W. M. Flinders. *Tell el-Amarna*. London: Methuen, 1894

Riefstahl, Elizabeth. *Thebes in the Time of Amenhotep III*. Norman: University of Oklahoma Press, 1964

Smith, W. Stevenson. *The Art and Architecture of Ancient Egypt*. Baltimore: Penguin, 1958

Weigall, Arthur. "The Mummy of Akhenaton". Article in *Journal of Egyptian Archaeology*, vol. 8, parts 3 and 4. October 1922

Wells, Evelyn. *Nefertiti*. London: Hale, 1965

Whittemore, T. "Excavations at Tell el-Amarna". Article in *Journal of Egyptian Archaeology*, vol. 8, parts 1 and 2. April 1922

Wilson, John A. *The Culture of Ancient Egypt*. Cambridge: Cambridge University Press, 1956

Winckler, Hugo. *The Tell el-Amarna Letters* (Translated by J. M. P. Metcalf). New York: Lemcke and Buechner, 1896

Woolley, C. Leonard. "Excavations at Tell el-Amarna". Article in *Journal of Egyptian Archaeology*, vol. 8, parts 1 and 2. April 1922

Chapter Eleven

PAPYRI

Baikie, James. *Egyptian Papyri and Papyrus-Hunting*. London: Religious Tract Society, 1925

Bratton, F. Gladstone. *The Heretic Pharaoh*. London: Hale, 1962

Breasted, James H. *Ancient Records of Egypt* (5 vols.). Chicago: University of Chicago Press, 1906

Breasted, James H. *The Edwin Smith Surgical Papyrus*. Cambridge: Cambridge University Press, 1930

Bryan, C. P. (ed.). *Papyrus Ebers*. London: Bles, 1930

Cobern, Camden M. *The New Archaeological Discoveries* (Sixth edition). New York and London: Funk and Wagnalls, 1922

Dawson, Warren R. "Medicine." Article in *The Legacy of Egypt*, ed. by S. R. K. Glanville. Oxford: Clarendon Press, 1942

Deissmann, Adolf. *Licht vom Osten*. Tübingen: Mohr, 1923

Deuel, Leo. *Testaments of Time: the Search for Lost Manuscripts and Records*. New York: Knopf, 1965

Ebers, Georges M. *Papyros Ebers* (2 vols.). Leipzig, 1875.

Erman, Adolf. *The Literature of the Ancient Egyptians* (Translated by A. M. Blackman). London: Methuen, 1927

Gardiner, Alan H. *Hieratic Papyri in the British Museum* (Third series). London, 1935

Gardiner, Alan H. *Berlin: Staatlichen Museen, Hieratische Papyri*. Leipzig, 1909

Goodspeed, E. J. and Colwell, E. C. *A Greek Papyrus Reader*. Cambridge: Cambridge University Press, 1935

Grenfell, Bernard P., Hunt, Arthur S. and Hogarth, David G. *Fayum Towns and their Papyri*. London: Egypt Exploration Fund, 1900

Grenfell, Barnard P. and Hunt, Arthur S. *Sayings of Our Lord*. London: Oxford University Press, 1904

Guillaumont, A., Puech, Henri-Charles, Quispel, Gilles, Till, W., Masih, Y. A. *The Gospel According to Thomas*. London: Collins, 1959

Hunt, A. S. "Papyri and Papyrology." Article in *Journal of Egyptian Archaeology*, vol. 1, part 2. April, 1914

Hunt, A. S. "Twenty-five years of Papyrology." Article in *Journal of Egyptian Archaeology*, vol. 8, parts 2 and 4. October 1922

Lahib, Phalor. *Coptic Gnostic Papyri in the Coptic Museum at Old Cairo* (Ed. F. L. Cross). 1956

Lietzmann, Hans. *Griechische Papyri*. Bonn, 1910

Milligan, George. *Selections from the Greek Papyri*. Cambridge: Cambridge University Press, 1910

Petrie, W. M. Flinders. *Egyptian Tales Translated from the Papyri* (2 vols.). London: Methuen, 1895

Prideaux, Tom and Mayer, Josephine. *Never to Die*. New York: Viking, 1938

Pritchard, James B. (ed.). *Ancient Near Eastern Texts Relating to the Old Testament* (Egyptian material translated by John A. Wilson). London: Oxford University Press, 1955

Puech, Henri-Charles. *Coptic Studies in Honour of W. E. Crumm*. Boston, 1950

Reisner, George A. *The Hearst Medical Papyrus*. Leipzig: Heinrichs, 1905

Roberts, C. H. "The Greek Papyri." Article in *The Legacy of Egypt*, ed. by S. R. K. Glanville. Oxford: Clarendon Press, 1942

Umnik, W. C. van, Puech, Henri-Charles, and Quispel, Gilles. *The Jung Codex*. London, 1955

Winter, J. G. *Life and Letters in the Papyri*. Ann Arbor: University of Michigan Press, 1933

Chapter Twelve

NUBIA AND THE NEW HIGH DAM

Arkell, A. J. *A History of the Sudan to 1821*. London, 1955

Budge, E. A. Wallis. *The Egyptian Sudan* (2 vols.). London: Kegan Paul and Co., 1907

Dunham, Dows. *Royal Cemeteries of Kush I. El Kurru*. London: Oxford University Press, 1951

Edwards, Amelia B. *A Thousand Miles Up the Nile*. London: Routledge, 1889

Emery, Walter B. *Nubian Treasure*. London: Methuen, 1948

Emery, Walter B. *The Royal Tombs of Ballana and Qustul.* Cairo: Government Press, 1938

Fairservis, Walter A. *The Ancient Kingdoms of the Nile.* New York: Crowell, 1962

Garstang, J., Sayce, A. H. and Griffith, F. L. *Meroe, the City of the Ethiopians.* Oxford, 1911

Greener, Leslie. *High Dam Over Nubia.* London: Cassell, 1962

Keating, Rex. *Nubian Twilight.* London: Hart-Davis, 1962

Little, Tom. *High Dam at Aswan.* London: Methuen, 1965

MacQuitty, William. *Abu Simbel.* London: Macdonald, 1965

Randall-Maciver, D. and Woolley, C. Leonard. *Buhen* (2 vols.). Philadelphia, 1911

Steindorff, G. and Seele, K. C. *When Egypt Ruled the East.* Chicago: University of Chicago Press, 1942

The UNESCO Courier. Articles: November 1962; October 1962; February 1960; October 1961

INDEX